HALEY'S HINTS

GRAHAM *and* ROSEMARY HALEY

Illustrations by DAVID McNIVEN

NEW AMERICAN LIBRARY

New American Library
Published by New American Library, a division of
Penguin Group (USA) Inc., 375 Hudson Street,
New York, New York 10014, USA
Penguin Group (Canada), 90 Eglinton Avenue East, Suite 700, Toronto,
Ontario M4P 2Y3, Canada (a division of Pearson Penguin Canada Inc.)
Penguin Books Ltd., 80 Strand, London WC2R 0RL, England
Penguin Ireland, 25 St. Stephen's Green, Dublin 2,
Ireland (a division of Penguin Books Ltd.)
Penguin Group (Australia), 250 Camberwell Road, Camberwell, Victoria 3124,
Australia (a division of Pearson Australia Group Pty. Ltd.)
Penguin Books India Pvt. Ltd., 11 Community Centre, Panchsheel Park,
New Delhi - 110 017, India
Penguin Group (NZ), 67 Apollo Drive, Mairangi Bay,
Auckland 1311, New Zealand (a division of Pearson New Zealand Ltd.)
Penguin Books (South Africa) (Pty.) Ltd., 24 Sturdee Avenue,
Rosebank, Johannesburg 2196, South Africa

Penguin Books Ltd, Registered Offices:
80 Strand, London WC2R 0RL, England

Published by New American Library, a division of Penguin Group (USA) Inc. Previously published
in a 3H Productions edition.

First New American Library Printing, January 2004
10   9   8   7   6   5   4

Congratulations! You have just done yourself a great favor.
By purchasing *Haley's Hints*, you've more than simply added
another good book to your home library. You now own a complete
household reference book that'll become indispensable to you.
On a daily basis, no matter what you are doing, in the house, garden,
workshop, office, or even on vacation, *Haley's Hints* will provide
you with money-saving ideas, timesaving tips, shortcuts…and lots
of plain old good advice!

However you wish to read it, be it from cover to cover in one sitting, a
chapter a week, or whenever you need help on a specific topic, we
know you'll find your new book fascinating. We have help for everyone,
from homemakers to office workers, gardeners to do-it-yourselfers,
infants to seniors, pet owners to picnickers. We've included chapters on
car maintenance, sporting equipment, camping in the great outdoors
and a section devoted solely to pampering yourself. And so you don't
miss anything, we've even added a chapter called "Hint Grab Bag,"
dozens of really clever hints for virtually every occasion.

And finally, we felt it was extremely important to provide a way for
the readers to find the exact hint they needed, quickly! To this end, we
have created an index that is so detailed and cleverly cross-referenced,
you should be able to find the tip you want in seconds.

Enjoy!
Graham and Rosemary

OUR GRATEFUL THANKS TO...

Every one of our local and international **television viewers** who supplied us
with such a variety of handy hints...

— ♦ —

Our North American **radio listeners,** for their many submissions...

— ♦ —

The **readers** of our first book, newspaper columns and cartoons,
for taking the time and effort to send us
all those clever personal tips...

— ♦ —

The **companies**, **organizations** and **individuals** who provided
information and advice essential to the research for this book...

— ♦ —

Gale, for planting the **first seed**...

— ♦ —

David, our gentleman **illustrator**, for bringing the pages to life...

— ♦ —

Michael, Margie and Cyndie, our **business partners**,
for keeping us on the straight and narrow...

— ♦ —

Our many **friends** who understood why we couldn't
play with them while we wrote the book...

— ♦ —

Our **family**, for their help and encouragement...

— ♦ —

Our three wonderful **kids**, Erin, Kerry and Anna,
for not disowning us...

— ♦ —

Each other, for the love and support.

TABLE OF CONTENTS

1. KITCHEN MAGIC

*"Hundreds Of Nifty Food
Tricks To Make Life In
The Kitchen A Breeze!"*

Oops! I've Run Out Of. 13

Cakes, Cookies, Pies & Frostings 16

Breads, Rolls & Crackers 23

Dairy Products 27

Fruitful Tips 32

The Produce Counter 36

Meats, Fowl, Fish & Shellfish 46

Soups, Stews, Sauces & Gravies 52

Perfect Pasta 54

Herbs, Spices & Condiments 56

Just Desserts & Beverages 58

What To Do With Leftovers 62

Freezing Tips 64

Catchy Kitchen Hints 70

2. ORDER IN THE HOUSE

*"How To Organize &
Clean Almost Everything
Around The Home!"*

Plan Ahead 80

Happiness Is A Clean & Tidy Kitchen 80

Bright Bathroom Tips 94

Furniture: Its Care & Cleaning 100

Getting The "Royal Carpet" Treatment 108

Floors, Walls & Woodwork 113

Tips For Windows 116

Around The House 119

Home Safe Home! 126

3. LAUNDRY-DAY HELPERS

*"A Hamperful Of Hints To
Delight Even The Most
Experienced Launderer!"*

Washing Away Those Laundry Blues 131

See Spot Run! 138

All About Drying 146

Ironing Out Your Pressing Problems 149

4. A STITCH IN TIME

*"Sewing, Mending & Knitting
Tips To Save You Time,
Money & Aggravation!"*

Sewing & Notions 154

Mending & Darning 160

Knitting Yarns 162

5. KIDS' KORNER

*"Great Ideas For Infants,
Toddlers, Schoolkids...
& Especially Moms!"*

Tips for Tots 165

Keeping Them Busy. . .Indoors & Out! 168

Order In The Kid's Room 174

Safety First 176

Kid Hint Catchall 177

Grandma's Remedies 180

6. 'SPECIALLY FOR SENIORS

*"Helpful Tips To Make
Life Easier For Those In
Their Golden Years!"*

Pointers For People In Their Prime 185

7. THE HOME HANDYPERSON

*"Tips & Information To
Help You Do-It-Yourself!"*

Tricks Of The Tool Trade 194

Walls, Floors, Windows & Doors 199

The Painter 205

The Plumber 212

The Electrician 215

The Carpenter 218

The Energy Saver 224

The Jack-Of-All-Trades 227

The Appliance Troubleshooter 232

8. PET PARADE

*"Tips Your Pets
Will Love You For!"*

Grooming, Raising & Picking Up After 236

9. PEST PEEVES

*"Getting Rid Of
What's Bugging You!"*

Controlled Pest Control 241

10. THE CAR MECHANIC

"All You Want To Know About Cars But Were Afraid To Ask!"

Preventive Maintenance 248

Driving, Parking & All The Rest 256

Hot Tips For The Cold 259

11. GARDENING WITH A GREEN THUMB

"Wonderful Ways To Improve A Garden...Both Indoors & Out!"

Seeing To Your Soil 264

Branching Out To Leaves & Stems 266

The Watering Hole 267

Perfect Potting 271

Cut Flowers 273

The Best Veggie Crop In Town 276

General Garden Tips 281

12. ROUGHING IT... THE EASY WAY

"Tips When Camping, Picnicking, Or Entertaining In The Backyard!"

Camping & Picnic Tips 286

Backyard Entertaining 291

13. SPORTING LIFE

"Taking Care Of Your Sporting Equipment!"

Keeping That Equipment In Good Shape 296

14. NINE TO FIVE

"Hints For The Third Of Your Life You Spend At The Office!"

Tips For The Workplace 303

There's No (Work)Place Like Home 305

15. JUST FOR YOU

"A Collection Of Tips To Pamper You, Relax You & Keep You Looking & Feeling Great!"

Masks & Scrubs To Make At Home 310

Toners, Astringents, Moisturizers, Etc. 312

Hair Dos...& Don'ts 314

Baths & Showers 317

Your Dressing Table 320

Your Wardrobe 322

Jewelry Gems 332

16. HINT GRAB BAG

*"A Host Of Helpful Hints
For Every Occasion!"*

Handy Hints From A To Z 336

17. INFORMATION AT
A GLANCE

*"Useful Charts On
Measurements,
Metric & Substitutes!"*

Measurements...In Other Words 351

18. EASY-FIND INDEX

*"The Most Important Part Of
The Book! Find the Exact
Hint You Want Instantly!"*

Easy-Find Index 361

CHAPTER 1

KITCHEN MAGIC

HUNDREDS OF NIFTY FOOD TRICKS TO MAKE LIFE IN THE KITCHEN A BREEZE!

OOPS!
I'VE RUN OUT OF...

SUBSTITUTES IN ALPHABETICAL ORDER...

Allspice... To make up 1 tablespoon of allspice, mix 1½ teaspoons of ground cloves with 1½ teaspoons of ground cinnamon.

Baking Powder... Use 1 teaspoon cream of tartar plus ½ teaspoon baking soda to replace 2 tablespoons baking powder.

Butter... In a pinch you can replace 1 cup of butter with ⅞ cup of ordinary kitchen lard.

Buttermilk... An equal amount of yogurt will replace buttermilk.

Celery... To fool your guests, replace celery in a salad with finely cut crisp cabbage. Sprinkle with a little celery salt.

Chicken... Short of chicken? Replace with cubed veal or pork. Believe it or not, tuna fish can also pass as chicken in a pinch!

Chocolate... Replace 1 square of chocolate with 3 tablespoons cocoa and 1 tablespoon shortening.

Chocolate Frosting… Combine sweetened condensed milk with powdered cocoa until frosting consistency is reached.

Cornstarch… Flour can be substituted for cornstarch if you double the quantity.

Corn Syrup… One cup of sugar dissolved in a quarter cup of warm water, will substitute for a cup of corn syrup. An equal amount of honey should also do the trick.

Cream, Sour… Should you need 1 cup of sour cream, substitute a blend of ¾ cup sour milk and ⅓ cup butter.

Cream, Whipped… If your recipe calls for 1 cup of whipped cream and you don't have any, try using 1½ cups of chilled evaporated milk with 1 teaspoon of lemon juice added. Whip as normal.

♦ Another handy substitute for whipped cream is to puree a banana, then whip with a beaten egg white. Add a drop or two of vanilla extract and sugar to taste.

Eggs… If the recipe calls for more than 2 eggs, 1 egg can be omitted, but add 2 tablespoons milk and ½ teaspoon baking powder to replace it.

♦ For a clever scrambled-egg extender, add a cupful of crumbled crackers if you don't have an extra egg or 2!

Flavor Fill-ins… A sherry flavor may be obtained by combining the flavors of rose and almond extracts. Pistachio flavor may be created by mixing vanilla and almond extracts.

Flour… A handy replacement for 1 cup of flour is 1½ cups of fine bread crumbs.

♦ Or to obtain 1 cup of all purpose flour, substitute with 1 cup plus 2 tablespoons of cake or pastry flour.

Food Coloring… When frosting a cake, you can substitute food coloring by adding some unsweetened flavored drink mix to your icing sugar.

Honey… For sweet success, replace a cup of honey with either a cup of molasses or corn syrup.

Ice Trays… If you run out of ice cube trays, a handy substitute is a foam egg carton.

Ketchup… Here's a quick replacement for ketchup to keep the kids happy. Combine ½ cup sugar, 2 tablespoons of malt vinegar and one 250 ml tin of tomato sauce.

Lemon… If your recipe calls for the juice of 1 lemon, use ¼ cup of lemon juice.

Mayonnaise… Here are two handy substitutes for mayonnaise when cooking. Use an equal amount of sour cream or pureed cottage cheese.

Milk… If you run out of milk while baking or making puddings, believe it or not, if you peel, then liquefy 1¼ lb. of zucchini, the liquid will substitute for about 2 cups of milk.

♦ Instead of mixing milk with eggs when making omelets, substitute ice-cold water. They'll come out fluffier too!

Mushrooms... It's said that mushrooms can often be replaced by cooking diced celery instead.

Oil... If a cake recipe calls for cooking oil and you have none, mayonnaise will substitute for the oil in a pinch. Use the same amount of mayonnaise as you would oil.

Salt... A healthy replacement would be a mixture of garlic powder, onion powder, oregano, basil, white pepper and lemon pepper.

Sugar... Use 1 cup honey plus ¼ teaspoon baking soda to replace 1 cup of white sugar. Remember to deduct 3 tablespoons of liquid from the recipe.

♦ Or use 1¼ cups of fruit sugar or brown sugar to substitute for 1 cup of white sugar.

Tomato Paste... If you require a small amount of tomato paste, try substituting an equal amount of ketchup.

Yogurt... A handy stand-in for plain yogurt is an equal amount of sour cream or pureed cottage cheese.

CAKES, COOKIES, PIES & FROSTINGS

CAKES...

Cutting And Slicing... Before cutting fresh, moist cake, run a thin-bladed knife under hot water and dry. Slices without crumbling.

◆ Or wrap some unwaxed dental floss around your fingers and slice through the cake with the floss as you would with a cheese wire. Crumble-free slices!

◆ After the cake has been cut, keep it moist by slicing fresh bread to the size of the exposed cake. Secure with toothpicks.

Sticking... Cake won't stick to the pan if you grease beforehand with unsalted fat and dust with flour.

◆ Another stick-free method is to thoroughly grease a piece of clean brown paper that has been cut to fit the cake pan. Foolproof!

◆ Save your butter wrappers in the refrigerator. They'll come in handy for greasing your pans when baking.

◆ To remove a cake that is stuck in the cake pan, invert the pan over the cooling rack. Take a hot steam iron and place it on the underside of the cake pan for a few seconds. You should find you can now lift the pan off the cake.

Moist Cakes... If you add a teaspoon of vinegar to the baking soda when baking a chocolate cake, you'll get the most moist chocolate cake you ever dipped your fork into!

◆ To keep fruit cakes moist while baking, place a pan of water alongside it in the oven and keep replacing the water until the cake is done.

Light Cakes... To make your cakes really light, add a teaspoon of lemon juice to the butter and sugar.

Cooling Cakes... If you find yourself without a wire-tray cake cooler, simply take a large mixing bowl and stretch some muslin or net curtain over it. Affix with clothes pegs and lay your cake on top!

COOKIES...

Sticky Dough!... Dip plastic cookie cutters in warm salad oil to prevent dough from sticking.

♦ To get cookie dough to slide off the spoon easily, dip the spoon in some milk first.

Emergency Cookie Cutter... The insert from a metal ice cube tray or an individual ice cube maker, makes a great emergency cookie cutter.

No Cookie Cutter!... For a quick way to form cookies without using a cookie cutter, try this. Form the dough into small balls and arrange on a cookie tray. Cut out a sheet of wax paper and lay it over the cookie balls. Take a flat-bottomed glass and press down on each cookie ball. Remove the wax sheet and you'll have perfectly formed cookies with no waste.

Ingredients... Before using raisins when baking cookies, let them sit in warm water for a few minutes to make them plump and juicy.

♦ When baking chocolate chip cookies, instead of using preformed chocolate chips, buy a good quality chocolate bar and cut it up into chunks.

Storage… To keep cookies fresher longer, store them in an ice bucket.

♦ Keep soft cookies separate from crisp cookies. Otherwise the crisp cookies will lose their crispness.

Next-Day Muffins… Revive stale muffins. Sprinkle with drops of water, place in a paper bag and warm in a hot oven for 5 to 10 minutes.

PIES…

Pastry Pointers… For an exact measurement when measuring sifted flour, never shake the flour level. Instead, use the back of a knife to scrape it level.

♦ Toss the ingredients with a fork lightly and quickly, rather than stirring them, which creates a tough pastry.

♦ Don't use too much water. For 2 cups of flour use only ¼ cup of iced water.

♦ Try rolling some grated cheese into pastry dough when making apple pie.

Pie Geometry… When sharing a round pie between 5 people, cut the pie into the shape of a Y. Then cut the large pieces in half!

Crusts… Eliminate soggy crusts when baking fruit pies by brushing the bottom crust with egg white before adding fruit. This helps prevent the juice from soaking through.

♦ For the flakiest upper crust on pies, brush lightly with cold water just before popping in the oven. Melts in your mouth!

♦ To avoid burned pie edges, try this tip. Take a foil pie plate and cut out the center, leaving just a one-inch rim. You can now place the rim over the pie and bake normally. The rim will reflect the heat from the pie edges and prevent them from burning.

Fast Fillings... To speed up the process when baking fruit pies, such as apple or peach, try this. Slice your fruit into a strong plastic shopping bag first. Then, add the filling ingredients and give the bag a good shake. Now you can simply add it to your pie.

Juice Spills... To prevent juice spills when baking pies, cut several 3-inch lengths of macaroni and poke them into the pie crust before placing in the oven. Heated juices will rise up into the hollow macaroni, instead of spilling over and messing your oven.

Sticky Meringue... Prevent meringue from sticking to the knife by adding a pinch of cream of tartar to the egg whites when beating them.

FROSTINGS...

Unique Toppings... Place a layer of chocolate mint patties over a baked cake and return it to the oven until the patties have softened. Spread with a spatula for a delicious icing.

◆ To spiff up plain frosting try shaving multicolored gumdrops on the top of the frosting with a coarse grater. They'll shave easier if you chill them well before you begin. They'll look like pretty flower petals.

◆ Or sprinkle cinnamon and sugar right on top of the cake batter for an "instant" sweet topping.

◆ For a quick topping, just lay a paper doily on top of the cake and dust it with icing sugar. Lift the doily off carefully and you'll have an elegant design.

Making Your Job Easier... A pinch of salt and a tablespoon of cornstarch for every two cups of icing sugar will help take away that "too sweet" taste.

◆ Before frosting your cake, cut triangles of waxed paper to cover the cake dish. Let several inches overlap. Place pointed ends of the triangles in the center of the dish. Place the unfrosted cake on top. 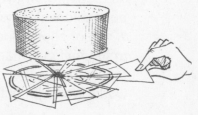 When the frosting is completed, slide each piece of waxed paper out slowly. You will have a sparkling-clean cake dish.

◆ Fudge frosting will stay soft and workable if you place the frosting bowl in a pan of hot water.

◆ No cake decorating utensil? Cut the end off an empty quart milk bag and wash it out. Clip a small opening at the opposite end. Fill the bag with frosting and squeeze through the small hole to decorate!

♦ To prevent the frosting from slipping when icing your cake, dust the surface of the cake with cornstarch before you begin.

IN GENERAL...

Measuring The Easy Way... Honey, syrup or other sticky liquids will slide out of the measuring cup with ease if the cup is oiled lightly before use.

♦ To measure awkward ingredients, like shortening, first pour cold water into your measuring cup. If you need ½ cup of shortening, fill the measuring cup with water to the half-cup mark. Then put your shortening in until the water level reaches the full-cup mark. This also works well with butter and hard margarine.

Softening Brown Sugar... A slice of fresh bread placed with the hardened brown sugar in a plastic bag and sealed tightly, will soften the sugar in about three hours.

♦ Or simply place a few slices of apple in the bag of sugar.

♦ If you really need brown sugar in a hurry, try running it through a hand grater.

♦ Or put hard brown sugar in an ovenproof bowl. Alongside, place another bowl filled with water. Set in a low-heat oven for about an hour.

Cloudy Honey?... To restore your clouded honey to it's clear liquid form, simply place the honey in the microwave on medium for a short while until you see it clearing. However, make sure the container hasn't just come out of the fridge when you do this...it could crack!

The Nuttier Side!... To make shelling Brazil nuts easier and faster when baking, always store them in the freezer. This keeps them fresher longer, and when you come to crack them, the shell will be brittle. You'll also have more chances of removing the kernels whole.

♦ If you need to chop nuts, pop them into the oven for a few minutes on a medium heat first. It'll make your job considerably easier.

♦ Did you know that a cup of almonds is equivalent in calcium to a cup of skim milk?

BREADS, ROLLS & CRACKERS

nice buns!

BREADS...

Bread Snacks... When your bread has turned stale, take a cookie cutter and cut the bread into shapes. Place in a plastic bag and freeze. When company arrives, top them with cheese spread and pop them under the broiler. Instant snacks!

♦ Take your leftover bread crumbs, add a little egg and shape into little balls. Drop them into hot oil and brown them. Sprinkle with sugar and cinnamon. The kids will love them!

A Few "Crumby" Ideas... Cut stale bread into ½-inch cubes. Place on a baking sheet and bake at 325°F for 15 minutes, stirring occasionally. If desired, sprinkle with seasonings such as garlic or celery salt before baking. Lovely salad croutons!

♦ Dry bread in an oven at 300°F for 10 minutes. Break into pieces and place in a paper bag. Secure end and crush with a rolling pin to make bread crumbs.

♦ Toss stale bread cubes and crusts into a blender to make quick bread crumbs.

Storage... Bread will last longer if you place a stalk of celery in the bag along with the bread.

Slicing... Bread you slice yourself stays fresher longer.

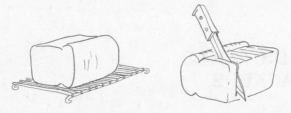

♦ When baking bread, cool the loaf on its side on the cooling rack. The rack will leave slight indentations, which happen to be a perfect slicing guide.

Rising... For a convenient method of getting your bread dough to rise, try popping it into the oven with just the oven light on. Generally, the light gives off sufficient heat to make the bread dough rise.

♦ Or take a small electric heating pad and place your dough on top of this. The even temperature is great for activating the yeast and speeding up the rising process.

Rejuvenating!... To restore bread to its original freshness, take a damp tea towel and wrap the loaf in it. Place in the fridge till the next day. When ready to serve, remove the tea towel and warm the bread in your oven.

Use Your Loaf... To sell your house! Real estate agents sometimes recommend that you bake bread when you hold an open house. The fragrance tends to make a favorable impression on prospective buyers!

ROLLS...

Bun Warmers... When heating your buns in the oven, heat an old ceramic tile along with them. Place a napkin in the breadbasket, pop the warm tile inside and put the buns on top. You'll find they keep warm a lot longer!

♦ If you're cooking vegetables on the element, turn the pot lid upside down and place your bread rolls on it. Sprinkle a small amount of water on them and cover with an inverted cake pan. The heat from the pot and element rises into the inverted pan and warms the bread!

♦ Or wrap the buns in foil and place them in your Crock-Pot. Turn the thermostat on low.

♦ Use large, foil potato chip bags to heat rolls and bread in the oven. Saves $$$!

Bun Revivers... Place your stale bread rolls in a brown paper bag. Sprinkle the bag liberally with water and place it in a warm oven for approximately five minutes. Watch carefully.

Bottom Of The Bun Bag!... Notice how many sesame and poppy seeds collect in the bottom of your plastic bun bag? Store them in an airtight container for later use. Added to regular bread crumbs, they'll enhance the flavor dramatically.

Burned Buns?... If you accidentally burn the top of your bread rolls when warming or baking them, simply rub the blackened part on a cheese grater. It works "grate"!

CRACKERS...

Crispy Crackers... Keep soda crackers in the bottom drawer of the stove. The heat from the oven will keep them crisp.

♦ If you have a gas stove, pop your crackers into the oven. The oven's pilot light will have the same crisping effect.

♦ Store leftover soda crackers, and their wax-wrap sleeves, in a cylindrical potato chip container.

♦ Crackers, pretzels and potato chips that have lost their crunch can be revived by placing on a cookie sheet and broiling for just a minute.

Born-Again Crackers!... For a new look for plain salted crackers, brush some melted butter or egg white on the crackers. Sprinkle with caraway, sesame or poppy seeds, perhaps some garlic or onion salt and toast in the oven. Yummy!

DAIRY PRODUCTS

MILK, BUTTER & CHEESE...

Milk...

Milk That Has Taken A Turn... Don't pour out sour milk—it can still go a long way. If it's just beginning to turn, a pinch of baking soda can restore freshness.

♦ If it's still a little too sour for your taste, you can usually use it in gravies and for baking by adding 2 teaspoons of baking soda for each cup of milk. (Reduce baking powder in your recipe by 2 teaspoons.)

But On The Other Hand... If your recipe calls for sour milk and you don't have any, add 2 tablespoons of vinegar or lemon juice to 1 cup of sweet milk and stir.

Storing Milk... Take note: Milk stored at normal fridge-operating temperature, 40°F (4.5°C), should keep up to 10 days. At 50°F (10°C), it should last about 2 days; at 59°F (15°C), only 1 day.

No More Scorching... Using pan rinsed in cold water before heating milk will help prevent it from sticking.

♦ Adding a pinch of salt to scorched milk removes much of the "burned" taste.

How To Whip Whipping Cream... Make sure cream and all utensils are cooled before starting.

♦ Keep the bowl in a pan of ice-cold water throughout the whipping process.

♦ Add a drop or two of lemon juice if the cream won't stiffen.

♦ Or add an egg white and refrigerate before whipping.

Butter...

Butter Extender... Stretch a pound of butter into two. Bring butter to room temperature and beat to a cream with a mixer. Slowly add 2 cups of evaporated milk and continue beating until the mixture is smooth. Chill as a solid.

Butter Balling... Take a melon baller, run it under a hot tap and scoop it through the butter. Immediately pop the ball into a bowl of iced water.

♦ Make sure that the butter is not too cold. Otherwise the balls will tend to crack and break.

Butter Storage... Butter may be stored in the freezer for up to 6 months. Wrap it well in airtight freezer wrap.

Hard Butter?... For a quick way to soften your butter, place it in a butter dish first. Then, using oven mitts, hold the lid under the hot-water tap for a minute or two. Replace the lid on the dish and leave for a couple of minutes.

Cheese...

Dried-Out Cheese... Cheese that has dried out can still be used. Simply grate and store for use with soups or vegetables.

  ♦ Make a delicious spread with dried-out cheese by blending with raw onions and your favorite seasonings.

  ♦ However, to prevent your cheese from drying out, soak a cloth with malt vinegar, wring it out and wrap it tightly around your cheese.

  ♦ The next time you slice cheese, spread a little butter or margarine on the exposed area. It'll stop it from drying out and getting hard.

Moldy Cheese... To keep mold from forming on your cheese, wrap a few cubes of sugar in with the cheese. It works!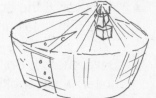

Hardened Cheese... A quick way to soften that piece of hardened cheese is to leave it for about 30 seconds in a bowl of buttermilk.

Cottage Cheese... They say if you want to almost double the life of your cottage cheese, keep the container upside down in your refrigerator. Worth a try!

EGGS, EGGS, EGGS...

Fried Eggs... The texture of eggs will be tough if you salt them during the frying process.

Poached Eggs... No egg poacher? Use the rims from preserve jars and lightly grease the inside of the rim to prevent eggs from sticking. Add a drop of lemon juice to the water to keep the egg whites from spreading.

♦ Or grease metal jar lids and place upside down in pan.

Boiled Eggs... Boiled eggs should never be boiled! Simmering to doneness will produce tastier results.

♦ To prevent boiled eggs from cracking, let stand in warm water for a few minutes prior to cooking.

♦ Eggs won't crack if you make a small hole with a needle in the large end of the egg before boiling.

♦ However, if the egg is already cracked before boiling, wrap it in tinfoil and then hard-boil normally.

♦ Save energy! Boil eggs in the bottom half of a double boiler, while cooking cereal in the top half.

♦ To keep yolks centered for decorative purposes, gently stir eggs throughout first two minutes of boiling.

Slicing Hard-Boiled Eggs... When slicing, dip your knife in water periodically to prevent the yolks from crumbling.

♦ When a piece of egg shell falls into the bowl, remove it by using the large broken half of the egg shell. The small piece will cling to the larger shell for easy removal.

Storing Eggs... Eggs should be stored with the large end up. This keeps the air pocket in the large end and the yolk in the center.

♦ Store your eggs in the carton. It tends to slow down moisture loss and helps stop them from picking up fridge odors.

♦ Always keep eggs refrigerated and remove a ½ hour before cooking, for best results.

Storing Egg Yolks... Egg yolks can be kept fresh for several days by covering with cold water and refrigerating.

Storing Egg Whites... Egg whites can be kept in the fridge for up to 7 days if you cover them with plastic wrap.

Beating Egg Whites... Just a pinch of salt added to egg whites makes beating a quick and easy job.

♦ Egg whites will whip better in a glass or metal bowl and at room temperature.

♦ To make sure egg whites are whipped enough, invert the bowl. The contents shouldn't slide out.

♦ When beating eggs separately, beat the whites first. They won't cling to the beater the way yolks will, saving you a washup.

Separating Whites And Yolks... When you only need the white of an egg and not the yolk, economize by cutting a ¼-inch square in one end of the shell and allowing the white to drop through. Seal the hole with a small piece of tape and cover the entire shell with foil. You'll have a fresh yolk when you need it.

♦ A small kitchen funnel is a handy tool when separating yolks and whites. The yolks will remain in the funnel.

Testing Freshness... The freshness of eggs can be determined by these simple methods. Fresh eggs will sink in water; shells should be rough and dull (if it's smooth and shiny, it's not that fresh); contents should feel firm, not loose, when shaken lightly.

Buying Eggs... Remember, white eggs are just as good as "wholesome" brown eggs. The color of an egg has nothing to do with the amount of nutrition it contains.

♦ However, if you buy brown eggs one week and white eggs the next week, you'll always know which ones are the fresher!

FRUITFUL TIPS

IDEAS THAT BEAR FRUIT...

Apples...

Nonbrowning Apples... When peeling a quantity of apples, place peeled apples in a basin of cold, slightly salted water to prevent browning. Or try coating them with a little lemon juice.

♦ When making a fresh-fruit salad, keep cut fruit from browning by placing it in a bowl of grapefruit juice. If you don't have grapefruit juice, lemon juice works too!

Bananas...

Buying Bananas... Look for unmarked and yellow bananas. If they have small brown specks it shouldn't affect the flavor. But remember, they last longer in bunches!

Don't Toss Out That Banana!... Save it for making banana breads and cakes. Mash the darkened banana with a potato masher and freeze in a plastic container.

◆ To hurry up the ripening process, wrap your bananas in a damp kitchen towel and place in a paper bag.

Cantaloupe...

Buying Cantaloupe... Look for ones that are an even beige to gray color. Avoid those that are hard and green. These tend to be picked before they are ripe and will not be as sweet as those left to ripen longer. Always sniff before buying, there should be a soft sweet scent.

Cherries...

Buying Cherries... Look for large ones, they tend to be the most flavorful. Next, find ones that are smooth and firm with a dark red to black color to ensure sweetness.

Grapefruit...

Buying Grapefruit... Look for grapefruit that is a consistent round shape, feels heavy for it's size and is fairly thin-skinned. Smell first; a sweet scent means freshness.

Honeydew...

Buying Honeydew... Look for ones that have a good round shape and feel heavy for their size. The texture of the skin should feel firm and smooth with a creamy color. There should be pleasant, fragrant odor.

Did You Know?... Honeydew is the only melon that continues to sweeten after it's been cut from the vine!

Kiwi Fruit...

Buying Kiwi Fruit... Look for ones that are firm, but not hard. If they are hard, they are probably not yet ripe. They should also have a sweet fruity scent.

Lemons...

Lemon Aids... Get almost twice the juice from a lemon by heating it first. Place lemon in a saucepan of water and bring to a boil, or microwave on high for 30 seconds.

♦ Before cutting lemons, roll gently on the cutting board using a little hand pressure as you roll. You'll be surprised at how much more juice is extracted.

♦ If you need only a small amount of lemon juice, instead of wasting a whole lemon, simply puncture a hole in it with a skewer.  Squeeze out the required amount and pop the lemon back in the refrigerator until the next time.

Oranges...

Buying Oranges... The smaller ones are generally sweeter. Look for those that feel heavy for their size. Also, check their scent for a sweet, pleasant odor.

When Making Orange Juice... You will get more juice from an orange if it is allowed to warm to room temperature first. To achieve the same effect quickly, hold oranges under hot running water for a few minutes.

♦ Save orange and lemon rinds. Grate, place in a plastic bag and freeze for use in drinks, breads, cakes, etc.

Peaches...

Peachy Keen!... To ripen your peaches in a hurry, try storing them in an old shoe box and cover with crumpled newspaper.

Buying Peaches... When you sniff the stem top of the peach, there should be a sweet scent. They've reached ripeness when there's no sign of green left on the fruit. The flesh should give slightly to the touch.

Pineapples...

Buying Pineapples... Should feel firm to the touch and have a sweet scent at the bottom. Check for soft spots and healthy green leaves.

Strawberries...

Cleaning Strawberries... Insert a thin plastic drinking straw into the strawberry from the bottom and push it up through the top of the berry. It should slide right through, taking the stem and leaves with it.

♦ Only *rinse* strawberries. They'll absorb water if left to soak.

In General...

Peeling Fruit... A 45-second blanching in boiling water is sufficient to ease the skin off most fruit.

Removing Fruit Stains From Hands... To remove strawberry or other fruit stains from your hands, rub with a paste of cornmeal and lemon juice.

THE PRODUCE COUNTER

BUYING, PREPARING & SERVING...

Beans...

Fixing "Has-Beans"!... To remove rust spots from yellow beans, cover them with a solution of 2 cups white vinegar and 1 cup water. Leave to soak for 2 hours, then rinse and cook.

Cutting Beans... A safer method of cutting string beans is to cut them with a pair of scissors instead of a knife.

Storing Beans... Store beans in the fridge the same way as you would peas.

Buying Beans... Always buy green beans that are no thicker than a normal pencil.

♦ If they bend freely instead of breaking sharply, avoid them.

Broccoli...

Fresh Broccoli... Select broccoli in a nice green bunch with a small head. Individual stalks should be small and thin and the clumps at the end should be tightly packed. The little particles should come off easily when rubbed.

Storing Broccoli... To keep your broccoli fresh, store it in the refrigerator in a plastic bag.

Broccoli Fact... Did you know that a single helping of broccoli will provide you with 3 to 4 times your daily requirement of vitamin C?

Brussels Sprouts...

Buying Brussels Sprouts... Look for them loose, rather than packaged.

♦ They should be firm to the touch.

♦ Avoid those that have a yellowish color to them. Bright green is best.

♦ Smaller sprouts are the tastiest.

Cabbage...

Is That Cabbage I Smell?... Placing a heel of bread on top of cauliflower, broccoli, cabbage or brussels sprouts while cooking, will help to eliminate cooking odors.

♦ A spoonful of sugar added to boiling turnip helps prevent odors.

♦ A whole walnut added to boiling cabbage will help eliminate odor.

♦ Or add a stalk or two of celery to the boiling cabbage water.

♦ Here's an easy way to core your cabbages. Use a tulip-bulb planter. It's fast, easy and efficient.

Cauliflower...

Cauliflower...White And Bright... Cauliflower will be snow-white if soaked in cold, salted water for ½ an hour prior to cooking.

Fresh Cauliflower... Fresh cauliflower has a nice, clear, white head. If there are a few small brown spots, they're probably water marks which can be cut off.

Corn...

Cooking Sweet Corn... A teaspoon of lemon juice added to boiling corn on the cob will keep the corn a bright yellow color.

Corn Hairs?... A quick way to remove those silky corn hairs from the cob is to simply brush it with a vegetable brush or toothbrush while holding it under cold running water.

Shucking Sweet Corn... To remove corn from the cob, rest the tip of the cob in the center of an angel food (or Bundt) pan. With a ordinary shoehorn, shave the kernels off with firm strokes. The corn will fall neatly into the pan!

Buttering It Up... Simply spread a generous helping of butter onto a slice of bread and rub or roll the cob on the bread!

♦ Fill a tall jug with hot water. Place several spoons of butter onto the water surface. Simply dip the corncobs into the water. As you remove them, the butter will coat the kernels beautifully!

Cucumbers...

Buying Cucumbers... Avoid cucumbers that are not firm and rigid.

♦ To remove the waxy film from your cucumber, simply rub with vinegar. The skin is a good source of nutrition and helps in the digestion of the cucumber.

Cucumber Sandwiches, Anyone?... For cucumber sandwiches that aren't soggy, dry the sliced cucumbers on a paper towel for 5 minutes or so before putting in the sandwich.

Cute Cukes!... Make an attractive scalloped edge on thinly sliced cucumbers by running the tines of a fork lengthwise over the cucumber before slicing.

Garlic...

Garlic Odor!... While garlic is great for cooking, it's not so great for socializing. To remove garlic odor from your hands, here's a quick tip. Take a handful of cool, used coffee grounds, rub them into your hands well, then simply rinse off. Similarly, to get rid of garlic breath, just pop a coffee bean into your mouth and chew.

Mushrooms...

Cleaning Mushrooms... Pop your mushrooms into a mesh onion bag and hold the bag under the cold-water tap. Knead gently and you'll soon have dirt-free mushrooms.

Slicing Mushrooms... For neat, even mushroom slices, use an egg slicer.

Storing Mushrooms... The best way to store mushrooms in the refrigerator is to wrap them in paper towels first.

Onions...

No-Tear Onions... Why do onions make you cry? A liquid ingredient in onions evaporates when the onion is cut and is exposed to the air. Liquid film in our eyes is especially sensitive to this and we produce tears to wash it away. Eliminate this problem by refrigerating the onion for an hour before cutting. (The cold substance evaporates more slowly.) Also be sure to use a very sharp knife so the onion is cut cleanly rather than torn.

♦ Or run the onion under cold water as you slice it.

♦ Some say the trick is to always cut the bottom root of the onion off first, and then cut the top off.

♦ You can also try burning a candle while cutting.

Storing Onions... Take an old pair of panty hose and drop an onion into the foot of each leg. Tie a knot immediately above each onion. Add more onions in each leg with knots between each onion, until both legs are filled and then hang behind a door. This helps prevent rotting by keeping them separated. Simply cut one off when you need it.

Onion Odor... It's said that to remove onion smell from your hands, place all five fingers on the handle of a stainless-steel spoon. Then run cold water over your fingers!

♦ Another method to remove strong odors from your hands is to apply some ordinary underarm deodorant to your hands. Rinse off after five minutes. They say this also works for bleach odors.

Peas...

Cooking Sweet Peas... Instead of adding sugar to sweeten fresh peas during cooking, try adding several empty pea pods to the pot. Economical and tasty!

Storing Peas... To extend the life of your peas, wash them in cold water, but don't dry them. Store in the refrigerator in a perforated plastic bag.

Peppers...

Pretty Peppers!... Coat green peppers with olive oil before stuffing and baking to maintain their original color.

Buying Peppers... They say that the freshest sweet pepper is one that has a firm and shiny skin.

♦ Remember, some peppers remain green, while others turn red, yellow or even a purplish black!

Potatoes...

Peeling... Pour boiling water over potatoes just before peeling to allow you to peel thinly and easily.

On The Other Hand... Instead of peeling potatoes, scour with a metal sponge and rinse well. It's quick, easy and saves valuable nutrients close to the skin. As a matter of interest, it's said that the average family's annual potato peels amount to the following nutrients: the iron provided by approximately 450 eggs, the protein of 50 steaks and the vitamin C you can get from 100 glasses of O.J.!

Slicing... For thin, uniform potato slices, use a cheese slicer (the kind that has a 2- or 3-inch slot and looks a bit like a cake lifter).

Baking Potatoes... Boil potatoes whole for fifteen minutes before placing in a hot oven; it saves half the baking time.

♦ When baking potatoes in the microwave, stick four toothpicks into the potato like little legs. This allows the air to circulate around the potato and it will cook more evenly.

Cozy Baked Potatoes!... To keep potatoes warm between cooking and serving, just slip them into your oven mitts. They'll stay nice and warm until dinner!

Creamy Mashed Potatoes... Mashed potatoes will be light and fluffy if milk is heated and added before mashing.

♦ If you find your mashed potatoes are too soggy or runny, stir in some powdered milk gradually with a whisk until you're happy with the texture and fluffiness.

Home Fries With Extra Zip!... Sprinkle potatoes to be fried with flour. They'll be deliciously golden brown. Try adding a little paprika and garlic salt for extra flavor!

Unfried Fries... To make healthier french fries without frying, try coating french-cut potatoes with egg whites. Add a little seasoning, like paprika, salt and garlic, and bake in a medium-heat oven until golden brown.

Buying Potatoes... They should have a good uniform shape.

♦ Size is unimportant, as long as they have a good weight to them.

♦ Look for potatoes that have a nice firm feel to them and a smooth texture.

♦ Watch out for "eyes," cracks, shriveling and a greenish texture.

Sweet, Sweet Potatoes... Add brown sugar and butter to mashed sweet potatoes and stuff in empty orange shells. Brown in the oven for a few minutes and watch those eyes light up!

Pumpkin...

When Buying... Look for the ones that have no signs of bruising and breaks on the skin. There shouldn't be any soft spots. The best size for eating are those the size of a small squash.

Tomatoes...

Turning Green Tomatoes Red!... Keep green tomatoes firm through the ripening process by storing stem-up in a shady place.

♦ Place them in a damp cloth and store in a paper bag.

♦ Put green tomatoes in a brown paper bag and throw an apple in with them.

Slicing Tomatoes... To keep your sliced tomatoes firmer longer, slice the tomatoes vertically, instead of horizontally.

♦ For the canned variety, empty the juice into another container. Then, take a pair of kitchen scissors and cut the tomatoes without removing them from the tin.

Peeling Tomatoes... Place your tomatoes in a bowl and pour boiling water over them. In about three or four minutes they should be ready to peel.

♦ Or stick the tomatoes on a long metal skewer and, using oven mitts, hold them over the open flame on your gas stove. When the skin starts to split, remove them and they'll be ready to peel.

♦ Another method of peeling a tomato is to stroke the skin of the tomato with the back edge of a knife. It's skin should crinkle and remove easily.

Ugly But Cheap Tomatoes... Save money by deliberately buying misshapen or scarred tomatoes. The taste is generally not affected.

Rice...

Tastier Rice... Add fruit or vegetable juice instead of water to rice for a great taste!

Rice That Won't Stick... Add a spoonful of lemon juice to boiling rice to keep grains from sticking together.

Rescuing Burned Rice... To rescue rice that is a little burned, first lay a slice of bread on top of the rice. Replace the lid and leave it to stand for about 10 minutes or so. The bread should soak up most of the burned taste. Next, remove the rice carefully, leaving the burned rice on the bottom of the pot.

IN GENERAL...

Crisping Wilted Vegetables... Add a few drops of lemon juice or cider vinegar to a bowl of ice-cold water. Add wilted lettuce and let stand for an hour.

♦ Don't throw away unattractive wilted lettuce leaves. Crisp them in cold water and shred them for use in sandwiches and salads.

♦ Or save them and place them around any unused part of your head of lettuce. Secure with a rubber band and you'll find this will keep your unused lettuce nice and fresh.

♦ Wash and wrap vegetables in paper towels before placing in the refrigerator.

♦ Add a few slices of raw potato to a pan of cold water and allow celery and lettuce to crisp for ½ hour. Better still, when cutting up your raw veggies like carrots, radishes, celery, etc., just pop a piece of raw potato in the water with them.

♦ Stand stems of wilted asparagus in cold water for a while and watch them come back to life!

Watch Those Nutrients!... Soaking fresh vegetables in water for too long a period reduces vitamin content.

♦ Similarly, using soda when cooking green vegetables may create an appetizing appearance, but most of the important nutrients will be decreased.

MEATS, FOWL, FISH & SHELLFISH

MEATS...

General Cooking Tips... Tender meat is best cooked with a dry heat, like oven roasting, barbecuing or panfrying.

♦ Tough meat is best cooked with moisture, like slow stewing, braising or simmering.

A Tender Tip... Here's a less violent way of tenderizing your meat. Instead of pounding it, simply run a rolling pizza cutter back and forth over each side of the meat.

♦ Or try rubbing your meat with kiwi fruit. It works!

Cooking Roasts... To ensure that your roast is moist, wait until it's nearly cooked before adding any salt, otherwise the salt will draw the juices out while it's cooking.

♦ Place several stalks of celery under your roast and you'll find that cleaning the roasting pan will be a snap. You'll also have some irresistible celery-flavored meat stock.

♦ If you're concerned that the roast is going to be tough, it's said that if you cook it along with either a banana or slices of pineapple, it tenderizes the meat.

Carving Roasts... When carving a roast, cut across, instead of with, the grain. This will give you more tender slices.

Baking Ham... If you're concerned that your baked ham is going to be too salty, bake it halfway, then pour all the juices off. Pour a can of ginger ale over the ham and bake it until it's done.

Look Ma, It's All Sliced!... Ask your supermarket to slice the next ham you buy. Tie it securely and bake it with your pineapple etc. in the oven. When you remove it, it'll already be sliced. No more mess!

Hamburger Stretchers... Crushed cereals or bread crumbs added to hamburger will make it go a little further.

Fast Hamburgers... Poke a hole in the center of the burger before frying. This helps to cook the center as quickly as the outside.

Moist Meatballs... To keep your meatballs moist, try this. When forming them, simply place a small ice cube chip in the center of each meatball. This will help prevent the center from drying out during the cooking process.

Reduce Sausage Shrinkage... And remove excess fats. Boil sausages for 5 to 10 minutes and roll in flour before frying or broiling.

Cooking Bacon... If your bacon curls up when you're frying

or broiling, try dipping the pieces in cold water first. They should come out nice and flat, which makes them easier in sandwiches. It also looks better on the plate!

♦ If you've just taken the bacon out of the fridge, roll the package on the counter. This will help separate the rashers.

Saving Your Bacon Drippings... Bacon drippings are an economical and delicious seasoning. Keep drippings in good condition by following these steps. Use small jars for storage so bottom layers are used before spoiling. Date jars as you use them, using the oldest jar first.

♦ Remove sediment from bacon fat by frying raw potato slices until brown. Potatoes will absorb most of the sediment while soaking up any extraneous flavors.

♦ And remember, when substituting bacon fat for shortening, always reduce the quantity by 25% to achieve the same effect.

Buying Meat... A general rule of thumb is to choose meat from the least-exercised part of the animal. Therefore, the further from the loin, the tougher the meat.

FOWL...

Buying Chicken... Look for the chicken that has a creamy, smooth but firm skin. It should also appear plump and white with no odor.

Stuffing Chicken... When stuffing chicken or turkey, place the stuffing in an onion bag first and then insert it. You'll find it'll come out easier and hold together better.

Roasting Chicken... To give roast chicken a lovely golden brown texture, rub mayonnaise over the chicken and place in the oven for the required period. For extra crispiness, uncover the pan for the last half hour.

Coating Chicken... For a great chicken crumb coating, place some stale bread and a package of seasoned dry-mix salad dressing in the blender and blend.

Defrosting Chicken... It's a good idea when defrosting chicken to thaw it in well-salted water. This will make the breast meat pure white, due to the salted water drawing the blood out.

Defrosting Turkey... To defrost your turkey naturally, place it in the refrigerator for 24 hours, for every 5 pounds. If you're in a hurry, place the bird in a basin and cover it with cold water. Don't forget to change the water often, allowing a defrosting time of ½ hour per 1 pound of turkey.

Buying Turkeys... If you are buying fresh, check that it has a firm, milk-white skin with no bruising, purplish marks. The flesh should be plump and clean smelling. If buying frozen, check the packaging, it should be airtight without any breaks or rips in the plastic wrap.

Roasting Turkey... Never roast a turkey in a brown paper bag. Even if the bag doesn't catch fire, the heat of your oven could cause the paper to release chemicals, resulting in an off-tasting turkey dinner.

Stuffing Turkey... Some people stuff their turkey ahead of time to avoid the rush. Don't. Bacteria growth could make the meat dangerous to eat!

Basting Turkey... One of the most common misconceptions is that to make a turkey tender and juicy, frequent hand basting is necessary. Not so. Basting only penetrates about an eighth of an inch into the turkey's surface. This could actually lengthen roasting time, because whenever you open the oven door, you get a drop in temperature.

FISH & SHELLFISH...

Fish...

Baking Fish... Place filets of fish on lettuce leaves when baking to prevent sticking to pan. Discard leaves after.

Thawing Fish... They say it's a good idea to thaw frozen fish in milk. Evidently the milk tends to draw out the frozen taste and gives it a more "fresh-caught" flavor.

Preparing Fish... When handling fish, moisten fingers and dip them in salt. This helps prevent fish from sliding out of your grip and cuts down on fish odor left on your hands.

♦ Remove fish odor by rubbing hands with liquid soap and toothpaste.

Fish-Buying Tips... Look for the fish with the shiniest eyes. If they're dull, stay away. They should also protrude from the head slightly. If they appear sunken in, be wary.

♦ Check the gills. Fresh fish have nice clean-looking red gills. If they are faded and brownish, keep looking.

♦ Check the flesh. It should be firm and springy, not soft.

♦ The skin should have a nice radiant sheen to it and the scales should not be coming off.

♦ Give it a good sniff. If it has a fresh, ocean-type smell to it, rather than a musty, fishy odor, that's your choice.

Shellfish...

Shucking Clams... Hard-shell clams can be easily opened by-pouring boiling water over them first.

Scrumptious Oysters!... Try rolling oysters in cracker crumbs seasoned with celery salt before frying. Delicious!

Fresh Mussels?... It's said that a quick method of testing if a mussel is fresh, is to see if you can twist the two halves apart. If they move, even slightly, then stay away! It's not worth the risk.

Buying Scallops... When buying scallops, ensure they are of a uniform size. This facilitates their cooking evenly.

♦ Look for scallops that are beige to pink in color and are relatively free of liquid.

♦ Fresh scallops should also have a pleasant, sweet sea smell to them.

Buying Lobster... It's generally agreed that when choosing lobster from a tank, the freshest are usually the liveliest.

♦ If you are not buying live lobster, it's a good idea to check all the joints. They shouldn't be discolored.

Shrimp Odors... To cut down on any odor when boiling shrimp, try adding some caraway seeds to the boiling water. They say it works.

SOUPS, STEWS, SAUCES & GRAVIES

SOUPS & STEWS...

Too Salty?... Add wedges of raw potatoes or apple to reduce saltiness in soups or stews. Remove wedges after cooking along with the stew for about 10 minutes.

♦ Or you could add a little sugar to counter the saltiness.

♦ Some people recommend adding a teaspoon of cider vinegar or a teaspoon of sugar to have the same effect.

Too Sweet?... If your soup or stew turns out to be too sweet, try adding a little salt or a teaspoon of cider vinegar.

Too Greasy?... To remove excess fat from soups and stews, toss in a lettuce leaf. It will absorb a lot of the fat and can then be thrown away.

♦ Another way to remove excess fat is to toss in a few ice cubes. Stir them around and you should find the fat will stick to the cubes. Remove them and the fat along with them.

SAUCES & GRAVIES...

Sauces...

Preparing Pasta Sauces... When preparing your vegetables to add to pasta sauce, sauté them first. The browning releases the natural sugars and flavors in the veggies and gives added color and character to your sauce.

Through Thick To Thin... When using cornstarch as a thickener in sauces, be careful not to beat the sauce too much. This can often cause the sauce to become thin. A gentle stir with a spoon or whisk is usually sufficient.

Overdue Sauces... When refrigerating sauces with eggs or milk in them, do not keep them for more than 2 days.

Tomato Sauces... To ensure a good, robust color to your tomato sauce, don't cook it too fast or for too long.

Rescuing Your Hollandaise... When preparing your hollandaise sauce, if you find it starting to curdle, gradually stir in a teaspoon of boiling water.

♦ Or try stirring the sauce into a beaten egg yolk.

Gravies...

Making Gravy... Creamy smooth gravy can be made by substituting ½ the amount of flour with cornstarch.

♦ When roasting meat, place a small pan of flour beside the roasting pan in the oven. The flour will brown for use when making gravy.

Browning Gravy… To make your gravy an attractive, brown color, darken it with instant coffee. Stir in a teaspoon and it will awaken the color without affecting the taste.

Gravy Too Thin?… Slowly add a mixture of cornstarch or flour and water to gravy. Bring to a slow boil, stirring constantly.

   ◆ Or gradually mix in some instant mashed-potato flakes until you have the right consistency.

Too Thick?… Add water. (For nutritious and great-tasting gravy, remember to use water in which vegetables have been cooked or canned.)

Too Greasy?… If the gravy turns out to be too greasy, try adding a pinch of baking soda. Sprinkle roasting pan with flour and brown well before adding liquid.

Too Burned?… It's said that a spoonful of peanut butter stirred into burned gravy will help remove that scorched taste. However, be aware of peanut allergies!

PERFECT PASTA

BUYING, COOKING, SERVING & STORING…

Buying…

Pasta-Purchase Pointers… Generally, when buying pasta, pastas that are thick and chunky are better served with thick sauces. Conversely, thinner pastas match thinner sauces.

Cooking...

Cooking Spaghetti... Place your deep-fryer basket into the pot of water before you add your spaghetti. Now you have an automatic strainer that lifts the spaghetti out easily and also prevents it sticking to the bottom of the pot.

Sticky Spaghetti?... Once your spaghetti is cooked, run it under hot water to prevent sticking. If you're not serving it immediately, you can let it sit in the hot water, but add a few ice cubes to stop the cooking process. Before serving, run it under hot water again.

Oil On Troubled Waters... A few drops of oil added to boiling water when cooking pasta will prevent spillovers on the stove and will also keep the pasta from sticking to the pot.

Serving...

Pretty Pasta... If you add a few drops of yellow food coloring to the boiling water when you serve your pasta, it'll have a delicious, rich, buttery look.

Pastapicks... Instead of using toothpicks to keep rolled hors d'oeuvres together while cooking, use small lengths of raw spaghetti. The spaghetti will cook right along with the hors d'oeuvres, becoming tender and blending in, while holding them together.

Storing...

Storing Pasta... To keep leftover spaghetti fresh and moist, put it in a plastic bag, seal with a rubber band to make sure it's airtight and place in the refrigerator. When you heat it up, it will have all it's moisture and less starch.

♦ Fresh, uncooked pasta should be cooked within 7 days of being stored in the fridge.

♦ To prevent the uncooked pasta sticking to itself, add some cornmeal to it and rewrap tightly in plastic.

HERBS, SPICES & CONDIMENTS

HERBS & SPICES...

Storing Herbs... It's a good idea to store fresh herbs in your freezer. When you come to use them, don't defrost them. Simply cut off the amount you require while they're still frozen. They'll retain their flavor longer this way.

Storing Spices... Spices hold their flavor longer if you store them in a cool, dark place, like a windowless pantry or a kitchen cupboard.

♦ Don't line your spice bottles on a shelf or rack that is near your stove. The heat will sap their strength and flavor.

♦ Write the purchase date on the labels of your ground spices. Most of them will only hold their potency for about a year.

Buying Spices... It's wiser to buy your spices whole, rather than in the ground form. They'll taste better.

Keep Salt From Clogging... If your saltshaker clogs up, try placing several grains of uncooked rice in the shaker. The rice will absorb the excess moisture that causes the clogging.

♦ Or place a small piece of blotting paper in the bottom of your saltshaker.

Taste Testing... When testing to see if food is too salty, don't limit your tasting to the tip of your tongue. Evidently the center and sides of your tongue are even more salt sensitive.

CONDIMENTS...

Lunch Containers... If you take a lunch to work, pour your condiments, like ketchup, salad dressing, chili sauce, etc., into empty pill bottles.

Ketchup Too Slow?... A drinking straw pushed into a slow-pouring ketchup bottle will speed up the process. Remove the straw and pour.

Vinegar Storage... Because of its acidic properties, never store vinegar, or foods pickled with vinegar, in containers made of brass, copper, iron or tin. It's always safest to use glass containers.

Homemade Wine Vinegar... For a quick way to make your own wine vinegar, simply add red wine to regular white vinegar. Experiment with quantities to suit your taste.

Homemade Pickles... Remember to always scald the vinegar first when pickling. Otherwise, the vinegar will deteriorate faster.

♦ White vinegar gives pickled vegetables a more natural color.

♦ When pickling in brine, it's best to use coarse salt. Table salt can discolor the brine solution and the pickles themselves.

JUST DESSERTS & BEVERAGES

EASY DESSERT RECIPES & KNOW-HOW...

Easy Recipes...

Baked Apples... An old favorite is to core the apple first and fill the center with plump raisins. A great dessert with whipped cream.

Stuffed Fruit... For a tasty dessert the kids will love, first core an apple or pear. Replace the core with some fresh marshmallows.

Banana Ices... For a quick dessert that's also good for your kids, put bananas in the freezer and make popsicles!

Easter Fondue... Once Easter is over and your child is left with all that chocolate, why not use it all in one fell swoop. For a tasty chocolate fondue, melt the chocolate eggs and bunnies in a fondue pot and add some milk. Cut up chunks of different fruits and you'll have a scrumptious dessert your kids will devour!

Instant Chocolate Mousse... If you're in a hurry for a chocolate mousse, try this: Open a package of instant chocolate-pudding mix and whip with a cup of whipping cream until thick. Chill and serve.

Dessert Know-How...

Quick Melted Chocolate... If you require a small amount of melted chocolate for baking, wash out a used plastic milk bag and simply place the chocolate squares in it. Pop the bag upright into a pot of very hot water and when the chocolate has melted to the right consistency, simply snip off a corner of the bag. Voilà!

Creamier Puddings... Waxed paper placed over pudding before it has had time to cool will prevent a top layer of film from forming.

Nonstick Jelly Molds... Lightly oil the mold and rinse with hot water before using. The mold will lift off easily once the gelatin has set.

Gelatin Tip... You should always soften gelatin first in cold water and then dissolve it in hot water. Don't let the water boil, or it could lose it's gelling properties.

Going Bananas?... When baking bananas for a dessert, to cut down on the chance of them burning, dip the bananas in fruit juice first.

Cracked-Up Apples!... Baked apples won't crack if you peel a ½-inch band around the middle of the apple prior to baking.

Recycled Coconut Topping... Shredded coconut that has dried out is delicious toasted and sprinkled over desserts. Sprinkle on a cookie sheet and bake in a medium oven, shaking occasionally.

Made-To-Measure Marshmallows... If your recipe calls for miniature marshmallows and you have on hand the larger variety, simply cut with scissors dusted with flour.

BEVERAGES...

Save That Coffee... Don't pour that last cup of coffee down the drain! Pour it into a thermos bottle and have it later.

Freeze That Coffee... Freeze your leftover coffee in ice cube trays, for use with iced coffee. The same can apply for tea.

Bitter Coffee?... If you find your drip or perked coffee is a little bitter, simply add a pinch of salt to your coffeepot.

Iced-Coffee Sweetener... Always dissolve sugar in a little hot water for use in iced coffee or tea to prevent sugar from sinking to the bottom.

Storing Coffee Beans... Coffee beans stay fresh if kept in the freezer compartment of your refrigerator.

Storing Tea... Whether you use loose tea or tea bags, always keep it in a tightly sealed container. This will help prevent flavor loss.

Iced Tea Foggy?... To make your iced tea a little clearer, pour in a small amount of hot water.

Tea And Vitamin C!... Try this tasty hint. Add a pinch of grated orange rind to tea when steeping for a delicious flavor!

Bubbly, Anyone?... If your sparkling wine has lost it's sparkle, just drop a raisin into the bottle. The concentrated sugar in the raisin will help make your bubbly bubbly again!

Wine Storage... Wine should be stored on its side and in a dark, even-temperature, draft-free environment.

Wine-Cork Bits... If you find you have small pieces of cork in your wine from opening, simply use a tea strainer when pouring it into the glass.

Use Those Liqueur Dregs!... Here's a way to make good use of those small amounts of liqueur that never seem to get consumed. Blend about ½ cup of liqueur with 1 cup of milk and 2 cups of ice cream. Milkshakes with a kick! Experiment with different flavor ice creams and liqueurs.

Cocktail Dictionary... Translate cocktail terms as follows:

A Dash. . . . . 5 or 6 drops
A Pony . . . . 2 tablespoons
A Jigger . . . . 3 tablespoons
A Large Jigger . . . . . . 4 tablespoons

Keeping Hot Drinks Hot... Believe it or not, the shape of your drinking container makes a difference to how long the contents remain hot. It's said that a tall, thin mug or cup will maintain the temperature longer than the wide-brimmed variety.

WHAT TO DO WITH LEFTOVERS

POULTRY, MEATS & FISH...

Chicken Livers... Use your blender and favorite recipe to make a lively pâté out of leftover chicken livers.

Turkey Carcasses... Boil leftover turkey or chicken carcasses to make a broth that you can store for soups and casseroles later.

Ham... Use ham slices to decorate and liven up muffins. Split the centers and stuff with rolled ham. Tasty!

♦ Dice cooked ham for use in salads or omelets.

Pork... Slice leftover pork and add to rice dishes or soups.

Meat Loaf... Add leftover meat loaf to your spaghetti sauce!

♦ Make a meat loaf salad for sandwiches by mixing with onions and mayonnaise.

Bacon... Fry up that last piece or two of bacon and crumble for use in salads or as a topping.

♦ Strain your bacon fat and store it in the refrigerator. It's great for frying potatoes, eggs, etc.

Tuna Salad... Leftover tuna salad can be added to cooked macaroni. Sprinkle with cheese and bake for ½ hour. Instant casserole!

PASTA, RICE & VEGETABLES...

Pasta... Add leftover noodles to chicken or beef broth for a delicious "next-day" soup.

♦ Toss pasta with oil, vegetables and seasonings for a delightful cold noodle salad.

Rice... Mix with kidney beans, your favorite seasonings and toss. Makes an interesting side dish.

♦ Add olives and pimentos for a cold rice salad!

♦ Turn leftover rice into a rice pudding.

Vegetables... Keep leftover corn, peas, carrots, green beans, etc. for use in a rice salad.

♦ Make an interesting "garden" omelet.

♦ Add to your homemade or canned vegetable soup.

♦ Reheat baked potatoes. Slice at ½-inch intervals and stuff with garlic butter.

♦ Grated potatoes make a great meatloaf extender.

♦ Panfry leftover boiled potatoes or boil some eggs and make a potato salad.

♦ Roll mashed potatoes into balls, dip them in egg, then bread crumbs and bake until golden brown.

♦ Try putting leftover salad into your blender. Add some water or tomato juice and blend. You'll have a delicious and easy cold gazpacho soup.

FREEZING TIPS

TAKING CARE OF YOUR FREEZER ... & WHAT'S IN IT...

Efficiency... To keep your freezer efficient, keep it well stocked, even if you top it up with plastic bags filled with water.

Moving... When moving, let your freezer sit for at least 2 hours before plugging it in at your new location.

Power Failure... When the power goes off, do not open the freezer. Cover the freezer with blankets and it should maintain 32°F for up to 3 days, if left unopened.

♦ If only the freezer power is affected, check the fuse box or circuit breaker panel and the plug.

 ♦ To make sure your freezer hasn't defrosted while you were away on vacation, before you leave, place a jar of ice cubes in the freezer. When you return, if the cubes have lost their form and have refrozen into a solid piece, then you can bet your boots your food has too!

Containers... Use coffee cans with plastic lids for freezer storage.

♦ Plastic milk bags with their tops cut off make great freezer storage bags. Economical too!

♦ Draw air out of plastic freezer bags by using a drinking straw.

♦ Avoid using glass bottles with narrow necks for freezing. Fluids expand when frozen and may cause glass to break.

Dating... Keep a package of adhesive-backed labels handy for labeling and dating freezer items.

♦ Be sure to rotate items by date in the freezer to avoid spoilage from stale-dated items.

FREEZING MEATS, FRUITS & VEGETABLES...

Meats...

Cooked Meats... Add sauce or gravies to cooked meats to avoid drying out in the freezer.

Raw Meats... You may want to remove any foam trays when freezing meat. We've heard it's healthier that way.

Soups, Stews And Sauces...
When freezing a soup or stew, first place it in a strong plastic bag. Put the bag inside a square plastic container and freeze. When frozen, remove the bag which will have taken on the shape of the container. Saves space, & containers!

♦ And for a mess-free dinner, simply pop the frozen bag into boiling water!

Hamburgers... Don't add salt to hamburger patties intended for the freezer. The salt may create spoilage when combined with fat and shorten its freezer life.

Fruits...

Four Fruit-Freezing Facts... Choose firm, fresh fruit.

♦ Don't freeze large quantities at the same time. Fruit should be frozen quickly and smaller amounts will freeze faster.

♦ Always leave a small space at the top of the container. Fruit tends to expand when it freezes.

♦ To prevent the fruit you are preparing from discoloring when freezing, mix a pinch of ascorbic acid with the sugar when preparing.

Vegetables...

Leftover Vegetables... Throw your leftover vegetables in the blender, puree them and pour into ice cube trays. When frozen, transfer cubes to a plastic bag. They can now be used to flavor soups and stews.

♦ Vegetables that we eat raw generally don't freeze well ... like radishes, cucumbers and lettuce.

Cabbage... If you make cabbage rolls, place the leaves in a plastic bag first and freeze. When defrosted they'll be limp, which will facilitate rolling when making the cabbage rolls.

Tomatoes... Peel some tomatoes; then puree them. Pour the liquid into ice cube trays and place them in the freezer. When frozen, transfer them into plastic bags and you'll have instant tomato flavoring for your cooking.

Tomato Paste... Spoon out leftover tomato paste onto a waxed baking sheet or an ice cube tray. Freeze and pop into a brown paper bag. You'll have handy premeasured amounts!

And Remember... Fried or breaded foods and vegetables tend to become soggy when frozen. This also applies to meats.

FREEZING BAKED GOODS & DAIRY PRODUCTS...

Baked Goods...

Cakes... Iced cakes should be frozen unwrapped to avoid damaging the frosting. As soon as the icing freezes, wrap the cake securely and return to the freezer.

♦ Instead of freezing an entire cake or pie, slice, wrap and freeze individual pieces or quarters for use in lunches or dinners for two.

♦ Cake frosting made with brown sugar or egg whites doesn't do well in the freezer.

Waffles Etc.... The next time you serve waffles or french toast, make extras and freeze them. Reheat in your toaster.

Dairy Products...

Eggs... Eggs should never be frozen in the shell. Beat them first.

♦ Egg whites don't need any special preparation. However, egg yolks will do better if you add the following: For every six yolks you freeze, add one teaspoon of salt or one tablespoon of sugar.

♦ Hard-boiled eggs turn rubbery when frozen.

Cheese... The most effective way to freeze cheese is to keep it in its original package so there are no air leaks. When you want to use it, thaw portions of about 250 grams (½ lb.) in the refrigerator slowly to get the best results. Soft cheeses generally freeze best.

FREEZING THE REST...

Coffee... Freeze leftover coffee in ice cube trays to be used as a browning agent in gravies, or as a liquid in spice cakes. Once cubes are frozen, remove from tray and place in a brown paper bag before returning to the freezer.

Ice Cube Trick!... When storing extra ice cubes in your freezer, place them in brown paper bags. Evidently the cubes are less likely to stick to each other this way.

Wine... Freeze leftover wine as above to enhance gravies, soups, stews and drinks.

Exotic Ice Cubes... For "cocktail" ice cubes, freeze your cubes with maraschino cherries inside. For martinis, freeze with olives, cocktail onions or twists of lemon. For a summery touch, try adding a sprig of mint!

♦ Another colorful look is to take flower petals, say from a nasturtium or a rose, and freeze them into the ice cubes.

♦ Make giant ice cubes for the cooler by cutting pop cans in half. Throw away the top half and fill the bottom with water and freeze.

Clearer Ice Cubes... They say that boiling water makes clearer ice cubes!

Spices... Foods seasoned with pepper, garlic or vanilla don't freeze well. The flavors tend to fade.

♦ Spices and flavors like salt and onion tend to get stronger when frozen. So cut back on those spices if you intend freezing the food.

"TV" Dinners... If you're single and find grocery shopping for one a chore, shop for two and cook for two. Make another serving and freeze in trays for a quick homemade dinner.

♦ Cooking and freezing extra portions is a great idea for working mothers too and saves a lot of time doing dishes.

CATCHY KITCHEN HINTS

HANDY SUBSTITUTES...

No Bread Tag?... Clip your bread bag shut with a child's plastic barrette.

No Tea Cozy?... Here's a neat substitute for a tea cozy. Just take an old woolen toque and cut holes for the handle and spout. To make it more permanent, bind the edges of the holes you made.

No Coffee Filter?... A great replacement coffee filter is a clean J-cloth. Simply fold it into several layers to fit your holder. Recyclable too!

♦ You can also fashion a coffee filter by folding a paper towel and placing it in your holder.

No Funnel?... Make a funnel quickly and easily by cutting an empty, clean plastic bleach or liquid detergent bottle in half. Using the upper half, remove the cap and invert. Be sure to clean thoroughly though!

No Shrimp Deveiner?... A hook-type can opener makes an excellent shrimp deveiner. Neat and quick!

No Splatter Guard?... A metal colander placed over a frying pan, rim down, will allow steam to escape while eliminating splatters.

No Corkscrew?... You could try placing the neck of the wine bottle under hot water for a few minutes. Often this will cause the cork to pop out. Make sure the bottle has not just come out of the fridge though or it could crack.

♦ In addition, you might try wrapping your hand in a dish towel and giving the bottom of the bottle a few sharp thumps. The cork will sometimes protrude enough to grasp.

No Sink Plug?... Just use a wet tea bag!

No Pencil Sharpener?... A potato peeler works quite well as a pencil sharpener. Don't forget to wash it thoroughly after using it!

TIME- & MONEY SAVERS...

Time-Savers...

Uses For Saltshakers... Keep a saltshaker filled with flour. It comes in handy when dusting rolling pins or boards.

♦ Buy spices you often use in bulk and purchase inexpensive saltshakers to store them in.

♦ Keep a saltshaker handy for quick sprinkling while you cook. Combine ¾ salt and ¼ pepper in the same container (or to your own taste).

Veggie Transferal!... When transferring a large amount of chopped vegetables from your cutting board to a wok or wide-rimmed pot, scoop them up into a dustpan you keep just for that purpose. Fast and easy!

Double Your Results... The next time you are boiling veggies or pasta, pop in a few eggs and let them hard-boil along with the contents. This way you'll always have hard-boiled eggs for sandwiches, salads, etc.

Good To The Last Drop... To make sure you get that last drop out of your spray bottles, place some marbles in the bottom of the bottle. This will raise the liquid to meet the suction tube.

Opening "Easy Open" Cartons... A hook-type can opener is great for opening cardboard cartons. Especially those that have that little area surrounded by dots, saying "press here for easy opening"!

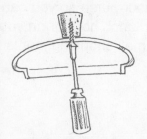

Insulated Pot Handles... If you lose the handle on your pot lid, take an ordinary cork and put it over the hole in the lid. Then, using a course-threaded screw, screw it from underneath up into the cork until it's nice and tight. A heat-resistant knob!

Time-Saver Dishes... Stock up on ovenproof baking dishes which allow you to go from oven to table without using more dishes and saving time as well.

Money Savers...

Recycled Cereal-Box Liners... Remove the wax paper from your empty cereal box and use it to wrap your kid's sandwiches in. Money saver!

Supermarket Smarts... Couponing is a great way to save $$$ galore on your regular grocery bills. Many books are available on the subject and most cities have traders clubs. Investigate what is available in your area, or start your own. Clip and save as many coupons as you can, trade with friends and neighbors for products you most often buy and keep a list of what coupons you have to help plan your weekly grocery list.

♦ Write your coupon list on the front of the envelope in which you store your coupons. Now you'll know exactly what coupons you have without having to sort through them. It's also more convenient to have them together.

♦ Some people attach their coupons to the matching product in their kitchen with a rubber band. When that product runs out, they don't have to search for the corresponding coupon.

♦ Keep a running grocery list in your purse so you can pick up items you need on your lunch hour or on your way to or from home. Several small shopping jaunts can take less time.

♦ To prevent your fruit from being bruised by other items when shopping, first place the fruit in plastic bags. Inflate the bags by blowing air into them, spin them and seal by tying a knot. Now your fruit will be protected from being bumped around.

♦ If you're single, invent an "imaginary friend" when shopping. Buy for two and cook for two. Freeze one portion for a quick homemade dinner.

♦ If you buy large quantities of canned goods, it's a good idea to mark the purchase date on the labels. This way you'll know if you've kept your cans too long.

NEAT IDEAS & GOOD ADVICE...

Neat Ideas...

A Simple Alarm... You'll know when the water boils dry by placing a spoon or jar lid in the bottom pan of your double boiler or steamer. The rattle of the spoon or lid will alert you.

No-Drip Creamer... Place a dab of butter or margarine under the spout of your creamer to prevent drips.

Opening Hard-To-Open Jars And Bottles... Wear a rubber glove to provide a good grip. It should open easily!

♦ A rubber band wrapped around the lid will also improve your grip.

Double-Duty Cooking Pot... If you find that you don't have enough pots or stove elements to go around, place a wire strainer in your cooking pot. Throw one vegetable in the strainer and the other vegetable in the bottom of the pot with the water. They'll cook along together.

Legible Measuring Spoons... If you find it difficult to read the raised markings on your measuring spoons, paint a strip of red nail polish over the measurements. Sand them lightly and the numbers will stand out clearly against the nail polish.

Blender "Shoes"... If you find that your blender is leaving black marks on your kitchen counter, glue some of those soft plastic medicine-bottle caps onto the feet of your blender. They make great little "overshoes"!

Static Whipping!... When whipping ingredients, place the bowl on a damp dishcloth. It won't move around as much as it would on the smooth countertop.

Taking Stock!... For those jars that are completely covered up with a large label, simply tear a strip off vertically down the entire label. Now you can see exactly how much of the contents are left in the jar.

"Grate" Tips!... To prevent grating your fingers on the cheese grater, here's an ingenious idea. Select three or four different size sewing thimbles. Place these on your fingers and you'll find you can comfortably grate much faster and closer.

♦ For neat and tidy grating, hold the hand grater (and whatever you're grating) inside a plastic shopping bag while you grate.

Food Wrapping Made Easy!... As you use up your food wrap, tearing it becomes harder, because there is less weight to the roll, so there is nothing to pull against. To fix this, stick a piece of lead pipe inside the roll to give you the weight you need to make it easier to tear.

The Indispensable Clothespin... It's a good idea to keep several clothespins in the kitchen, either the wooden or plastic variety. They're great for sealing just about any bag closed.

Recipe Tips... When you get a new recipe, first write it down on a piece of paper. Next, take out your favorite recipe book and tape the new recipe over a similar one in the book. Simply tape the top edge of the new recipe to the book so that you can read and compare both recipes. Next time you want to prepare that dish you only have to check the index to get the updated recipe.

♦ If you use recipe cards, try taking a cork and cutting a little slit across the top at a slight angle. Slip the recipe card into the slit. Not only will you be able to easily follow the recipe, but it'll keep the card from getting messy on the kitchen counter or table.

♦ To keep your paperback recipe book open and out of any messes, fetch a wooden pants hanger from your clothes closet. Now you can clamp the book open at the page you require and hang it up at eye level on a cupboard doorknob.

♦ Or place your loose recipes in a photo album. A binder-type album will facilitate organizing your recipes into categories.

A Reflective View... If you don't have a window above your kitchen sink, simply attach a framed mirror above your sink. Hang curtains from it to make it appear like a window. It'll make your kitchen seem larger and more cheerful!

Good Advice...

Poor-Fitting Pot Lids... When next you're boiling or braising, make sure your pot lid fits really snug. You'd be surprised how much cooking time and flavor is wasted by steam escaping through an ill-fitting pot lid.

Temperature Tips... Most nonstick pans will become discolored if they are subjected to heat above 450˚F.

♦ Ideal cooking temperatures are low to medium. Too-hot temperatures could cause:
~ meat shrinkage
~ scorched liquids (soup, milk, etc.)
~ rubbery dairy foods (eggs, cheese, etc.)
~ curdling
~ breakdown of essential nutrients (vitamin C, etc.)

Micro Magic... The best-shaped container for the microwave is a round one with low sides. Evidently this allows uniform  distribution of the waves throughout the food and thus cooks it better.

♦ Stir your food often when microwaving. But stir from the outside edge to the middle.

♦ Instead of using plastic wrap, cover your food in the microwave with one of those little container covers made of plastic (the ones that look like a miniature shower cap). In fact, if your bowl is large enough, a shower cap would be ideal!

Dishcloth Bacteria Buster... To remove bacteria from your kitchen dishcloth quickly and easily, try this method we heard about. Place your wet dishcloth in your microwave oven on high for about 30 seconds. Be careful when removing ... it'll be HOT! HOT! HOT!

Dishwasher Time-Saver... When loading the cutlery basket in your dishwasher, it's a good idea to give each of the basket's compartments its own item...like spoons in one, forks in another, etc. This will save you lots of time when transferring the cleaned cutlery to your cutlery drawer!

— ♦ —

CHAPTER 2

ORDER IN THE HOUSE

HOW TO ORGANIZE &
CLEAN ALMOST EVERYTHING
AROUND THE HOME!

PLAN AHEAD

- ♦ Clean one room at a time. If you are interrupted, at least one room is finished and you can continue cleaning later.

- ♦ When cleaning around the house, carry a bucket or basket filled with all the cleaning materials you might need. This eliminates trips back and forth, and saves time.

- ♦ Put on your leotards or exercise outfit when cleaning. The psychological effect will make all that bending and lifting seem like exercise instead of work.

HAPPINESS IS A CLEAN & TIDY KITCHEN

LARGE APPLIANCES...

Removing Dishwasher Film... The inside of your dishwasher will be film free if you do this occasionally. Fill washer with dirty dishes but make sure you have not included any silver or other metals. Place a bowl with ½ cup of bleach on the bottom rack and allow the machine to run through the wash cycle only. Fill the same bowl with ½ cup of vinegar and this time allow the machine to run through a full cycle.

Removing Dishwasher Stains... It's said that a quick way to get rid of those yellow stains in your dishwasher is to first allow your empty machine to fill for a wash. Then add a package of flavored orange crystals (the kind you make orange drinks out of) and allow the wash and rinse cycle to complete.

Hot Tips For Oven Spills... When spills occur, sprinkle with table salt. When the oven is cool, wipe up the salt. It will absorb the drippings.

♦ To dislodge baked-on spills, apply a paste of baking soda and water, with a little elbow grease!

♦ Or place a small dish of ammonia on the upper rack and a pan of water on the lower rack of a still-warm oven. Leave for ten to twelve hours or overnight. Air oven and wipe grease away with an all-purpose cleaner and warm water. An inexpensive way of oven cleaning.

♦ Prevention is better than cure! Avoid oven spills by placing casseroles and pies on a cookie sheet or in a larger pie plate.

Cleaning Oven Racks... Allow oven racks to soak in the tub while you're working on the inside of the oven.

And Oven Tops... Rubbing alcohol shines oven tops beautifully.

♦ Household ammonia diluted with water to half strength makes an excellent oven-top cleaner.

And Oven Window... To tackle that brown-stained oven window, make a paste of water and baking soda. Simply coat the inside of window with the mixture, leave for 10 minutes and then rinse off with water.

A Spotless Microwave Oven... For a quick and simple method of cleaning, wet a dishcloth and place in the center of your microwave. Turn on high and allow the cloth to sort of cook for about 30 to 40 seconds. The steam that this creates will help loosen any hardened spills and you can use the heated cloth to wipe the inside clean. Be careful. The cloth will be really hot!

A Fresh Microwave!... To freshen up and deodorize your microwave, place a bowl of water in the oven and add 3 or 4 slices of lemon. Cook on high for 30 seconds.

A Fresh Fridge!... Freshen up the inside of your refrigerator by wiping periodically with a cloth moistened with vinegar...a great way to prevent mildew.

♦ A little dab of vanilla, lemon or orange extract on a small pad of cotton will keep the refrigerator smelling sweet.

♦ Baking soda will keep odors away for several months. Just open the box and place on a middle shelf.

♦ Many common fridge odors may be removed by placing a small tub filled with charcoal briquettes in the middle rack of your fridge. Every so often, you might want to revitalize the briquettes by heating them mildly in a cast-iron pan on the stove.

Defrosting Your Freezer... Should you own a fridge whose freezer is not self-defrosting, try this. Wipe the inside of the freezer compartment with a cloth dampened with glycerin. When it's time to defrost again, the chunks of ice will drop without effort.

Whiter-Than-White Appliances... Keep white appliances sparkling clean and prevent yellowing by washing with a mixture of ½ cup of bleach, 8 cups of water and ½ cup of baking soda. Rinse well.

SMALL APPLIANCES...

Blender Cleaning... Add a small amount of dishwashing liquid to your blender. Fill halfway with hot tap water and blend. Instantly clean!

Messy Mixers?... Prevent messy splatters when using electric mixers by covering the bowl securely with foil. Punch holes in the foil for the beater shafts and beat away!

♦ Use vegetable oil to lubricate egg beaters for an easy cleanup.

♦ Or lubricate with glycerin before using.

Can-Opener Magic!... Run a piece of waxed paper through the can-opening process to keep it operating smoothly. Works with manual can openers too.

Kettle Kleaners... Clean your kettle periodically by boiling equal parts vinegar and water in it. Let it sit overnight and rinse well in the morning. The lime deposits will wash away.

♦ Or fill the kettle with water, sprinkle some cream of tartar into it and let it boil.

Coffeemakers... Give your coffeemaker a treat every so often. Clean it by filling the reservoir with water and adding 2 tablespoons of water softener. Run the machine through its cycle.

Electric Frying Pan... To remove caked-on grease, cover the surface of the pan with baking soda. Let it sit for 15 minutes or so and then rub with a wet cloth. Rinse with warm water.

Meat Grinders... A quick and efficient way to clean your meat grinder is to take a raw potato and run it through the grinder. Great for electric and hand grinders.

Garbage Disposer... To clean your garbage disposer and sharpen the blades at the same time, fill ice cube trays with equal parts water and vinegar. When frozen, drop the cubes into the disposer and turn it on.

♦ For garbage disposer odors, pour in a cup of vinegar and then immediately run the cold water tap for 2 or 3 minutes.

COOKWARE & FLATWARE...

Cookware...

Cleaning Enamel Broiling Pans... Remove tough-to-clean food and grease from broiling pans by  covering the bottom with a layer of powdered detergent or water softener. Cover with a wet towel and leave for several hours. This should loosen baked-on grease enough to wash without effort.

Nonstick Pots And Pans... To remove stains on nonstick finishes, mix 2 tablespoons baking powder, ½ cup chlorine bleach and 1 cup of water. Put the mixture in the stained pot and let it boil for about 10 minutes. Wash with soap and water, dry, then rub a little vegetable oil on the surface. Don't allow the mixture to boil over or it might leave spots on the exterior finish of the pot.

Saving Scorched Pans... Remove as much burned food as possible from the pan. Sprinkle the bottom with baking soda to form a good layer over the burned area. Add 1½ cups water and let it stand overnight. Use a rubber spatula to scrape and lift remains.

♦ To remove burned food from enamel pots, cover the bottom of the pot with water and add 4 or 5 tablespoons of salt. Let the pot soak overnight and then bring the mixture to a boil.

Tackling Cast-Iron Cookware... Commercial oven cleaners will clean the OUTSIDE of cast-iron cookware. Use as directed but make sure not to use it on the inside. Rinse well after cleaning.

♦ To clean the INSIDE of your cast-iron cookware, instead of washing after each use with soap and water, try shaking salt on the cookware and wiping clean. Keeps food from sticking when frying and needs only to be washed every other use. A light coating of cooking oil won't hurt either. Prevents rust!

♦ Pancakes won't stick if you rub the griddle with salt first.

Copper Cleaning... A little salt and vinegar will clean copper bottoms on pots and pans. Just sprinkle on, rub lightly and wash as usual.

♦ Or rub with a lemon dipped in salt. Wipe off with a wet cloth, dry and apply lemon oil, car or floor wax.

♦ In a pinch, you can sometimes clean copper with ketchup.

Rusty Baking Dishes?... Rust can be removed from metal baking dishes by scouring with a raw potato and your favorite detergent.

"Stainless"-Steel Teapot Stains... For a quick way to clean your stainless-steel teapot, simply pop a denture-cleaning tablet into the pot and top it up with warm water. Leave for an hour or two and then give the pot a good rinse.

The Gentle Scraper... To make a great scraper that is strong but won't damage the surface of your pots and pans, take

a wooden spoon and a handsaw. Square off the rounded end by cutting off half the spoon's bowl and sand the edge smooth.

Flatware...

Clever Cutlery Cleaning... Restore the shine to your kitchen cutlery by simply rubbing the item with an ordinary cork!

♦ Remove egg stains on flatware by rubbing with damp salt.

Collective Cutlery Cleaning!... When washing a lot of cutlery by hand, pop a colander into the soapy water. As you wash, put the cutlery into the colander. Now you can rinse all the cutlery at the same time by running the full colander under the cold water tap.

Six-Second Silver Cleaning... Run about a quart of hot water into your kitchen or bathroom sink (cool enough not to burn you). Dissolve 1 tablespoon washing soda* (or laundry water softener) and 1 tablespoon salt in the water. Place a  sheet of aluminum foil on the bottom of the sink and place your tarnished silver on the foil. The silver that's both touching the foil and covered by the water should become clean within 10 seconds. If badly tarnished, rub silver item with a cloth after removing it from the water. Works on silver and gold jewelry too.

♦ Or next time you boil potatoes, cool the leftover potato water and dip your tarnished silverware into it.

CHINA, GLASSWARE & KITCHENWARE...

China...

Tea Stains... Tea stains can be removed safely from fine china by rubbing gently with a cloth sprinkled with baking soda or salt.

---

* Important: Outside North America, see "washing soda" reference in glossary of terms on page 398.

Protect Your Borders!... China with gold borders needs special care when washing. Never use hot water, only warm and don't rub detergent on the gold areas.

Cracking Up?... To prevent your unbordered china plates from cracking when washing in hot water, slide them into the water sideways. This will distribute the heat evenly throughout the plate.

♦ To avoid cracking, china dishes and bowls should always be warmed before placing hot contents on them.

♦ If your fine china plates have developed thin, spider cracks in them, place them in a pan of warm milk for 30 minutes. The cracks should disappear!

Removing Scratches... To remove black cutlery marks from the glazed surface of your fine china plates, try this. Apply some toothpaste to a clean soft cloth and rub the marks gently.

Preventing Scratches... Place paper doilies or napkins between stacked fine china plates to eliminate scratching.

♦ The rubber rings from preserve jars also work well as dividers between your china plates.

♦ China cups shouldn't be stacked on top of each other. They'll chip that way. Instead, suspend them from cup hooks under your cupboard shelf.

Buying China... To check if china is flawed, hold the item in the palm of your hand and tap it lightly with a pencil. Unflawed china will have a clear bell-like ring. Flawed china will have a dull ring or no resonance at all.

Glassware...

Crystal Care... Always slip delicate glassware and crystal into hot water on its side. Place a rubber mat on the bottom of your sink for extra protection against cracking and chipping.

Crystal Clear!... Vinegar cleans crystal beautifully. Wash in a mixture of 1 cup white vinegar and 3 cups warm water. Allow to air-dry.

Stuck Glasses?... When two glasses are stuck together, fill the top glass with cold water and submerge the bottom glass in hot water. Gently pull the top glass away.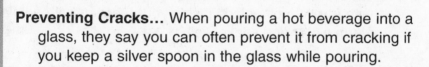

Preventing Cracks... When pouring a hot beverage into a glass, they say you can often prevent it from cracking if you keep a silver spoon in the glass while pouring.

Cleaning Heat-Resistant Baking Dishes... To remove burned remains from heat-resistant glass baking dishes, warm some liquid dish soap and allow it to sit in the item for 30 minutes or so. Rinse well with clean water.

Kitchenware...

Preventing Plastic-Container Stains... To prevent tomato-based foods from staining your plastic containers, soak the container and lid in cold water for 5 minutes or so before filling.

And Eliminating Their Odors!... Eliminate odors in plastic containers by placing ordinary newspaper, crumpled to a ball, inside the container before securing the lid. Odors should be gone overnight.

A Gleaming Grater!... Rub a small amount of salad oil or butter on the grater before using it. Cleaning up is a breeze.

♦ Keep a small toothbrush handy to remove foods from your grater.

Dental Solution!... A piece of dental floss comes in handy for cleaning awkward utensils such as pizza cutters and can openers.

Bright Thermos Tips... Freshen up thermos bottles or insulated coffeepots by filling with warm water mixed with 2 tablespoons baking soda.

♦ Save your egg shells and dry them out. Crush them with a rolling pin, place inside your thermos with a little warm water and shake well.

Wooden Cutting Boards... Slice a lemon or lime and rub the board vigorously. Rinse with cold water. Clean and fresh smelling too!

SINKS, COUNTERS & KITCHEN STORAGE...

Sinks...

Cleaning Stainless-Steel Sinks... Rubbing alcohol removes spots on stainless steel.

♦ Clean your stainless-steel sink by wiping with a warm, soapy cloth. Rinse in hot water. Wipe with a dry cloth.

♦ To remove remnants of food and dish-soap film, and deodorize your sink at the same time, scour with salt.

Kitchen Sink Plugged?... Pour in ½ cup baking soda and ½ cup vinegar. Flush with boiling water. For grease blocks, pour in ¼ cup washing soda and ½ cup hot water.

♦ Or mix together 1 cup baking soda, 1 cup salt and ¼ cup cream of tartar. Weekly, pour 5 tablespoons of mixture down the sink followed with a kettle of boiling water.

Curative Plumbing... Sometimes drains can be unplugged by simply pouring about 5 or 6 tablespoons of baking soda down the drain. Immediately add ⅔ cup vinegar and a kettle of boiling water once the bubbling stops.

No Plunger Plumbing... Try using a Frisbee and hot water!

Counters...

Removing Tea And Coffee Stains From Counters... If the tea stains are on your kitchen countertop, simply mix up a paste of baking soda and water and apply it to the mark. Leave for 15 minutes then rinse off.

♦ Fill a small squeeze container with equal parts laundry bleach and water. Use it for stubborn counter stains. Rinse immediately with clean water.

Everyday Counter Cleaning... For matte-finish counters, apply club soda. Rinse with warm water and dry well.

♦ Never use an abrasive cleanser on plastic laminate counters. It's too harsh. Simply wipe with a wet cloth. For persistent marks try cleaning with lemon juice.

Rusty Cleanser Cans?... To avoid cleanser-can rust marks on your kitchen counter, wrap a strip of plastic insulation tape around the bottom of the can.

Rusty Steel-Wool Marks?...

To prevent your steel wool leaving rust marks on your kitchen counter, make a decorative holder to keep by the kitchen sink. Cut an empty liquid detergent bottle 2 inches from the bottom, forming a small container. Make a lid to fit by cutting 2 inches from the top of the bottle.

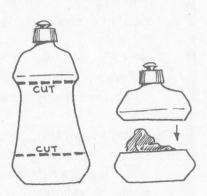

Kitchen Storage...

Cupboard Top Containers... Cover several boxes with wallpaper to match the decor of your kitchen and place them in the space between the top of your kitchen cupboards and your ceiling. They're great for storing things like plastic containers and recipe books you don't often use. Cut a handhold in the front of each box to make it easier to lift down.

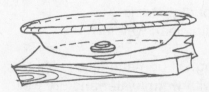

Spices At Your Fingertips!... By simply hammering a nail through the center of an old tin pie plate into your cupboard shelf and placing a couple of washers between the plate and the shelf, you'll have created a handy lazy Susan for your spice jars.

Clever Closet Storage... Shoe bags are handy when hung in the kitchen closet to hold cords, brushes, whisks and vacuum cleaner attachments.

Steel-Wool Storage... To prevent your steel-wool pad from rusting, store it in a bowl of water to which you've added 3 tablespoons of baking soda. Keep it in the cupboard under your sink for easy access.

Those Leaky Containers... Save your old plastic tablecloths and shower curtains. Cut them to size and line your kitchen drawers with them. Great for leaky containers!

Jewelry Hang-Ups!... Screw a cup hook beside the sink (not over it) to hang rings and watches when washing dishes.

IN GENERAL...

Instant Kitchen Deodorizers... Sprinkle cinnamon into a pan of boiling water. The aroma is truly appetizing.

♦ Lift cooking odors by placing some parsley in your cast-iron pan. Place over a low heat for five minutes.

♦ Wintergreen oil dabbed on cotton and placed out of sight, keeps your kitchen sweet smelling.

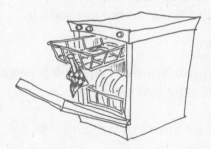

The "Ever-Clean" Dishcloth!... You'll always have a clean dishcloth on hand if you tie it to the rack of your dishwasher. It'll get cleaned right along with your dishes!

Easy Glass Pickup... Pick up those tiny pieces of broken glass by using a slice of fresh bread!

Easy Egg Pickup... If you accidentally drop an egg on the kitchen floor, sprinkle some salt on the broken egg. The salt will absorb the egg and allow you to mop it up with a cloth or paper towel.

Cleaning Straw Place Mats... Dissolve 1 cup of salt in a quart of warm water. Wash a section of the mat using a soft brush dipped in the solution. Air-dry in the sun before proceeding to the next section.

BRIGHT BATHROOM TIPS

BATHTUBS, SINKS & SHOWERS...

Bathtubs...

Bathtub Ring... If you're troubled with bathtub ring, it can often be prevented by softening your bathwater. Next time you run your bath, add ½ cup of baking soda to the water.

Getting Rid Of Enamel Bathtub Stains... Apply a paste of lemon juice and borax to badly stained areas.

♦ Remove old yellow water stains by rubbing with a mixture of salt and turpentine.

♦ Badly stained tubs need a special treatment. Scrub well with a scrub brush dipped in a mixture of cream of tartar and hydrogen peroxide.

Bathtub Mold... If you find mold forming around your bathtub, try scrubbing the area with vinegar. Rinse with clean water.

♦ If the mold persists, soak a cloth in laundry bleach and lay it on the moldy areas. Allow to sit overnight and then wash off with warm water and liquid detergent.

Bathtub Decals... Bathtub decals are great, unless you want them removed. Try soaking in mineral spirits and scrape until the decals are lifted. Sprinkle with cleanser and scrub with a mildly abrasive pad to remove glue. Once done, bring the shine back to the enamel by waxing the entire tub with car wax and shine with a dry cloth.

♦ Some say that decals may be removed by applying some rubbing alcohol and then scraping them off with a popsicle stick or similar implement.

♦ Some other suggestions are lighter fluid, nail-polish remover, baby oil or paint thinner.

Sinks...

Cleaning Porcelain Sinks... Porcelain sinks can be cleaned periodically with household bleach. Pour several capfuls over a cloth and rub the stains. Rinse well.

♦ Fill your sink with hot water and drop in a couple of denture tablets. Leave for a while and your sink should gleam! If you have any small porcelain items that need cleaning, throw them into the sink as well.

Keeping Soap Dishes Clean... Try cutting a sponge approximately ½-inch thick to fit the inside of your soap dish. The sponge will soak up any water left on the bar of soap, and prevent slimy buildup. Rinse the sponge every other day.

Showers...

Shiny Shower Walls... Some people say that you should apply car wax to the tiles in your shower stall. It has the same effect on shower water and tile as it does on rainwater and a car finish!

Shower Curtains... Soap film is quickly and easily removed from plastic shower curtains. Place several large bath towels in the washing machine along with the shower curtain. Add ½ cup vinegar. Remove curtain before spin cycle and hang immediately.

Shower Doors... Wash the doors with white vinegar. Rinse and wipe dry.

♦ To prevent those unsightly soap-scum marks, apply some lemon oil to the inside of the door.

Shower Tracks... To ensure your shower doors will operate smoothly, apply a light film of petroleum jelly on the inside of the tracks. Petroleum jelly will also help prevent your metal shower rods from rusting.

Showerheads... Remove lime deposits from showerheads by removing head and bringing to boil in a mixture of equal parts vinegar and water.

Shower Drains... Keep drains from clogging with hair by placing a piece of nylon netting in the drain. The netting dries quickly and when removed from the drain, so is the hair.

TOILETS & TILES...

Toilets...

Toilet-Ring Tricks... Remove toilet rings with a paste of lemon juice and borax. Allow to set before scrubbing away.

◆ You might also try this method. Pour a little white vinegar into the toilet bowl, let it stand for an hour, then brush and flush.

◆ Some say that if you pour cola into your toilet bowl, let it sit for an hour or so and then flush, it'll clean your toilet beautifully!

◆ Yet another environment-friendly toilet cleaner is vitamin C. Depending on how bad the stain is, simply place 2 or 3 tablets in the water. Let stand for 2 or 3 hours, and flush.

Toilet-Tank Condensation? No Sweat!... To stop condensation forming on the outside of your toilet tank, first shut the water off to the tank and drain it. Apply a thin coat of paste wax (floor or car will do) to the inside of the tank. Simple!

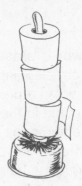

Keep A Handle On Your Toilet Rolls...
The next time you buy toilet rolls, slip
a few of them over the handle of your
toilet brush. So if your memory fails
you, your toilet rolls won't!

Tiles...

Cleaning Bathroom Tile... Mix a solution of 1 cup ammonia,
1 cup vinegar and ½ cup washing soda in a bucket of
warm water. Wash down the tiles and rinse thoroughly.

♦ Another method is to stir 1 ounce of unpasteurized
cider apple vinegar into a liter of water and, with a
clean cloth, rub the solution over the area.

♦ For quick rinsing, run the hot shower for a while with
the door closed. The steam will form beads of water
that can easily be dried with a soft cloth.

Cleaning Tile Grout... Use white toothpaste and an old
toothbrush to clean tile-grout stains. The pumice in
toothpaste is a sufficient abrasive.

♦ Or apply some bleach with a toothbrush. For caulking
between wall and tub, leave a rolled cloth soaked with
bleach on it for 3 or 4 hours.

THE REST OF THE STORY...

Chrome Cleaning... Chrome fixtures in your bathroom may
be brought to a beautiful shine simply by applying vinegar
and buffing with a soft cloth.

♦ Another quick chrome cleaner is rubbing alcohol.

♦ Or a quick spray and rub with your regular window cleaner.

Towel Tidiness... If your family bathroom seems to self-destruct daily, try this idea. Give each member of the family a towel rack of their own. Assign certain towels for each person to use (favorite colors is the easiest way). Presto! No more second-guessing when about to dry your face and you'll be pleasantly surprised at the decreased laundry load.

Instant Towel Rack... Make use of that old wine rack in the bathroom. Roll up towels and place in bottle slots for a creative and decorative touch.

Defogging Your Mirror... Next time, clean your bathroom

mirror by smearing shaving cream over the surface and then wiping it off well with a clean cloth. This will prevent your mirror from fogging up from the steam for several weeks or until you next clean it.

Those Hard To Reach Spots... Keep an extra toothbrush in the bathroom to use for cleaning those awkward places, like behind the faucets. It'll also clean bath-plug chains well.

Mat Mildew?... To prevent your bath mat from collecting mildew, keep a pant hanger in the bathroom. After you shower or bath, hang the mat up in the hanger. This way it'll air on both sides and discourage odor and mildew.

Shampoo Leftovers?... If you find that the shampoo you've bought is not a family favorite, why not pour it into your pump dispenser for washing your hands. It works well and is milder on your hands than regular hand soap.

Wastebasket Wisdom... The next time you remove your wastebasket liner, and before you put the new liner in, slip 5–6 liners in the bottom of the basket. This way you'll always have one on hand.

FURNITURE: ITS CARE & CLEANING

WOODEN FURNITURE...

Homemade Polishers... A great homemade polish can be made from equal parts of vinegar, turpentine and boiled linseed oil. Bottle it and shake well before using. Apply with a soft cloth and polish with another clean cloth.

♦ Or mix one part lemon juice to two parts olive or vegetable oil for another great polisher.

♦ A soft chamois does a great job of dusting and polishing at the same time.

Homemade Polish Remover... A solution of equal parts vinegar and water will serve as an economical polish remover. Moisten a cloth with the solution and wipe until dry.

Reaching Those Tiny Crevices... To clean tiny crevices in carved furniture, use a cotton-wrapped orange stick or cotton swab.

♦ Or spray the bristles of an artist's paintbrush with furniture polish to dust and polish at the same time.

Applying Extra Elbow Grease... Getting a perfect shine is sometimes tough work. Try wrapping a brick or heavy piece of wood really well with buffing cloths. The extra weight means you won't have to press as hard.

Remember... Don't polish any wooden surface when it is damp or white patches may appear.

Getting Rid Of Sticky Marks... Here's a good homemade furniture cleaner for wiping up sticky marks. Mix 1 tablespoon turpentine and 3 tablespoons boiled linseed oil in a quart of hot water. Mix well and allow to cool. Wring a soft cloth in the solution and wipe where needed. Dry at once with a clean soft cloth and rub to polish.

And White Spots... Remove white spots on mahogany by covering the spot with a thick layer of petroleum jelly. Wait 48 hours before wiping off.

And Water Rings... Try applying a paste of cooking oil and salt. Wait 15 minutes and wipe off. Polish as usual.

♦ Or apply a small amount of toothpaste and baking soda to a damp cloth and rub the stain lightly.

♦ Another good idea is to apply mayonnaise liberally over the water ring and leave overnight; wipe off with a soft dry cloth the next day. That should do the trick.

Remedy For Graying Wood Surfaces... When a whitish-gray film appears on wood furniture, mix a small amount of vinegar (1–2 tablespoons) with a pint of water and soak a soft cloth in it. Wring the cloth lightly and let remaining mixture in the cloth drip onto the wood surface. Rub lightly. If this doesn't take, sanding may be required.

Cleaning Black Lacquer Items... Make a really strong pot of tea and let it cool. Dip a soft cloth into the tea and rub it on the surface gently. Wipe off with a soft, dry cloth and you should end up with a smudge-free luster on your black lacquer furniture.

Cleaning Antiques... Here's an antique-cleaning tip. Mix a solution of 2 parts turpentine to 1 part boiled linseed oil, or use equal parts turpentine with boiled linseed oil and vinegar. Apply with a soft cloth and rub with another clean, soft cloth to polish.

Deodorizing Antiques... To remove musty odors from antique cupboards and drawers, take some oil of wintergreen and rub it sparingly on the inside of the item. When the wintergreen smell disappears, so should the musty odor.

♦ Or apply fabric softener to a cloth and rub it on the inside of the piece.

♦ If you place a piece of charcoal in an old container, you should find odors will be kept to a minimum.

♦ A last resort is to apply some boiled linseed oil to the inside and allow it to dry. Then take a good lacquer or shellac and brush over the area.

♦ To remove odors from old boxes or trunks, take a slice of bread, soak it in vinegar and place in the container for about 12 hours.

Unsticking Paper From Wood... Try soaking the paper in cooking oil for a few minutes. Rub with a cloth to "roll" paper off.

Unsticking Wax From Wood... To remove candle-wax spills from wooden furniture, soften the wax first with your hair dryer set on medium heat. When it starts to melt the wax, wipe the wax off with a soft cloth. Then wipe the area with a mild vinegar solution and polish as usual.

Treating Heat Marks... Remove heat marks from varnished or shellacked wood surfaces by dabbing spirits of camphor on the spot with a soft cloth. Allow to dry and then polish.

♦ For lacquered wood surfaces, apply a paste of powdered pumice and linseed oil. Rub in direction of the grain, and polish. Rub with toothpaste if the mark persists.

Burns On Wooden Furniture... Mix vegetable oil with powered pumice or rottenstone to make a paste. Apply paste to burned area only, rubbing it gently into the grain. Wipe clean and polish as usual. For minor burns, try toothpaste.

Invisible Scratches!... You can conceal scratches in dark wood by dyeing the scratch with iodine. For lighter wood, rub with the cut surface of walnut or Brazil-nut meat.

♦ Crayons also work well. Select the right color and melt a small amount. Work the melted wax into the scratch or nick until concealed.

Did You Know... If you keep any wood furniture too near a heat source, it may crack or warp. Alternatively if you keep furniture in a damp atmosphere it may swell, making drawers difficult to open. For the latter, try using a little soap along drawer runners for a smooth glide.

CANE, WICKER, PLASTIC & LEATHER FURNITURE...

Cane...

Cleaning Cane... To clean cane, add a little lemon juice and salt to some warm water. Then take a stiff brush, dip it into the solution and scrub the cane well. This method will also help to prevent the cane from yellowing.

How To "Raise Cane"... Tighten up sagging cane seats by sponging both sides with hot soapy water to which you've added a few spoonfuls of salt. Rinse with a clean wet cloth and allow to dry in the sun. When almost dry, cover caning with a towel and run a hot iron over it.

Wicker...

Dos & Don'ts For Wicker Furniture... Don't leave wicker outside in freezing weather. The coldness will cause wicker to become brittle and split.

♦ Wicker furniture requires moisture to prevent dryness, so turn the humidifier on occasionally, especially during winter months.

Cleaning Wicker... Clean wicker furniture by scrubbing with a stiff brush dipped in warm salt water. The salt prevents wicker from yellowing.

Plastic...

Shining Outdoor Plastic Furniture... Apply a small amount of toothpaste to the plastic surface and rub in. Buff with a clean cloth. This tip helps remove scratches from plastic as well.

♦ Or rub with a mild metal polish to remove any marks. Then rinse and buff with a soft cloth.

♦ Never use harsh abrasive cleaners or strong bleach to remove stains or marks. Acetone or gasoline is also a no-no!

Leather...

Cleaning... Saddle soap cleans leather beautifully.

♦ Leather shouldn't be wet too much. Simple marks can often be removed with a cloth dampened with the foam from a mild soap-flake detergent and water solution.

♦ Some people say that to restore leather's luster, try wiping the leather with a cloth dampened with milk.

♦ To remove those unsightly grease stains from leather, you may want to try dabbing a little stiffened egg white to the leather and then rub with a soft cloth.

Leather Softener... Several drops of olive oil wiped on with a soft cloth may help soften hardened leather upholstery.

Leather Preserver... Some say that to preserve your leather after cleaning it, rub on a layer of petroleum jelly, and leave it on for 3–4 hours. Wipe off with a soft cloth.

Remember... Always test on an inconspicuous area of the leather item you are treating first.

UPHOLSTERY CARE...

What To Do About Grease Stains On Upholstery...
Sprinkle liberally with salt as soon as the accident occurs. Allow salt to absorb grease, then brush off.

Bloodstains... As soon as possible, cover bloodstains with a paste of cornstarch and water. Allow to dry and brush off. Repeat if necessary. Not for velvet or velour upholstery.

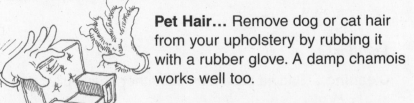

Pet Hair... Remove dog or cat hair from your upholstery by rubbing it with a rubber glove. A damp chamois works well too.

Back To Front Cushions... If you find the front of your seat cushions are getting a little worn, but you can't turn them around because of a zipper in the cushion cover, try this tip. Using an invisible mending stitch, sew the flaps that cover the zipper closed. Now you can reverse the cushions.

Sliding Seat Cushions?... To prevent your couch seat cushions from sliding forward, pin or sew some hand towels on the base of the couch under the cushions. This will provide a slip-resistant surface for the seat cushions.

Repairing Couch Rips And Holes... Snip a section of matching fabric from the back, bottom flap of your couch and sew it over the damaged area using an invisible thread, like hair or thin fishing line.

DUSTING...

Instant Dusters!... Use old woolen or terry socks as dusters.

- ◆ Or, sew a pair of mitts out of an old hand towel. Great for dusting venetian blinds because you can clean both sides of the slat with one movement.

Dust Cloth Treatment... Dip cheesecloth squares in a mixture of ½ cup lemon oil and 1 pint hot water. Squeeze out excess moisture and dry thoroughly. Store cloths in clean coffee cans with secure lids.

- ◆ Or mix 3 teaspoons ammonia, 3 teaspoons laundry soap powder, 5 tablespoons of boiled linseed oil and 5 cups of slightly warmed water. Drop a soft cloth into the mixture and let it sit overnight. Hang dry and use.

Washing Your Dusters... Replace your cloth dusters after a couple of washings. After that they tend to lose their ability to pick up the dust.

Dusting And Deodorizing At The Same Time... For a twofold use of your duster, spray it with your favorite air freshener.

Dusting Your TV... When dusting your TV or venetian blinds, use a soft cloth that has been dampened with fabric softener. This will reduce the static, which collects dust.

GETTING THE "ROYAL CARPET" TREATMENT

CARPET CLEANING...

Sounds Corny, But... You'll liven up a solid, light-colored carpet by brushing in cornmeal before vacuuming.

♦ Another way to brighten up your carpet is to apply a mixture of 3 parts hot water to 1 part vinegar. Dip a cloth into the mixture, squeeze any excess liquid out, then rub the carpet thoroughly and allow to dry. Once it's dry, heat some bread crumbs and rub them into your carpet gently. Finally, vacuum the carpet well.

Homemade Carpet Shampoo... Use ½ cup powdered detergent, 1 teaspoon ammonia and a quart of warm water. Mix in a bowl, stirring constantly to work up a layer of froth. Using froth only, rub lightly with a sponge or cloth over the entire carpet. When necessary, continue stirring solution to get additional froth. Allow carpet to dry. Vacuum entire area.

Protecting Furniture During The Shampoo... Keep furniture legs free from damage when shampooing the carpet by slipping plastic baggies over the legs. This will also protect

your carpet from rust stains caused by metal legs and from smudges from dampened furniture oil.

Removing Carpet Stains... If the carpet stain is still wet, try pouring a little club soda on the stained area. Wait a moment and blot until moisture is absorbed.

♦ If you don't find the stain right away, mix a diluted solution of vinegar, soap and water. Dampen a cloth with this solution and press firmly against the stain for several moments. Blot dry with a rinse cloth.

♦ Shaving cream is a great emergency carpet-stain remover. Use on ketchup, chocolate, tea, coffee, wine, even blood.

♦ Salt is also a great pepper-upper for tired carpets and is a terrific absorbing agent for mud stains. Sprinkle it liberally on fresh stains and allow to soak up the moisture. Then vacuum.

♦ Never rub a carpet to soak up liquid that has been spilled. Using as much dry cloth as you need, blot the area until most of the liquid has been absorbed.

♦ If your first treatment fails, let the carpet dry before you try something else. You'll have a better idea how much of the stain remains once the carpet is dry.

Homemade Carpet-Stain Removers... Add 1 teaspoon of vinegar to a pint of Homemade Carpet Shampoo (see earlier tip) and together to form a lather. Rub stain very gently with a lathered sponge and rinse with clean water.

♦ Mix equal parts salt and baking soda, add several drops of white vinegar and enough water to make a paste. Check carpet for color fastness, then apply the paste to the stain and let it set. When it's dry, brush it away and the stain should go with it. For a particularly nasty stain, scrub it when you first apply the paste.

Pet "Accidents"... Pour liberal amounts of club soda on the area and blot immediately with paper towels. If odor is there the next day, cover the area with about ¼ inch of baking soda and let it sit for 2 days, then vacuum.

♦ If stain or odor persists, try this method. Add 1 cup of hydrogen peroxide to 1 tablespoon of baking soda. Add ½ teaspoon of dish soap and stir well. Apply solution to the stained area with a sponge. Let dry and vacuum.

Vomit Stains... Remove as much as possible with a spoon, spatula or paper towel. Then sponge with a solution of 1 tablespoon of borax and 2 cups of water. If any stain remains, rub with some foamy shaving cream.

Removing Candle Wax... Place a folded paper towel over the hardened wax. Hold a warm iron on the paper towel for a few seconds. When you lift the iron you will see the paper has absorbed the melted wax. Several applications with fresh paper towels are usually necessary.

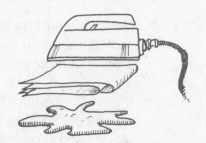

♦ Any residual dye stains from colored candles can often be removed by dabbing with paint thinner.

Removing Chewing Gum... Hold an ice cube against the chewing gum until it hardens. Then chip the gum away.

Removing Soot... Vacuum excess soot then sprinkle table salt liberally over the area. Leave for a few minutes and vacuum again.

Glue On The Wrong Side Of The Carpet?... Remove with a cloth dipped in vinegar.

GENERAL CARPET & RUG CARE...

Drying Rugs... After you've washed your rugs, the best way to dry them is to hang them on the clothesline. However, the normal clothespins are generally too small to hold the rug in place. So use 2 or 3 pant hangers instead. They'll hold the rug well.

Static Treatment... Put an end to carpet static with this simple treatment. Combine ½ liter of fabric softener with 5 liters of water. Decant it into a spray bottle and spritz your carpet with it until it is fairly moist. Don't soak the carpet or you could damage the backing. Let it dry overnight and that should do the trick for several weeks.

Raising The Pile... Raise the flattened carpet pile by holding a steam iron over the area. Allow the steam to penetrate the pile and brush the spot immediately. Remember not to touch the carpet with the iron!

♦ Dampen a chamois and fold several times. Place it over the flattened nap and leave for several hours. The nap should lift right up.

Cigarette Burns... Snip away the singed edges with fine manicure scissors or a razor blade. If it's still noticeable, remove several strands of carpet yarn from another area. Use tweezers to pull out the severely burned fibers and discard. Apply glue to the burned area and press down the clean fibers into the spot. Place a heavy object over the burned area and allow several days to dry completely, before walking on it.

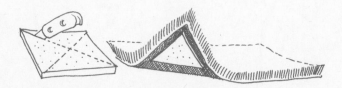

A Carpet That Curls?... Try cutting a triangle of tile or linoleum and applying it to the underside of each curled corner using double-sided carpet tape.

Frayed Carpet... Instead of fretting over a fraying braided carpet, glue the pieces together with fabric glue.

Throw Rugs That Throw You!... Use rubber rings from preserve jars to end sliding rugs. Glue three together and then glue to each corner. The rings will form a kind of suction cup to help keep the mat in its place...and you in yours!

♦ Also try using heavy-duty two-sided tape to stop your rug from moving.

♦ You can also solve this problem by sticking several bathtub decals to the back of your rug.

♦ Or simply not polish the floor under the throw rug.

Carpet Sweepers And Beaters... To remove thread wound round the rotating brush, slice the threads with scissors and pull the shortened threads out.

♦ For nonelectric carpet sweepers, try wetting the bristles to help pick up lint quicker.

FLOORS, WALLS & WOODWORK

FLOORS...

Prevent Scratched Floors When Moving... Slip a small scatter rug under heavy dressers and place old socks on furniture legs when rearranging a room.

And When Rocking... Prevent marring on wooden floors by placing a long strip of adhesive tape along the bottom of each arc of your rocking chair.

♦ Or glue strips of felt to the arcs.

But If It's Too Late!... Remove scratches in wooden floors by sanding very gently with fine steel wool that has been dipped in paste wax.

Polisher Pad Buildup... Remove excess wax buildup by placing brown paper over pads and pressing with a warm iron. The wax will melt and adhere to the brown paper. Paper towels work well too.

Cleaning Linoleum Floors... Linoleum floors should never be scrubbed with strong abrasive cleaners or cleaning tools. Simply wash with a wet mop that has been dipped in warm, soapy water. Wring well.

♦ To restore old linoleum, often a mixture of equal parts milk and turpentine will work.

Wax Crayon On Linoleum... Remove wax crayon marks from vinyl or linoleum flooring by rubbing with silver polish.

Scuff Marks On Linoleum... Persistent scuff marks can often be removed from linoleum by applying a small amount of toothpaste to a dry cloth and wiping the scuff firmly. Once the mark has been removed, clean off with a wet cloth.

♦ Some scuff marks can also be removed by simply using a gum eraser as you would on paper.

Heel Marks On Linoleum... Heel marks and small dents can be sometimes disguised by applying some porcelain glaze (the type you repair chipped bathtubs with). Match the color of your floor and apply with a small artist's paintbrush. Allow to dry and buff the area smooth with some very fine sandpaper.

A Clean Sweep!... When sweeping up, dip the tip of your broom in water to help pick up the dust.

♦ Also, to minimize dust, make sure you never lift the bristles of the broom more than 1 inch above the floor.

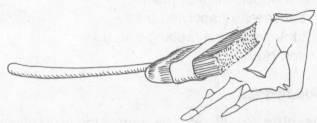

♦ To keep your corn broom in shape, cut a 4-inch band from one of the legs of a pair of panty hose. Slip it over the broom so that it sits about 3 or 4 inches above the end of the bristles.

Broom Storage... To extend the life on the bristles of your broom, never rest the broom on the brush end when storing.

Registers And Vents... Place a piece of screening inside floor vents and registers to catch small objects that fall and dust that collects.

WALLS & WOODWORK...

Walls...

No Streaking Please!... When washing painted walls, always start at the bottom and work your way up. This prevents streaks from dripping water that are difficult to remove.

Whitewashed Walls... It's always best to simply paint over any marks. Washing will just remove the paint.

Easy Wallpaper Cleaning... Cleaning marks on wallpaper is often easy if you rub the stain with rye bread or an Artgum eraser.

Pint-Size Picassos... To remove marker or crayon marks from wallpaper, walls or painted surfaces, try applying a little toothpaste and rubbing with a soft cloth.

Woodwork...

Cleaning Woodwork... Squeeze the juice of one lemon into one quart of water for use as a rinse after washing woodwork or linoleum. The surfaces will maintain their high-gloss finish.

♦ Use cold tea to clean woodwork.

Removing Candle Wax From Woodwork... The trick is to soften the wax enough to wipe it up with an absorbent cloth. Try using a hair dryer. Wash woodwork afterward with a mild vinegar solution to remove all traces of wax.

A Swell Tip!... If your wooden doors expand and seem impossible to close, check the position of your humidifier or its setting. Wood absorbs moisture and then swells slightly.

TIPS
FOR WINDOWS

CLEANING & CARE...

When To Wash Windows... Wait for a cloudy day to wash normally "sunny" windows. The sun will cause the glass to dry too quickly, leaving unsightly streaks.

How To Wash Windows... Always wash your windows with

horizontal strokes on the inside and vertical strokes on the outside, or vice versa. This way, if there are any streaks, you'll know which side of the glass they're on!

Homemade Window Cleaner... Mix ¼ cup of white vinegar and ¼ cup of ammonia into a bucket half filled with warm water. Fill several spray bottles or plant misters and you'll have an excellent cleaner as well as a long-lasting supply.

- ♦ To give your homemade window cleaner a "professional" appeal, try adding a drop of blue food coloring to each container and shaking well.

- ♦ Or, wash your windows and mirrors with a mixture of ½ cup of cornstarch to a gallon of warm water.

Frost-Free Windows... Add 2 tablespoons of rubbing alcohol to a container of Homemade Window Cleaner to help prevent frost forming on the inside windows.

The Final Shine... Keep a lamb's-wool mop pad in your cleaning basket to be used for giving glass a final buffing.

Save On Paper Toweling... Use crumpled newspaper to dry windows.

Softening Your Window Chamois... Soak in a bucket of warm water and a capful of olive oil.

Window Wipers... Recycle your car's worn-out wiper blades. You can use them as squeegees on windows at home.

Cleaning Window Screens... Use a soft paintbrush to dust screens before cleaning.

♦ Dip paintbrush in kerosene and brush both sides of the screen. Dry with a clean cloth.

Stubborn Window?... For slider windows that won't open easily, lubricate the frame grooves by rubbing them with a wax candle.

♦ To remove cobwebs, dirt and dust, etc., from the window tracks, use a 1-inch paintbrush. It's firm, yet able to access awkward areas.

DRAPERY CARE...

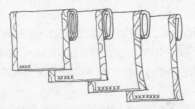

Which One Goes Where?... Mark your drapery panels before they go to the cleaners. You'll know exactly where they belong when returned home. On the underside of the individual panel hems, place a single long stitch in contrasting thread on the panel closest to the left side of the window. Increase by one stitch for every panel, moving in a counterclockwise rotation around the room.

♦ Mark the location of drapery hooks with a dab of colored nail polish when removing them. The polish will remain throughout the dry-cleaning process and will make reinserting the hooks a simple task.

Hooks And Weights... Drapery hooks are easily inserted into fabric if you first push the pointed end of the hook into a bar of soap.

♦ Use old keys as drapery weights.

♦ Or raid the toolbox for several heavy nuts for weights.

AROUND THE HOUSE

FIREPLACES, WOODSTOVES & CHIMNEYS...

Fireplaces...

Cleaning Fireplaces... Keep an Artgum eraser handy for removing soot from your stone fireplace fronts. If discoloring remains, use a solution of trisodium phosphate and water. Follow directions on package.

♦ For big jobs, prepare by sweeping all the ashes up and vacuuming thoroughly. Place newspapers in and around the hearth. Make sure you have on hand rubber gloves, a bucket of water, a cloth, a bowl of vinegar and a scrub brush. Dip the brush in the vinegar and scrub a section of tile. Rinse and wipe with cloth and water. Continue until all sections have been cleaned.

Woodstoves...

Cleaning Woodstoves... To clean your woodstove window, dip a moist rag in some cold wood ashes and rub well into the window. Wipe off with a clean, wet cloth and then rub with crumpled newspaper.

◆ A quick way to see if your stovepipe needs cleaning is to rap the pipe with your knuckle...when it's cold! A tinny sound means the buildup is minor. A heavy, dull tone indicates more extensive buildup.

Polishing Your Woodstove... At the end of the winter season, give your woodstove a good polish with some regular vegetable oil. Simply rub on a light coating. This will not only polish the stove but deters rusting over the spring and summer.

Using Your Woodstove As A Humidifier/Deodorizer... For a pleasant room humidifier/deodorizer, place a pot of water on the top of your woodstove and add some orange and lemon peels.

"Fossil" Fuel?... It's said that bones give off a substantial heat in a woodstove. So you might want to save your leftover dinner bones to add to the evening fire.

Chimneys...

The Chimney Sweep!... To clean your chimney yourself, wait  for it to get cold and then place several tire chains in a burlap bag. Tie a rope to the bag and lower it into the chimney. By moving it up and down it will dislodge the soot and creosote which can be collected from the stove itself. This works best with a straight up and down chimney.

Warning!—Dangerous Cleaning Method... Never try to remove creosote by letting your fire get so hot as to burn it off. Not only is it unreliable, it can damage the insulation inside the chimney...not to mention the risk of starting a chimney fire!

Soot Seeking!... If your chimney is vertical, you can check for soot buildup by shining a flashlight up the chimney while holding a mirror at a 45-degree angle at the base.

HOUSEHOLD ITEMS & FIXTURES...

Items...

Candleholders... Candle wax can be removed by freezing the holders until the wax is easily chipped off.

Compact-Disc Cleaning... If your CD skips, rub the surface with some toothpaste on a soft cloth. Rinse with water and dry well.

Gilt-Frame Preserver... Twice each year, apply a small amount of lemon oil to frames to prevent cracking.

Cleaning Gilt Frames... When cleaning gilt frames, pat on the cleaner, never rub. Mix together equal parts of ammonia and denatured alcohol. Dampen a soft cloth with this solution and apply to a small area of the frame, dabbing gently. Repeat with a soft, dry cloth to pick up the dirt.

Oil Paintings... To clean your favorite oil painting, try blotting it with a piece of soft bread.

♦ Another method is to carefully dab the painting with a sliced cucumber or potato.

Vases... Add a capful of ammonia and fill vase with hot water. Rinse thoroughly.

♦ Or drop two denture tablets in and fill with hot water.

Ashtrays... Coat the inside of your ashtrays with a thin layer of floor wax. The wax will keep the ashes from sticking to the ashtray. Simply wipe them out with a cloth or paper towel and they're ready to be used again.

Cleaning Silk Lampshades... Before cleaning, check for colorfastness and to ensure that glue was not used to affix trimming. Working quickly, dip the shade up and down in lukewarm, soapy water. Use a soft brush on stained areas. Rinse several times. Towel-sponge until most moisture is removed. Do not place in the sun or near heat, but dry in a well-ventilated shaded area. Turn upside down to even drying process occasionally. Remember, the trick is to dry the shade as quickly as possible without using heat.

Artificial Plants And Flowers... Clean by spraying with an all-purpose cleaner and rinsing in warm water.

♦ Or clean artificial flower centerpieces by holding the container and dunking in warm, soapy water, then clear water. Let it sit upside down on a towel until moisture has run off.

♦ Spruce up your silk flowers by placing them in an ordinary paper bag with a third of a cup of salt in it.

Playing Cards With A Full Deck... Old playing cards can be rejuvenated by applying a little spirits of camphor, dabbed lightly with cotton balls. Just wipe and polish.

Piano Keys... To clean ivory keys, rub with a lemon-half. Or use a paste of lemon juice and salt. Wipe with a clean cloth.

♦ Or clean with a cloth moistened slightly with denatured alcohol. Wipe dry. Never use soap to clean ivory. It will stain.

♦ For plastic keys, buff with toothpaste on a soft cloth.

Top Brass... Shine brass items with Worcestershire sauce! Dip a damp rag or toothbrush into the sauce and rub the brass well. Wipe off with a clean, damp cloth, then buff with a dry cloth.

♦ Toothpaste, rubbed on with a dry, soft cloth will also clean brass.

♦ Lemon juice and salt works well too!

Mopping Up... Here's a "pollution-wise" method for shaking mops. Place a plastic or paper bag over the mop head and secure with a twist tie or rubber band. Shake vigorously and discard the bag filled with dust. Especially useful for apartment dwellers.

Fixtures...

Dusty Radiators... Hang a damp tea towel behind radiator and use your blow-dryer to blow the dust onto the towel.

Removing Stains From Marble Fixtures... Scrub with a paste of baking soda, water and lemon juice. Rinse and dry.

Crystal Chandeliers... Place a plastic cover over a kitchen table along with a few layers of newspaper. Position the table under the chandelier. Fill a glass with lukewarm water and add 2 ounces of alcohol or vinegar. Hold the glass up to the individual crystal teardrops until totally immersed. Let them drip dry.

Cleaning Chrome... Dampen a cloth with ammonia or vinegar to clean and shine chrome in a single step.

♦ Straight vinegar is also a great chrome cleaner!

♦ Nail-polish remover is another chrome cleaner to try!

♦ Leftover tea that has been steeping in the pot will also bring a lovely shine to your chrome faucets, etc. It cuts grease as well!

Pristine Porcelain!... Clean porcelain fixtures and items by rubbing with a soft cloth sprinkled with salt.

HOUSEHOLD ODORS...

Tobacco Smoke... Burn several decorative candles to lift.

♦ They say that you can absorb tobacco odor by placing a few saucers of vinegar in strategic spots.

♦ Activated charcoal will also remove stale smoke odors. Place small amounts in saucers around the room.

Oh No, It's Burned!... For a quick way to disperse smoke from burned food, take a wet bath towel and swirl it around the room for a few minutes.

Humidifier Odor... Simply add a teaspoon of laundry bleach to the humidifier water. That should do the trick.

Vacuum-Cleaner Odor... Freshen up your vacuum by removing the outside bag and washing it with some lemon juice in your washer. Dry thoroughly outside.

Confined Odors... To remove odors from confined areas, leave an open tray of cat litter in the offending area.

Homemade Air Deodorizer... Take a spray mister with 2 cups of water in it, add 2 teaspoons of baking soda and spray those odors away!

Eau Du Incandescence!... To hide odors (such as cooking odors, etc.) simply place a drop or two of your favorite perfume on the lightbulb of one of your table lamps. Turn the lamp on and soon you'll have a pleasant fragrance throughout the room.

AND FINALLY...

Avoid Closet Dampness... Place a box of chalk on the shelf of your closet to eliminate dampness.

♦ Charcoal also absorbs dampness. Place in a container that has several air holes in it and set it on the floor of your closet.

Front Door Storage... String two lengths of cord on the inside of your hall closet and attach several clothespins along each string. When your kids come in, they can pin their mittens together on the lower string and hats on the upper string. Not only will you know where they are, you'll know they're drying as they hang.

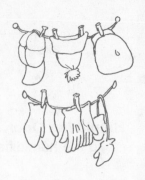

♦ A simple trick to help you find your own boots at the front door when going to a party is to take along a clothespin with your name printed on it. When you take your boots off, clip them together with a clothespin.

HOME SAFE HOME!

HELPFUL HINTS TO KEEP YOU SAFE & SECURE...

Fire Prevention!... Never run lamp wires under a carpet. Eventually ridges are worn into the fabric and you may have a potential fire hazard underfoot.

♦ When you can smell gas, never strike a match. Open windows immediately and call your local utility company.

Ornamental Smoke Alarm... Next Christmas, get the kids to decorate a smoke alarm to look like a star and attach it to the top of your natural Christmas tree. If there's a problem the ornament will be the first to know!

Battery Anniversary!... It's a good idea to make it a habit to replace the batteries in your smoke detector each year. You might find it easier to remember if you make point of changing them on a special day, such as your birthday, anniversary, the first day of spring, etc.

Firefighting... Keep your emergency numbers updated and on a wall near your phone.

♦ Even if the fire is small, limit your firefighting efforts to less than one minute before evacuating the building.

♦ Never use water on grease, oil or electrical fires.

♦ Familiarize yourself with the type of fire extinguisher you have. Certain types may only fight certain fires.

Emergency Light... If you have to call for help, time is of the essence. Instead of having an ordinary white bulb in your outside light, screw in an unusually colored one. It will be easier and quicker for the emergency service to find you.

 **Prevent A "Shocking" Experience...** To make sure electrical cords can't be plugged in, take a paper clip and stick it through the holes at the tip of the plug prongs. This will prevent the plug from going into the outlet.

Household Inventory... It's always practical to keep track of household possessions and their value for insurance purposes. If this is a task you have long put off, try taking a walk through the house with a small cassette recorder. Describe the articles you see as you walk through each room and any particulars that may help identify it in case of theft. Also note the value of the item. Keep the cassette in the car or at the office, and let's hope you never need it.

♦ If you own a video camera, use that. This way you have a visual record of your inventory.

Telephone Safety... It's said that you should never talk on the telephone while you're in the bathtub, or during an electrical storm.

Baffling Burglars... Before you leave on your next vacation, ask your neighbors to clear your mailbox every day and on garbage day, have them leave one of their full garbage cans in front of your house for pickup.

♦ If possible, leave a parked car in your driveway.

♦ Turn the volume on your telephone ring right down.

♦ If you live in a house, leave a heavy dog chain hanging on the outside knob of the back door, or a large dog food dish close by. Most thieves will not go near a house that has evidence of a dog, let alone a very large dog.

Identifying Keys... Many hardware stores now carry various colored keys which will help you identify the key you want in a hurry, but for existing keys, try marking with nail polish or acrylic paint in bright colors. Write down which keys are painted what colors should you require reference.

♦ Another way to keep keys identified is to trace the outline of each key on a card and write down where it fits—e.g., the front or back door, etc. File cards in a safe place. Tape unused keys to cards with an appropriate description of where it belongs.

Watch Your Head... Try not to hang very heavy pictures or mirrors above the head of your bed.

— ♦ —

CHAPTER 3

LAUNDRY-DAY HELPERS

A HAMPERFUL OF HINTS
TO DELIGHT EVEN THE MOST
EXPERIENCED LAUNDERER!

WASHING AWAY THOSE LAUNDRY BLUES

THE BASICS...

Keep Those Labels!... Never remove the manufacturer's washing-instruction label from clothes, or you may be in trouble when it comes to laundering the garment. If it interferes with the wear by scratching, or it's visible, cut it out, but mark the instructions on a piece of paper and keep it in a recipe box above the washing machine.

Separation Savvy... Before washing anything, sort laundry into convenient piles and wash separately: white cottons and linens; nylon and synthetics; silks and rayon; woolens; and noncolorfast articles. Use very hot water for whites and reduce water heat for synthetics, silks, woolens and noncolorfasts, respectively.

♦ Remember to wash colored sheets and towels separately for the first few washes to remove any excess dye.

Prewash Pointers... Take a few minutes while sorting the wash to check for unusual stains or seams that have come apart. Mend seams before laundering to ensure that a small rip won't get caught in the dryer and ruin your garment completely.

 ♦ Check for grease stains before washing as well. Once a stain has been laundered it is virtually impossible to remove.

Overload!... Avoid overloading your washing machine. The clothes will wash a lot better if there is room for them to circulate.

Prevent Soap From Sticking... Remember to always dissolve soap powder detergents in warm or hot water before placing garments in the washer. Undissolved soap particles may lodge in corners of clothing, damaging the fabric.

Reducing Suds... Salt sprinkled on suds will reduce the amount of lather and keep the machine from overflowing. But prevent this accident from happening by measuring detergent carefully!

Penny-Wise, Pound-Foolish... One place you really can't save is laundry water. Using dirty water over again to do the next load may seem economical, but it will show in the color and feel of your wash. Always use clean, soapy water and rinse until the water is clear.

Washer Washing!... Washing machines need to be cleaned too from time to time. Pour a gallon of distilled vinegar into the washer and using warm water, let the machine run through a wash and rinse cycle. The vinegar will cut through built-up soap residue in hoses and leave your washer sparkling clean.

Treating Hard Water... Soft water is much easier on fabrics than hard water. Repeated hard-water use will weaken fabrics and sometimes turn whites gray. Use a commercial water softener or washing soda. As well as saving garments, it saves money because you need less detergent.

♦ Add washing soda to hard water before adding soap flakes to prevent a soap scum from forming.

♦ Washing soda turns hard water to soft and reduces the amount of detergent required. If you are trying washing soda for the first time, go easy on the detergent.

Laundry-Powder Scoop... Cut a plastic bleach jug in half. Use the top portion, with its handle and cap secured, to scoop soap powder. Measure one cup of powder and mark the level with red nail polish for future accurate measuring.

Lazy Laundromatting!... If you use a laundromat, don't lug along all those detergent boxes and bleach bottles. Instead, make up a load of laundry in a pillowcase, add the required amount of detergent and DRY bleach and when you get to the laundromat, empty the prepared load right into the washer.

THE SPECIFICS...

Silks... Launder your silks safely by washing in a little tepid water with some baby shampoo. Wash the garment carefully and squeeze the excess water out gently so as to avoid breaking any fibers. Then hang it out to dry. Finally, if necessary, press with an iron set on low.

Hosiery... Hand washing is the best and safest way to get the longest wear out of hosiery. It takes about as much time at the end of the day as washing your hands. Keep a bar of soap or a container of "weak" detergent in your bathroom cabinet just for the hosiery and watch how long they last!

♦ Nylon stockings that are dried in the dryer will create a lot of static cling. Another reason to hand wash.

Socks... To prevent disappearing socks, when you wash them, pin each pair together or use a clothespin.

♦ For whiter socks, soak in hot water to which the juice of ½ lemon has been added.

♦ Soaking white socks in baking soda and water before washing also works well.

♦ Or instead of adding detergent, try adding about half a cup of water softener and wash on the warm cycle.

Washing Woolens... Woolens are usually washable but take care. Use lukewarm water, never hot, with adequate sudsing. Don't leave it in the wash water longer than 15 minutes and rinse several times in cool water. Dry on a form or flat surface.

♦ For softer, fine woolen hand-washables, try adding a small amount of cream rinse to the final rinse water.

♦ Several drops of glycerin added to the final rinse water will soften woolens and make them less scratchy.

♦ After washing and rinsing, place your white woolen washing in your freezer for about an hour and a half. The cold will have a harmless bleaching effect on the garments. Just let them thaw naturally and dry as usual.

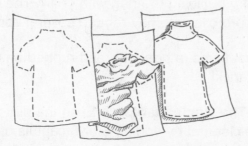

♦ Keep your hand-washable sweaters in shape by using this simple shape preserver. Place the unwashed sweater on a clean, large sheet of paper. Affix straight pins around the outline. After the sweater has been washed, shape it within the outline, pinning the garment to the paper. It should dry to exactly the right form.

♦ When your favorite woolen sweater is tossed in the wash by mistake, you may be able to reshape it. Try soaking in lukewarm water with a mild hair-shampoo lather.

♦ If the ribbing on your sweater waistlines and cuffs get stretched out of shape, you can often bring them back in line by dipping the ribbing, but not the rest of the sweater, in very hot water. That should shrink the ribbing back to normal.

Collar Rings... Apply a paste of baking soda and vinegar. Work in with fingers around the shirt-collar ring; then wash as usual.

♦ Rub a small amount of hair shampoo along the collar ring to loosen oils. If the ring doesn't fade while rubbing, try a small, soft brush. Launder as usual.

♦ An abrasive hand soap will work wonders as well.

♦ Or try outlining the ring with chalk. The chalk will absorb oils, but may require several applications.

♦ Sometimes, a heel of bread rubbed on the collar does the trick!

Cleaning The Uncleanables... Even the dirtiest of clothes can be cleaned by adding 5 or 6 capfuls of household ammonia to the wash water.

Washing Noncolorfast Garments... Epsom salts will help prevent running and fading of noncolorfast items. Add 1 teaspoon Epsom salts per gallon of wash water for the first washing.

♦ A teaspoon of ammonia added to the wash water will also help keep colors from running.

Setting Colors... To set the colors in new cottons and keep them bright, soak them overnight in lightly salted water, or a weak solution of vinegar and water.

Brilliant Brighteners... It's said that if you add about 1/3 of a cup of white vinegar to your rinse cycle, you'll find that your clothes will come out brighter and softer. Any vinegar scent should vanish after the clothes have dried.

♦ Another nifty clothes brightener is cream of tartar. It's easier on the fabric than many bleaches are, which is great for washing delicates. Simply mix 2 teaspoons cream of tartar in 1 gallon of hot water and leave the garments to soak overnight. Wash as usual.

Delicate Laundry... Those precious little garments can be washed gently and safely if you place them in a pillowcase and knot the open end before washing in your machine.

♦ Delicate washables should not be laundered using a harsh all-purpose laundry detergent. Make your own "weak" detergent, by dissolving a cup of powdered soap flakes in a cup of warm water. Keep in a bottle for later use.

♦ Here's a natural recipe for cleaning delicates: Take 1½ cups of bran and tie it up in a piece of cotton cloth. Put it in a pan with 1 quart of water and bring to a boil. Let simmer for 30 minutes and then strain it. Add 2 cups of warm water and stir it all up. You now have a cleaning solution for those special, brightly colored garments that would fade with soaps. Because of the fibre there is no need to add any starch.

♦ To remove the yellowing from old lace items, wash them in hot water on a gentle cycle. Make sure there is no bluing in the detergent. If the yellowing persists, try mixing a ¼ cup of baking soda with some detergent in water. Drop the lace item in and boil it on the stove.

"Lintless" Laundry... Try adding ½ cup of white vinegar to the final rinse.

♦ Before you place your garments in the washing machine, turn them inside out. Any lint buildup will collect on the inside of your clothes!

♦ After drying, dampen a clothes brush and brush clothes downward in even strokes.

Mothers Beware!... When laundering children's sleepwear, use a phosphate detergent. If you don't, you may find that the flame retardents required by law on children's clothing will have lost their resistance. If you do use a nonphosphate detergent, make sure you add a cup of vinegar to the cold rinse water and allow garments to soak for ½ hour before starting the spin cycle.

Old-Fashioned Sugar Starch For Grandma's Doilies... Boil one cup of granulated sugar in one-third cup of water for two minutes. Immerse doily until thoroughly soaked. Allow the doily to drip dry, shaping as it dries.

Starching Pillows... Did you know that by lightly starching your pillowcases, you can help prevent stains from hair oils and face creams?

SEE SPOT RUN!

LAUNDRY STAIN-REMOVAL TIPS...

NOTE: The following stain-removal tips are only for use on washable fabrics unless otherwise indicated. In all cases use your own discretion and caution.

General Stain Strategy... When applying stain-removing solutions to fabric, it's best to attack the stain from the back of the fabric and not the front. This way the stain won't spread deeper into the fabric.

♦ Use a dabbing motion rather than a rubbing one, working from the outside in, when applying solutions.

♦ For nongreasy stains, use cold water. Hot water tends to set the stain.

Homemade Spot Remover... Make your own commercial spot remover. Simply add 1 part rubbing alcohol to 2 parts water. Simple as that!

Suede... Removing a stubborn stain on suede can be very simple. If ordinary brushing doesn't do the trick, try rubbing the spot lightly with an emery board, then steam over a boiling kettle. Just like new. Be careful with that steam though!

♦ Sometimes makeup stains can be removed from suede collars by rubbing with a heel of bread.

Bloodstains On Clothing... Bloodstains can often be removed by applying a paste of meat-tenderizing crystals and cold water. Allow ½ to ¾ hour to set. Rinse in cool water.

♦ Or dab immediately with soda water; then treat with cornstarch paste.

♦ For dried blood, try a little ammonia.

♦ Foamy shaving cream, rubbed with a sponge, often works too.

Gum Removal... To get rid of chewing gum, even from hair, put the white of an egg on it and leave for a few minutes. Work the gum out.

♦ To remove gum from clothing simply place the item in your freezer compartment for an hour or so, this will harden the gum enough to allow you to dislodge it easily. Works for candle wax too!

Wax Removal... Crayon marks and candle wax can be easily removed from fabric. Place 2 folded paper towels on both sides of the stained area and press with a warm iron. The paper towels will absorb the melted wax.

Mud Stains... Slice a raw potato in half and rub the mud stain. Soak the item in cool water for a while; then launder as usual.

Grease Stains... Try pouring club soda over grease stains.

♦ Waterless hand cleaner rubbed into the stain usually works well.

♦ Baby powder or cornstarch rubbed into the stain often works. Launder as usual.

♦ Dab with eucalyptus or tea-tree oil before washing.

♦ On delicates, washing with baby shampoo often works.

Oil Stains... Stubborn oil stains can often be removed by dabbing with eucalyptus oil. Wash with warm soapy water.

◆ As a last resort, try spraying the stain with automotive "engine-start" spray. The ether in the spray usually does the trick. Be careful not to breathe the spray; also be aware it can be highly flammable.

Ballpoint Pen Ink... A great way of removing ballpoint ink stains is to use hair spray (pump or aerosol). Douse the stain with the hair spray and then rub hard with a bar of soap (bath or laundry). Rinse the garment in cold water. Remember hot water can set nongreasy stains. Launder as usual.

◆ Rubbing alcohol dabbed on the stained area may also lift the ink.

◆ You can sometimes remove ink stains on colored garments by soaking the garment in milk.

◆ Remove ink stains on white fabrics by rubbing the area with a mixture of lemon juice and salt. If possible, hang to dry in a sunny place.

Lipstick Stains... You can often get rid of lipstick stains by applying some toothpaste to the mark. Rub the toothpaste well into the garment, then wash as normal.

◆ Or try dabbing the lipstick stain with petroleum jelly and then washing.

◆ Hair spray often works as a prewash spray for lipstick stains.

Rust Stains...
Remove rust from clothing or fabrics by applying lemon juice and salt. Hang outside in the sun to dry.

♦ Or cover the area with cream of tartar. Roll the item tightly and soak in a bucket of hot water. Launder as usual.

Mildew Stains... Dampen the stain with salt and lemon juice and let it sit in the sun.

♦ Or soak in weak solution of water and ammonia. Sponge with vinegar.

♦ Or dab with some hydrogen peroxide and launder as usual.

♦ Salt and milk works too, they say. Soak overnight; then place in the sun.

♦ For mildew on leather, apply a little antiseptic mouthwash to the area with a soft cloth.

Perspiration Stains... Place garment in a bucket of warm water with 1 cup of vinegar added. Soak for an hour or so before laundering.

Tar Stains... Rub the area with kerosene before laundering, but be sure to check for colorfastness before applying the kerosene.

Tea and Coffee Stains... Spray the area with hair spray. Rub with a bar of soap and rinse in cold water.

Mustard Stains... Wash item in cold water while rubbing with laundry bar soap. Soak 12 hours in the soapy water. If necessary, use bleach.

♦ Or apply rubbing alcohol and launder as usual.

♦ Glycerin applied to the stains may also do the trick.

Scorch Stains... Dampen a piece of cloth with a weak solution of peroxide and press over the scorched area.

♦ Cut an onion in half and rub it on the scorched area. Then soak the item in cold water.

Red-Wine Stains... Treat a wine stain immediately. For fabric or carpets, sprinkle salt liberally over the area to absorb the spill. For fabrics, wash in cold water with regular detergent. For carpets, rub with foamy shaving cream, dab/rinse with cold water and vacuum when dry.

♦ Or immediately soak the area with club soda and blot with paper towels.

♦ On fabrics, we've also had success with waterless hand cleaner.

♦ If carpet stain persists, you can try dabbing the area with a little hydrogen peroxide. Dab/rinse with cold water and vacuum when dry.

♦ Sometimes a paste of cream of tartar spread on fabric or carpet wine stains will do the trick. Again, wash as above.

Chocolate Stains... Remove any excess chocolate first then immediately run club soda through the fabric and rinse with a mild detergent and cold water. If the stain persists, follow up with a mixture of 1 tablespoon ammonia and 2 cups cold water. Dab the solution on the fabric working from the outside in. Rinse well and wash as usual.

♦ Waterless hand cleaner also works well!

Grass Stains... Persistent grass stains can often be removed by dabbing with eucalyptus oil and laundering as usual.

♦ Also, try using denatured alcohol as a prewash.

Tomato-Based Stains... For ketchup and spaghetti-sauce stains on garments, try the following. Blot the area with some denatured alcohol and then launder in a cool wash.

♦ For similar carpet stains, apply a generous amount of foaming shaving cream and rub it well into the stain with a sponge. Rinse with water, let dry and vacuum.

Curry Stains... Good luck! What you might try is rubbing a mixture of 3 tablespoons of glycerin and 4 tablespoons of warm water. Let sit for 1 hour, then launder in warm water.

♦ Soak in diluted ammonia (1 tablespoon ammonia, 2 cups water) or dab with borax and water. Launder as usual.

Oil Paint Stains... Mix 2 tablespoons ammonia and 1 tablespoon turpentine. Rub into the stain and launder in warm water. Several applications may be necessary.

♦ Waterless hand cleaner rubbed into the stain often does the trick. The older the stain, the longer you leave it before laundering.

Acrylic-Paint Stains... Dab the area with some denatured alcohol. Launder as normal.

Latex-Paint Stains... Fresh latex paint is usually easy to remove with soap and cold water. However, dried latex paint is extremely difficult to remove. Try soaking the stained area with rubbing alcohol and launder as usual.

♦ You may also want to try applying natural yogurt. It sometimes works.

Fruit Stains... Sprinkle some salt on the garment and then rinse in cold water. Wash it in warm water with liquid detergent, preferably biodegradable, and if the stain persists, try applying a little hydrogen peroxide, or borax.

Mystery Stains... For stains of unknown origin, try following these steps: First, rinse the stain in cold water. Pretreat it with a prewash—spray or soap—then rinse again. Now wash the garment in chlorine bleach or an all-fabric bleach, in water that's as hot as the manufacturer recommends, adding extra detergent to the wash. Let it air-dry, and if the stain is still there, soak it in cold water for half an hour. Sponge it with a cleaning solvent, let it sit for 5 minutes and then rinse again. Repeat all of the above if stain persists.

♦ If all else fails, try brushing with toothpaste on a toothbrush.

ALL ABOUT DRYING

PUTTING IT ON THE LINE!...

Solar Substitute... We've all heard about solar heating, but if you have a backyard and haven't considered solar drying your clothes on a line, think about it now. Clothes dryers use a lot of electricity to dry several loads. Line drying is a terrific way to conserve energy, and it really does leave clothes fresh-smelling and static-free.

Trousers... When line drying trousers, hang them by the cuffs. The weight of the trousers will usually keep the legs wrinkle free, making pressing a simple job.

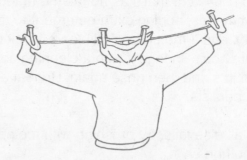

Sweaters... To prevent your sweaters forming clothespin "points" when hanging up try this. Thread the legs of a pair of panty hose through the arms of the sweater and pull the waist through the sweater neck. Now you can attach the clothespins to the feet and waist of the panty hose instead of to the sweater.

Dresses And Coats... When hanging a delicate dress or heavy coat outside on the line to dry, use two plastic coat hangers hooked in the opposite direction. This will prevent the wind from blowing the garment off the line.

Lingerie... Fine undergarments can usually be washed in the washing machine without damage but automatic dryers might turn the fabric gray. Keep a small clothesline in your laundry area or bathroom to hang dry lingerie.

Panty Hose... If you find your panty hose and leotards get twirled around your clothesline, just drop a teaspoon into each leg.

Timing Is Everything!... A strong sun will weaken cotton fibers over a period of time, and intense cold will break fibers. So keep an eye on that clothesline, and bring clothes in as soon as they are dry.

Clothespin Mitts... Save your old cotton gloves and cut the fingers off. Slip these fingers over the arms of your old and weathered clothespins. They'll prevent them from marking your clothes.

TUMBLING TIPS...

Dryer Care... You should check dryer filters often for signs that may indicate a bit of repair work is needed. Damp lint on the filter may mean a clogged vent. Check outside vents periodically.

Lint-Free Drying... Nylon netting will catch lint if placed in your dryer along with the regular load.

Static Free!... Instead of using costly sheet fabric softeners in the dryer, buy a budget liquid softener. Moisten an old facecloth and place in the dryer. Repeat for every load. Works just as well!

♦ Or for light fabrics and delicates, put a wet towel in the dryer with them. The towel will stay wet longer than the garments, eliminating static caused by overdrying.

♦ Static can also be reduced by placing a ball of aluminum foil in the dryer.

Oops, I Forgot!... If you forget your clothes in the dryer and they're a mass of wrinkles, try this. Wet a towel, wring out the excess water and throw it into the dryer along with the wrinkled clothes. Let it tumble another cycle and you should be the owner of a relatively wrinkle-free wash!

Fluffy Feather Pillows... Tumble in a cool dryer for about 10 minutes. For a really fresh lift, add a cloth dampened with liquid fabric softener to the dryer.

♦ Another method is to pop them into the tumble dryer on a low-heat setting along with two or three clean tennis balls. Works great!

Noniron Jean Drying... To avoid ironing your jeans or cords, let the dryer do the work for you. Fold the wet jeans as you would normally fold them when dry. Then lay them as flat as possible in the dryer. When they come out they should be almost as neat as if they were ironed!

Reducing Drying Time... When your washing cycle is completed, remove your lightweight garments and place them in the dryer. Allow your heavier items to run through the spin cycle one more time. While this is reducing the moisture in the heavy items, the light items are drying faster on their own. You'll find you can press and fold the light-weight washing while the heavier items are in the dryer.

♦ If you only have a few items to dry, pop a thick, dry towel into the dryer with them. The thick towel will absorb a lot of the moisture.

IRONING OUT YOUR PRESSING PROBLEMS

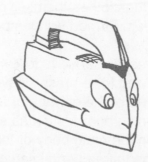

DASHING AWAY WITH THE SMOOTHING IRON!...

Pamper Your Iron... Tap water may cause mineral buildup in your steam iron. Instead, buy demineralized water and use that in your iron. If you're thrifty, simply melt the frost from your freezer or even collect rainwater, or snow.

♦ Keep a plastic mustard or ketchup bottle filled with the water for your iron. You can now squeeze water in without spilling a drop.

Cleaning Your Iron... Remove brown spots by rubbing with fine steel wool dipped in warm vinegar.

♦ Polish with toothpaste! That's right. Apply and allow to dry. Buff with a soft cloth.

♦ Remove deposits from the steam system by filling with equal parts vinegar and water. Allow the iron to steam for 2 or 3 minutes. Let it cool for an hour. Rinse well.

Efficient Ironing Ideas...
"Insulate" your ironing board with foil. The foil will reflect heat back to the underside of the item you're pressing.

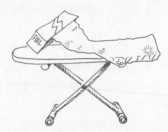

♦ If you dampen the cover of your ironing board, instead of the clothes themselves, you should find that the steam formed will dampen the clothes more evenly.

♦ It makes sense to follow a few simple rules to avoid having to re-press sleeves and collars. First press all parts of the garment that can hang from sides of the ironing board, such as sleeves cuffs and belts. Then iron the main body of the garment without disturbing those already-pressed pieces. Make sure you iron fabrics until completely dry.

♦ Ironing predampened garments is much easier if they are folded lightly after sprinkling. Tight folding creates extra wrinkles and work.

♦ Here's a great idea for ironing rough, dry garments in a hurry. Sprinkle with lukewarm water, roll tightly and place in a plain paper bag. While the iron is heating, place the bag in a warm oven. Within 2 or 3 minutes, the garment will have warmed and will be thoroughly damp.

♦ If you don't plan to iron your clothes immediately, dampen with water and slip them into a plastic bag and place it in your freezer until ironing time. When the clothes thaw out, they will be moist and ready for ironing.

Emergency Ironing... When you don't have time to iron a garment, try popping it into the dryer along with a damp towel. It removes most of the wrinkles in a few minutes.

Oops I've Scorched It!... If you accidentally scorch your cotton garment while ironing, it can sometimes be salvaged if you immediately soak the item in cold water and leave overnight.

Smoother Collars... When pressing shirt collars, work from the corners into the back of the collar, to prevent wrinkling along the front edges of the collar.

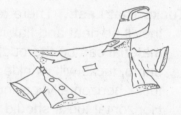

Glazed Chintz... Glazed chintz should be ironed on the right side in order to bring out the luster of the fabric.

Shoulder Pads... Shoulder pads are in and out of fashion, but when laundering, follow the old-fashioned rules: remove pads before laundering if at all possible. If not, make sure they are completely dry before ironing sleeves, to avoid ugly rings.

Ironing Wool Blends... Blended fabrics of wool and rayon should be ironed as if 100% wool. Steam-press using a damp cloth.

Ribbons... When ironing an unruly piece of ribbon, don't think of it as pushing the iron. Instead, think of it as pulling the ribbon. Works great!

Two "Bright" Ideas... A quick way to press ribbons is to run the ribbon over a clean warm lightbulb. Saves getting the iron and ironing board out.

♦ When you've forgotten the travel iron, a warm lightbulb will help get light creases out of cottons and woolens. Dust and wipe the bulb, turn on and allow to warm. Turn off before passing the creased area over the bulb.

Tucks That Last... There really is a trick to ironing tucks so they'll be neat and flat. Make sure you iron slowly so that material can be thoroughly dried. If they are still somewhat damp, tucks will wrinkle soon after ironing. Press vertical tucks horizontally, pulling the material taut as you iron. Horizontal tucks should be pressed by starting at the top and working slowly to the bottom.

Embroidery Magic... Place a turkish towel on the ironing board and iron embroidery work facedown on the towel. This will guarantee a smooth finish, even in the tiniest of spaces.

Restoring Velvet... Restore velvet garments by brushing thoroughly with a soft brush in the direction of the nap. Then steam it on the wrong side and hang to dry.

— ♦ —

CHAPTER 4

A STITCH IN TIME

SEWING, MENDING & KNITTING
TIPS TO SAVE YOU TIME,
MONEY & AGGRAVATION!

SEWING & NOTIONS

CRAFTY SEWING SOLUTIONS...

Time-Savers... Being organized is the first key to saving time when sewing. Find a small area in your home where you can set up your machine and leave it. Convert an unused closet into a sewing room, or screen off a small corner of a large room. Being able to leave your sewing without having to pack up, saves valuable time.

♦ When buying fabric for a new outfit, buy everything you'll need to complete the project all at once and avoid trips to the store later.

♦ Try leaving your hand sewing in a decorative basket by the telephone or your favorite chair. You can have a chat with friends or watch television and get a few hems and buttons done as well.

♦ You must press garment pieces as you go, but why not collect a few pieces and press at one time. Remember though, never sew across a seam unless it has first been pressed.

♦ If you are interrupted just as you're ready to press garment pieces, set them aside and iron along with your regular ironing. When you next have some time to sew, your pieces will be ready.

♦ Do all topstitching at one time to avoid having to re-thread your machine.

♦ Make a simple sewing apron with pockets to wear when sewing or mending. Tape a cloth tape measure to the hem for a quick rule and store your mending equipment in the pockets.

Beach Blanket And Pillow... Towels have many uses long after they are ready to be discarded. Try sewing three or four together for a family beach blanket, or make beach pillows out of old facecloths stuffed with shredded nylons or discarded material.

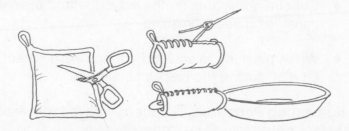

Cast-Iron Handle Holders... Cut an old pot holder in half. Using the half with the little loop for hanging, sew a seam to join two edges forming a tube. Slip over the handle of your cast-iron pan and double the life of that old pot holder!

Ski Pants... Make cross-country ski pants from a pair of old corduroy pants. Cut the legs off below the knee and sew on wide knit sleeve cuffs to finish. Hemming with elastic also works well. Spray with fabric protector.

Quilts... Make a patchwork quilt by saving your children's clothing and cutting pieces to fit your pattern. The little ones will love it.

♦ Use pinking shears to cut squares out of an old quilted crib cover and use the pieces as pot holders.

Lovers' Mittens... For brisk winter walks with someone you love, try making a pair of lovers' mittens. Simply use an old pair of mitts, or buy an inexpensive woolen pair. Cut the thumbs away and, working from the inside, stitch openings of both mittens together. Holding hands in cold weather—with a personal touch!

Quick And Easy Pattern Cutting... Instead of pinning your pattern to fabric, tape it. It's much easier and keeps the pattern from tearing. When cutting out, the tape is easily cut and removed from the fabric.

♦ Cut ¼-inch snips into seams instead of notches.

♦ Cut straight seams on the selvedge and eliminate time-consuming seam finishing.

♦ When planning to sew more than one garment, save time by cutting the pieces all at once.

Long-Lasting Patterns... A pattern sprayed with sizing, before pressing, will last longer.

♦ If you really love that pattern and plan to use it often, make all the necessary adjustments and cut it out on a heavier paper (kraft parcel-wrapping paper is ideal). Punch a hole in a corner of each pattern piece and store your new pattern on a coat hanger. Remember to write down any instructions you need on one of the pieces, or clip the manufacturer's instruction sheet to a large piece.

♦ To store your patterns, take some cardboard tubes (from wrapping paper) and wrap your patterns around them. Start with the small pieces and then roll the larger pieces over them. Secure with a rubber band and identify them by the name and number on the plastic core at the end of the tube. Store the tubes in a closet where they won't get torn easily.

Pattern Pinups... Place a 2 ft. x 2 ft. piece of Peg-Board on the wall over your machine for a handy place to pin up pattern instructions.

Pattern Money Saver... A lot of money can be saved by using your local library as a source for knitting and crochet patterns. Most libraries have a good selection of instruction books. Don't forget to note the publication and page before returning the book to the library.

Tailor's "Soap"... When a bar of soap is down to a thin piece, allow it to dry and use it in place of tailor's chalk to mark darts, pleats, hems, etc. The mark is easily erased with a light brush of the finger.

Knotless Thread... After threading the needle, be sure to knot the end that was cut closest to the spool to help eliminate tangles.

No More Knotting... Eliminate the need to knot thread ends of seams, by backstitching at the beginning and end of each piece.

♦ Never knot ends when thread basting. One pull will then remove the entire length of thread.

NOTIONS & FABRIC...

Notions...

Threading Needles Made Easy... A bit of hair spray or starch rubbed on the end of thread before threading through the needle, will make the task much easier.

♦ Or take a small piece of white paper and push the needle through it until only the eye is sticking up above the paper. Threading will be easier because the thread will stand out against the white paper. If you're using white thread, use colored paper.

♦ Some people simply wet the end of the thread. But how about this? Try wetting the eye of the needle, not the thread!

Keeping Sharp Scissors... Sandpaper puts the fine sharp edge back on your scissors. Simply snip through a piece of sandpaper several times.

And Sharp Needles!... Sharpen your machine needle by running it through a piece of sandpaper several times.

Needle Storage... Sewing-machine needles are easily kept in a small scented soap bar. They'll sew more smoothly when used and will add a nice fragrance to your work area.

Pin Storage... Cut a piece of corkboard the size of your pin box and stick the pins in upright. This saves having to delve down into the box all the time.

♦ Wrap a piece of flannel around the main arm of your machine. When sewing, pins can be removed and stuck into the flannel without stopping.

♦ An old ice cube tray makes a great storage container for things like pins, buttons, thimbles, etc.

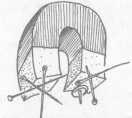

Pin Pickups... Straight pins on the floor? Keep a small magnet handy for quick pickups.

Portable Needle And Thread Case... Old lipstick tubes can be used to store emergency needles and thread. Clean out the tube thoroughly using an old mascara brush and soap. Rinse and dry. Place a small amount of cotton in the bottom of the tube to serve as a lining. Store a threaded needle and several lengths of white, black, blue or brown thread in the tube and carry in your cosmetic bag.

Cheap Storage Containers... Use old adhesive-tape containers to wind and store measuring tapes, bias tape, hem binding and mending wool.

Matchbook Uses... Push several pins into match stick stubs on the inside cover and wind thread around the closed matchbook for a traveling sewing kit.

♦ Use the cover to hold razor blades when ripping seams or removing button threads.

Tidy Thread... Use cellophane tape to keep spooled thread from unraveling and knotting.

Fabric...

Warehousing Fabric... Storing material for projects you plan to do is a great idea, as long as you remember for which pattern you bought the fabric. Pin a slip of paper to the folded fabric, noting its measurements and the pattern number you plan to make.

♦ If you want to take advantage of fabric sales, keep a list in your wallet with the various yardages required for your favorite patterns.

MENDING
& DARNING

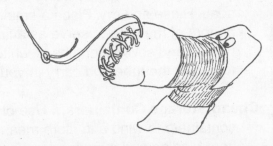

ON THE MEND...

Invisible Mending... To repair a tear, lay the item out flat with the wrong side facing up. Take some egg white and spread it over the area. Cut a piece of linen just a little larger than the tear and place it over the damaged area. Press it with a hot iron to make the egg white stick. Invisible mending! This method only works if you catch the tear before it's frayed too much.

♦ A long hair, used to stitch up a tear is much more invisible than thread. Especially when mending tweed.

Net Curtains... Use clear nail polish to rejoin tears in net curtains. You may have to repeat the procedure after each washing.

Adjustable Hems... Avoid letting down the hems on your kids' pants and resewing. Sew two strips of velcro vertically, inside the bottom of each pant leg. Now you can fold the leg to the desired length and adjust it when you wish. It also does away with fold marks because you undo the fold before washing.

Zipper Recycling... Before you throw away that old garment bag, remove the zipper. It's just the right size for replacing the zipper on your duvet cover.

Zipper Repairing... Often the teeth of zippers on dresses and skirts break off at the bottom. You can salvage the zipper by simply sewing the zipper together with strong thread at the bottom.

Handbag Recycling... Recycle your old handbags by cutting up the leather and using it for knee patches on jeans or elbow patches on jackets.

Buttons And Buttonholes... Buttons will stay on longer if you sew through only two holes at a time. Break the thread and knot before starting on the next pair of holes.

♦ Dab a bit of clear nail polish on the center of each sewn button to help prevent threads from breaking.

♦ For extra strength, try sewing buttons on with dental floss.

♦ When making buttonholes, prevent frayed centers by painting the buttonhole mark with clear nail polish. After it has dried, cut with a razor blade.

DARN THAT HOLE...

Darn Gloves!... When darning a very small rounded area such as the tip of a glove finger, drop one of the children's marbles into the finger and you'll have a perfect darning egg.

Darn Socks!... Use the lighted end of a flashlight as a darning egg when mending dark-colored socks. Turn it on, and see every stitch!

Darn Trick!... Place a piece of netting over the area to be darned and, using the net as a guide, darn through it.

KNITTING YARNS

KNEAT KNITTING TIPS...

Yarn That Won't Tangle... Use handy food-storage baggies for keeping wool clean and tangle free. Place the skein of wool in a bag, punch a hole in the bag and thread a strand of yarn through. Seal with an elastic band.

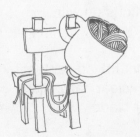

♦ Cut the bottom off a plastic milk or juice jug. Place your balls of wool in the container and thread the wool through the neck of the jug. Hook the container by it's handle over your chair or nearby doorknob keeping it safe and secure from tangles and playful pets.

♦ Another clever method is to put a clay flowerpot over the ball of yarn and pull the yarn through the hole in the bottom of the pot.

Recycling Sweaters... Old woolen sweaters can be recycled. Simply unravel all your cast-off sweaters and roll the yarn into balls. Now you can use the wool for making winter mitts and hats.

No Moths!... Place a mothball in the center of woolen yarn as you're winding to keep the moths away.

Keeping Count... To avoid tedious recounts of your rows when knitting, keep count by using a cribbage board. It's simple and fun!

Knitting Needles... You can improve your knitting speed by spraying some furniture polish on your knitting needles.

♦ Don't throw away your empty tinfoil boxes. They make great storage containers for your knitting needles.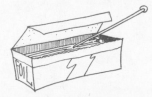

Pearls And Plains Made Easy... If your knitting pattern has a lot of repetitive instructions, record them onto a tape recorder at the approximate speed you would knit at. You can then play it back and knit at the same time without having to stop and read the instructions.

♦ When knitting consecutive rows differently, use a plastic hair clip to mark the row you've just completed. Simply move it down as you go.

— ♦ —

CHAPTER 5

KIDS' KORNER

GREAT IDEAS FOR INFANTS, TODDLERS, SCHOOLKIDS… & ESPECIALLY MOMS!

TIPS FOR TOTS

A BOUNTY OF BABY HINTS...

Bottled Hints... When cleaning bottles in your sterilizer, place some marbles in the sterilizer. They'll gather a lot of the corrosion.

♦ To free baby bottles from mineral deposits, add lemon juice to the water when boiling the bottles.

♦ Make a baby-bottle holder from a six-pack cardboard soft-drink container. Very convenient when traveling.

♦ Try holding the bottle in an oven mitt to keep it warm while feeding baby.

Rub A Dub Dub, Baby And The Tub... Put a small piece of soap into a cotton sock and tie the end. Perfect for small hands and it won't slip away!

♦ Keep those bath toys organized by placing them in a plastic bicycle basket. You can slip the little hooks over the side of the tub or soap dish and the water will just drain from the basket into the bathtub!

♦ Use your infant seat for bathing baby in the tub. Remove the pad, buckle the strap and put a folded towel in the seat. Place baby in the seat and into the water. This way you keep both hands free!

Teething... Stale bread is the perfect thing for your little one to chew on.

Bedtime Stories... When baby is up for his night feedings, turn a heating pad on warm and place it on his mattress. Remove the heating pad before returning the baby to his warm bed. He will settle down much more quickly.

Cribs To Beds... Your child is graduating from his crib to a bed. Put his crib mattress on the floor next to his bed. If your child accidentally falls out, he won't be hurt.

Toy Town... Small children have less trouble holding on to the strings of toys if you attach a large button or bead to the end of them.

Baby Noisemaker... Here's something that'll keep baby amused for ages. Wrap several crumpled pieces of cellophane paper in a cloth napkin. Secure the corners by knotting them tightly. Baby will love the crinkly sound the cellophane makes.

Inexpensive Baby Wipes... Instead of buying baby wipes, buy some cheap flannel diapers. Cut them into small squares and store them next to your baby's change table, along with a thermos of warm water. After use, throw them into the wash with some fabric softener.

Diaper Saver... Cut regular square diapers in half and use them as liners inside your baby's cotton or disposable diapers.

Diaper Rash... Try sprinkling a little cornstarch on the rash. They say it gently soothes sore bottoms.

Baby Powdering... Instead of sprinkling powder on baby from a container, use a powder puff. Baby will love the attention!

Baby Spit-Ups... Soda water will remove the odor caused by baby's spit-ups. Gently rub the area with a cloth dampened with soda water.

Sleeper Stretchers... Here's a money-saving tip. If your child is growing out of her sleepers too quickly, simply cut the feet off the sleepers and sew on a pair of socks, preferably the type with rubberized soles.

 **Baby Sleeping Bag...** Cut the arms off an old ski jacket and sew the arm holes and bottom closed.

Thank-You Photos... Instead of just sending a thank-you note for a baby gift, take a snapshot of baby playing with, or wearing, the gift and send that with the note. It'll be really appreciated!

Baby-Sitting Aid... Here's a clever way to keep your baby calm while in the care of a baby-sitter. Record your voice, or your spouse's, onto a tape. The sitter can then play the recorded lullaby or bedtime story to baby after you've gone.

KEEPING THEM BUSY...INDOORS & OUT!

INDOOR CRAFTY IDEAS...

Making Paste... Dissolve 2 tablespoons of laundry starch in a little cold water and add a cup of boiling water. Boil until thick. It won't gum up children's fingers, but if any should get on their clothes, let it dry and then simply brush off.

Play Dough... Make your own!
4 cups flour
½ cup salt
4 teaspoons alum
2–2½ cups boiling water
Food coloring

Mix boiling water and food coloring. Then add the other 3 ingredients and mix well. Let cool. Keep in your refrigerator uncovered for one day, then cover.

Finger Paint… An old-fashioned recipe.
½ cup powdered laundry starch
¾ cup cold water
1 package gelatin
¼ cup cold water
2 cups hot water
½ cup powdered detergent
Food coloring

Mix the first 2 ingredients and in a separate container, allow gelatin to soak in the ¼ cup of cold water. Add hot water to the starch mixture and boil until the solution is clear, stirring constantly. Remove from heat and stir in gelatin mixture and soap until fully dissolved and thickened. Pour 1 cup into each of 3 containers (old coffee tins with plastic lids are great) and add food coloring to each.

Homemade Paint Roller… To make a neat paint roller for your kids to paint with, all you do is pry the top off an old roll-on deodorant bottle and fill it with thinned finger or poster paint. Replace the top and away you go!

♦ Here's another handy poster paint organizer. Take a foam or cardboard egg carton and turn it upside down. Using an X-Acto knife, cut three holes in the bottom, centering each hole within four of the raised compartments. The holes should be large enough to allow a baby food jar to fit  through snugly. Now you can fill the jars with paint, and you won't have to worry about them being knocked over. When through painting, replace the lids on the jars, and store them in your egg-carton organizer until next time!

Messing Around... Cut old shirts off at the sleeves and use as coveralls when your child is eating or painting.

Easy Paint Cleanup... Before you give the paints to your kids, pour a small amount of liquid dish soap into the paint first. It doesn't effect the paint, but it sure helps cleaning up.

Handy Paint Tray... Use a plastic ice cube tray, or a foam egg carton. Great for mixing colors.

Homemade Painting Easel... Take an old chair and attach a  strip of wood across the seat. Lean a piece of plywood against the chair back. It'll be held in place by the strip of wood. You could also make a plywood shelf and attach it under the seat across the chair bars. Your child can store paints and brushes there.

Preserving Artwork For Posterity... Save your child's artwork. Apply a coating of hair spray to the drawing. This keeps colors from fading. Make sure the drawing is not done with ink though, because the hair spray could cause the ink to run.

Baubles, Bangles And Beads... Keep children amused for hours by giving them things like macaroni, beads, spools, buttons, yarn and other odds and ends you may have around. These things can be strung to make necklaces or bracelets or glued on paper plates to make an interesting collage.

Bird Feeder… Take a plastic bleach jug and cut a 5-inch square out of the side opposite to the handle and starting about 2 inches from the bottom. Turn the jug upside down and insert a broom handle into the neck. Have the kids decorate and fill their very own bird feeder. If you have an extra jug, get them to decorate one for you to use as a clothespin holder. You can hang it by the handle on your clothesline.

Emergency Sand Shovel And Pail… Cut a clean plastic bleach jug in half. Give your child the top half with the handle to use as a shovel and the bottom half as the pail.

Buttering Up Your Children… You and your child can make homemade butter easily. Pour a pint of whipping cream into a quart-size covered jar and shake until the cream thickens. Add a little salt to make salted butter.

Pancake Patterns… When next making pancakes, put the batter in a plastic ketchup bottle. Cut the tip off to make a larger opening and let the kids use the squeeze bottle to write their names or create shapes. It will make breakfast a lot more fun!

Porridge Put Over… If you have trouble getting your kids to eat porridge, try this. Instead of using just water or milk when cooking it, add some hot chocolate or cocoa powder to the milk or water. They'll eat it for hours!

INDOOR & OUTDOOR GAMES…

Indoor Games…

Trace-A-Friend!… Lay large pieces of brown paper or bristol board on the floor and get one child to lie down on it. Another child draws around them and the form can then be cut out. Have the kids draw in their own faces or each other's. It should keep them busy for hours!

Secret Messages… Have the children write messages or draw pictures on pieces of white paper using a candle or white crayon. Have them paint over it with some weak watercolor paints and their artwork or message is magically revealed!

Outdoor Games…

Garden Maze… Kids love mazes. Create your own by placing garden furniture in different positions and have them crawl through it. Tie ropes between the furniture to increase the difficulty, or have them hold a potato in each hand while they're negotiating the maze.

Space-Saving Sandbox... Get hold of an old truck tire and lay it in your back yard. Dump clean sand in it and you have an instant, custom-made sandbox.

Spoon Fishing... Attach small magnets onto some fishing line and tie the line to fishing poles. Scatter some old metal spoons on the lawn and let the kids "fish" for them. Prizes could be given for the most "fish" caught.

Short-Distance Calls!... Take your garden hose, remove the head and slip a plastic funnel into each end. Secure the funnels to the hose with adhesive tape. You now have a great "hose telephone" that the kid's will spend hours on, with no busy signal!

Forever Blowing Bubbles... For a fun slant on bubble blowing, let your kids use a variety of household items to create different sized and shaped bubbles. Here's a few ideas: garlic press, slotted spoon, plastic berry basket or a yogurt cup with the bottom cut out.

ORDER IN THE KID'S ROOM

TOYS, FURNITURE & CLOTHING TIPS...

Toys...

Stuffed-Animal Farm... Rub dry cornstarch into the toy. Let it stand briefly and then brush the cornstarch off.

♦ For unwashable stuffed toys that need cleaning, try this. Mix 1 tablespoon of liquid detergent with ½ cup of liquid fabric softener in a quart of warm water. Brush this on the toys (use an old, soft toothbrush), but do not saturate the article. Rub them with a clean, soft towel.

Art Gallery... Brighten your child's room by covering an entire wall with brightly colored felt or burlap. Your child can tape up his favorite paintings and pictures without damaging the fabric.

♦ Or hang a fishnet in your child's room and use colored clothespins to hang the pictures on the fishnet!

Games Organizer... Here's an idea for storing all those small game pieces and rules that always disappear mysteriously. Simply glue a small resealable plastic freezer bag on the inside of the box lid. It'll provide safe and secure storage.

♦ Freezer bags are also great for storing your jigsaw puzzle pieces. Place the pieces in the bag and leave the bag in the puzzle box.

Small Toy-Storage... Wash out your used cardboard and plastic ice cream containers. They're great for storing small toys in. Decorate with cartoons and pictures.

Furniture...

Nursery Ideas...Room For Improvement... Replace ordinary dresser knobs with small wooden alphabet blocks or wooden 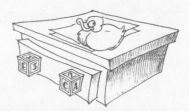 animal toys. Just remove the knobs and glue on the new drawer pulls with epoxy glue.

♦ Save the drawers from that old dresser and paint them colorfully. They make great toy boxes. You can even attach little wheels underneath so you can slide them into a closet or under the bed.

Clothing...

Bedroom Hang-Ups... Recycle your old towel rack by  attaching it to the footboard of your child's bed. It's a handy place for your kids to hang their clothes, especially if they're too small to reach their closet rod.

Shoe Things... Avoid falls in new shoes. Sand or scratch the soles lightly on pavement 2 or 3 times.

♦ Before polishing children's shoes, rub them with rubbing alcohol.

♦ Or get your children to rub their shoes with a raw potato before polishing and then polish with an old nylon stocking. They'll find it fun!

♦ When undoing knots in your child's shoelaces, save your nails by using a crochet hook.

♦ Teach your child to put his shoes on. Mark or tape the right shoe only. He'll be able to identify it quickly.

SAFETY FIRST

KEEPING THEM OUT OF HARM'S WAY...

Pool Safety... A great way to help prevent your children from slipping in their splash pool is to stick a bunch of bathtub decals on the bottom of the pool. Let the kids do it themselves…they'll have fun arranging them!

What's Your Number?... To teach your child their phone number, and make sure they remember it, have them recite it repeatedly to their favorite tune. The simpler the tune the better.

Paintbrush Handles... Cut all your child's paintbrush handles down to about four or five inches long. Not only will this make them easier to use, but it will keep your little Rembrandts much safer.

Prevent Your Child From Sneaking Out... Tie a small bell to your door. When your child tries to open the door, you will hear the bell ring.

♦ To prevent your child from turning a doorknob you don't want him to, try this. Fetch one of those odd socks lying around and slip the sock over the doorknob and attach with a rubber band. You'll find that when the child tries to open the door, the sock slips, because the child's grip is not strong enough.

Red Means Danger!... Teach your children that red means danger. Paint harmful bottle caps with red nail polish.

Keep Off The Glass!... To avoid toddlers walking into sliding glass doors, place a piece of colored tape on the glass at eye level. This will alert him.

KID HINT CATCHALL

NIFTY NOTES FOR NIPPERS...

The 3-Minute Toothbrushing... To get your kids to brush their teeth for the recommended 3-minute minimum, place a 3-minute egg timer in the bathroom. Turn it over and get them to brush until the sand runs out.

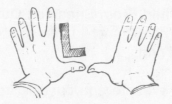

Left, Right, Left, Right!... To teach your children left from right, ask them to hold their hands up in front of them with palms facing away and fingers pointing upward. Next, tell them to spread their thumbs downward and the left hand then forms the shape of an L...which represents their left-hand side.

♦ To avoid the crush when exiting from a crowded concert or sports event with your children, always bear to the left. Most people tend to gravitate naturally to the right. You'll be going in the opposite direction to most of the crowd.

Traveling The Tidy Way... Hang a shoe bag over the backseat of the car and store all your traveling knickknacks and children's toys.

♦ Use small paper plates to slip your popsicle and ice cream sticks through to avoid messy drips.

♦ Why not collect a few of those fast-food vinegar packets to clean the kids greasy hands? They're useful and convenient. Just leave a few in your glove compartment.

♦ To avoid constant washroom visits when on a long drive, give the kids a cup of crushed ice instead of a soft drink. It will last a lot longer and will be less messy.

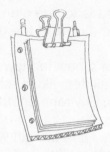

Back To School... To make sure your children don't lose their pens and pencils, make a little clipboard out of cardboard and a large paper holder. Attach their pens and pencils to it and punch holes in it to fit in their three-ring binder.

Yuletide Tips... To keep kids (and pets) at arm's length from the presents under the Christmas tree, recycle your old children's playpen. Paint it with bright Christmasy colors and place the tree and the presents inside it. Make sure the bars of the pen are the regulation distance apart.

♦ Here's what to do to prevent your kids from rummaging through to find their particular presents before the big day. Instead of writing the name on the present, put a number corresponding to a family member's name. The key to the numbers and names is kept safely hidden until Christmas morning.

Fun Wrapping Paper... Get the kids to make a special birthday wrap for their friend's birthday gift. Give them a road map and let them identify with a marker, familiar landmarks...like his school, your house and of course  his own home, etc. Include a tiny game piece, preferably in the shape of a car. You'll find he'll have as much fun with the wrapping paper as he will the gift!

◆ Another great wrapping idea is to use old magazines or comics. Tie them in with the theme of the gift.

◆ You could also wrap a gift in a new tea towel or scarf. Instead of a bow, use a small item like a mini egg whisk, or a colorful hair clip. Environment friendly too!

◆ And in place of a ribbon, try tying the gift with a skipping rope instead. An extra gift!

A Candle For Everyone!... When it's time for blowing out the candles on a birthday cake, a nice idea is to give a cupcake with a candle to each guest. This way everyone gets to blow a candle out!

Balloon-A-Grams... When sending out invitations to your child's next party, write the message on inflated balloons, deflate them and put each balloon in an envelope. Your child's friends will have to blow the balloon up to read the invitation!

Baby Bloomer!... A wonderful and unusual baby gift to give would be a flowering bush or tree seedling. The parents can plant it and watch it as it grows along with the child. A constant reminder of that happy occasion.

GRANDMA'S REMEDIES

FAMILY FIRST AID...

Ouches!... Saturate a piece of cotton with baby oil and rub over adhesive tape on your child's skin. No ouch!

Bitter Pill To Swallow?... Before you give your child that nasty-tasting pill or medicine, try giving him a flavored frozen popsicle to suck on. It'll help to anaesthetize their sense of taste long enough to make the swallowing a little easier.

♦ If your baby doesn't want to take the liquid medicine, simply wait until the next feeding. Pour the dose into a baby nipple and you'll find he'll be so intent on satisfying his appetite that the medicine will be devoured in no time.

Cuts... To make your child's experience with a cut a little less traumatic, try this idea. Use a dark-colored or red facecloth when first dabbing the injury. This way your child will not be alarmed by the sight of their own blood on the cloth.

Toothaches... Apply clove oil or a whole clove against the aching tooth to relieve pain.

♦ You can often reduce toothache pain by holding an ice cube against the stretch of skin between the  thumb and forefinger. Make sure it's the hand on the same side of the body that the toothache is.

Canker Sores... They say that if you soak an ordinary black tea bag in a sugar-water solution for a minute or so and hold it against the canker sore for a short while, it should relieve some of the pain. Evidently the tannin acts as a pain-relieving astringent.

Earaches... For temporary relief, hold a slice of warm bread over the offending ear. They say it works!

Chapped Lips Or Hands... Apply glycerin and lemon juice in equal amounts and leave overnight.

Sunburn... To bring relief from sunburn, whip an egg white and beat in a teaspoon of castor oil. Apply to the affected areas.

 ♦ Or add a handful of baking soda to a bathtub of warm water and soak in it for a while. It's also very relaxing!

Splinter... Apply rubbing alcohol to area and remove with eyebrow pluckers. If imbedded totally, sterilize a needle with alcohol and work the splinter out from the bottom. If necessary, numb the area first with an ice cube.

 ♦ To remove splinters easily, soak area in olive oil.

 ♦ If you're having difficulty locating the sliver, dab some iodine over the general area. The iodine exposes the sliver which makes it easier to remove.

Bee Stings... Apply a paste of baking soda and water. Also, dab with lemon juice.

 ♦ They say that if you cut a green onion and hold it on the sting, it should help relieve the pain.

 ♦ Or try holding a banana peel on the sting.

 ♦ Also, hemorrhoid cream can sometimes help too!

Mosquito Bites... Soak a cotton ball with vinegar and apply to the bite to relieve the itch.

 ♦ Or crush some of the leaves from the herb feverfew and mix it with a little petroleum jelly. It's very soothing.

♦ Another method is to make a paste of ¼ cup meat-tenderizing powder and 1 or 2 teaspoons of water. Apply it to the bite to relieve the itch.

Poison Ivy... If you rub the inside of a banana peel on a poison ivy rash, it should reduce the irritation within a few days.

♦ They also say that the impatiens plant will help reduce poison-ivy itch.

Pimples... A quick cure is to dab some lemon juice on the pimple. It should dry it up quickly.

♦ Or mix 1 cup of hot water with ¼ teaspoon of salt and apply to the pimple with a cotton ball. Evidently, the heat opens the pore and the salt tends to draw out the infection.

Emergency Ice Pack... Simply wrap a dishcloth around a tin of frozen juice. A bag of frozen vegetables works well too!

Did You Know... People with a high acidic diet tend to smoke more than those with an alkaline diet. Evidently, fruits and vegetables help sustain an alkaline condition, which causes nicotine to stay longer in the body. This, in turn, helps reduce cigarette cravings which can help you give up that nasty smoking habit. It's worth a try!

— ♦ —

CHAPTER 6

'SPECIALLY FOR SENIORS

HELPFUL TIPS TO MAKE
LIFE EASIER FOR THOSE IN
THEIR LATER YEARS!

POINTERS FOR PEOPLE IN THEIR PRIME

Taking Medication... If your medication is in a liquid form, it's a good idea to hold the spoon over a cup when pouring it from the medicine bottle. If the spoon overflows or spills, you'll still save every last drop.

♦ To keep track of when you have taken your medication, keep a small calendar on the fridge and mark down the time you take it.

♦ If your eyesight isn't that good, you may want to try this clever tip. Draw a picture with a bright-colored pen on the label, corresponding to the ailment you're taking the medication for.

♦ To avoid the prescription on your medication getting faded or blurred, stick a piece of scotch tape over the label. Or paint over it with clear nail varnish.

♦ If you have difficulty in seeing the little arrows on pill bottles and lids, you'll find it easier to line them up if you first paint the arrows with bright red nail polish.

♦ To make a safety cap easier to open, remove the cap and make 2 or 3 cuts in the side of the cap. This will loosen its grip substantially. Keep out of reach of the grandchildren though.

♦ It's a good idea to cut a piece of white cardboard from an old shoe box and write down all your medical information on it. Include your doctor's name and phone number, your blood type, medical insurance numbers and medication, complete with dosage. In an emergency, all your information is close at hand.

Orthopedic Towel!... For a handy, makeshift neck support when sleeping, simply roll up a bath towel and slip it inside your pillow case.

Easy-To-Read Telephone Book... Write all the important phone numbers you need on index cards, one to a card, in large print. Place them alphabetically in a photograph album or scrapbook and you have a handy, easy-to-read directory.

Magnifying Glasses... In a pinch, your eyeglass lens can act as a magnifying glass. Remove your glasses and hold the one lens over the item or word you wish to see. By adjusting the distance you can magnify it.

Time-Zone Tip... The next time you travel anywhere that is in a different time zone, you may want to take along a second watch or small clock, set to the time in your hometown. This way you'll know the exact time back home when you call friends or relatives. They'll appreciate it!

Safe Luggage... Keep a self-addressed letter in your luggage in case it goes astray. It makes identifying easier should your luggage tag come off.

Sweet-Smelling Luggage... Here's a way to prevent your clothes in your suitcase from smelling musty when traveling. Save your old soap slivers, pop them into an onion mesh bag and leave it in your suitcase.

    ♦ Fabric-softener sheets work well too!

Swollen Feet... When traveling by plane, your feet tend to swell. It's a good idea not to remove your shoes or you may have difficulty getting them on again.

Finding Your Way Back... It's a good idea when visiting strange cities to keep one of the hotel's matchbooks with you. This way if you can't find your way back, a local will be able to easily direct you.

Silence Is Golden!... When on a vacation at a hotel, you appreciate your beauty sleep. For extra silence, roll up a bath towel and lay it over the crack at the bottom of the entrance door and any door to the next room.

"Do Not...Rob"!... When staying in a hotel, it's a good idea to leave a "do not disturb" sign on the door when you go out for a while. This will usually discourage thieves.

Quick Address... Before you leave on vacation, write down your friends' and relatives' names and addresses on self-adhesive labels. This will save you valuable vacation time.

Pickpocket Prevention... To prevent pickpockets from removing your wallet from your back pocket, try this. Fold your wallet over your comb (teeth-side up) and return it to your back pocket. The teeth will snag if removed, unless you lift  one side of the comb and remove at a 45-degree angle.

Keeping Your Cool... If you plan to be out in the hot sun for a period of time, wear a cool straw hat, with a damp cloth under it.

Help At The Touch Of A Button... Pick up a cheap door chime and install the button in the room of anyone who might need help in a hurry. The chime should be placed centrally in the house where it can easily be heard.

In The Bathroom... If you have difficulty reaching certain areas when drying yourself after a bath or shower, instead of using a towel, use a hair dryer. It can reach spots you would normally find difficult to get to. Make sure you're not standing on a wet bath mat though!

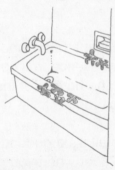

♦ Place a few bathtub decals on the top of the sides of the tub where you grip when lifting yourself out of the tub. It'll prevent your hands slipping.

Baby-Sitting Bath Time... If you're looking after your baby grandchildren and it's time for their bath, try this back-saving tip. Bathe the child in the laundry tub. It's just the right height!

Sugar Shake?... If you're on a sugar-restricted diet, pour some artificial sweetener into a saltshaker. You'll find it really handy for sweetening things like cereal, etc. Make sure you mark it "sweetener" though!

Easy-Grip Cutlery... To make cutlery easier to grasp, wind several rubber bands onto the handles.

Easy-Grip Zip!... Fit a small curtain ring through the hole in your zipper tab. You'll find it a lot easier to grip than that tiny metal tab.

Easy-Grip Playing Cards...
Sew two plastic tub lids at the center, back-to-back. This makes a great holder for playing cards. They fit snugly between the lids.

Easy-Grip Cash!... If you have a hard time removing silver coins from your change purse, try leaving a small fridge magnet in with the coins. You'll find everything except the pennies will adhere to the magnet, making it easier to remove them. This also works well for small change in your pockets.

See The Light (Switch)!... Often twist or push lamp switches are hard to turn on if you have arthritis. Have the light sockets changed to those with a pull chain. It'll be a lot easier to use and you may want to paint the knob at the end of the chain with luminous paint to make it visible in the dark. Another, more expensive, solution is to replace all your lamps with those that go on and off by just touching the base.

Detergent Cutlery!... Save plastic detergent scoops. They make great receptacles for small quantities of food or drink for people suffering from arthritis. The handles are easy to hold. Make sure to wash them out well.

Handy Limb Warmers... If you suffer from arthritis pain, buy some cheap woolen leg warmers. Slip them over your legs and arms for that extra warmth to ease the pain.

Emergency Identification... If you use a wheelchair, walker or even a walking stick and go out on your own, make sure you attach onto the item the phone number of someone to contact should there be an emergency.

The Perfect Gift... For a unique gift to a senior that will always be appreciated, arrange for a cleaner to clean their home from top to bottom.

Visitor Etiquette... The next time you visit someone overnight who is a senior, bring your own bed linen. They'll appreciate not having the laundry.

Clothesline Backache... To avoid the pain of bending over to pick up your clothespins when hanging clothes on the line, put an apron on and keep the clothespins in the pocket. Your back will thank you for it!

Footwear Fact... It's a good idea to remove the laces from your shoes and replace them with thick sewing elastic. This way you won't have to worry about tying those shoelaces again!

♦ If you have difficulty putting on boots, try sprinkling some baby powder in the boot first for an easier glide in.

♦ Or place a plastic shopping bag upright in the boot so that the top end drapes over the top of the boot and the bottom end hangs down to the foot of the boot. Slip your foot in and you'll find that the bag allows easy entry of your foot. Simply pull the bag out once your foot is in place.

Button Down Your Purse!... If your purse has a tendency to slip off your shoulder while shopping, try this. Sew a button under the collar of your coat or jacket. The purse strap will be held in place by the button.

Purse Penholder... Keep your pens and pencils in a toothbrush holder instead of carrying them loose in your purse. This prevents ink leakage and broken pencil tips. It also prevents the inside of your purse and items getting marked, not to mention the fact that the holder is easily visible in your purse.

Crochet Anyone?... Here's a clever idea for a crochet-ball holder. Attach a toilet-roll holder to the edge of a small side table. Simply slip the crochet ball onto the holder.

Skateboard Dolly... Pick up an old skateboard at a yard sale and use it to move heavy things around instead of carrying them. Garbage cans for instance.

Gardening Made Easy... If you have an old golf bag and golf cart, place your gardening tools in it. It makes it a lot easier to move your garden tools around the garden.

♦ A grocery buggy works well too!

Ring Around The Garden... Here's a clever way to protect your wedding ring from getting scratched when gardening. Cut the finger off a rubber glove and slip it on your wedding finger.

♦ To avoid stooping and grasping weeds, try this little trick. Take a broom handle and screw a large cup hook into one end. You'll find if you dampen the soil around the weeds first, your handy weed remover will do the rest.

Better Safe Than Sorry... When returning to an empty house after a period of time, it's a good idea to ring your own doorbell and wait for a minute or so before opening the door. This could scare off any intruder that might be inside.

Cooking Tips... To prevent the wide sleeves from your house coat catching on pot handles etc., while in the kitchen, slip a pair of cyclist trouser clips over the sleeves.

♦ If you are a little hard of hearing, instead of using the timer on your stove when cooking, use your microwave timer. The lighted numbers are easy to see.

♦ Remember, a whistling teakettle is essential for seniors. It remembers when you forget!

Finding A Needle In A Haystack... If you lose something tiny on the carpet or floor, like an earring back, or a contact lens...or, heaven forbid, the diamond from your ring, you could spend ages on your hands and knees trying to find it. To locate that errant item in a hurry, simply cut a leg from a pair of old panty hose (or a knee-high) and slip it over your vacuum-cleaner wand. Vacuum the floor area and in no time at all that lost item will stick to the panty hose at the mouth of the vacuum wand...ready for you to pluck it off and return it to its rightful place!

━ ♦ ━

CHAPTER 7

THE HOME HANDYPERSON

TIPS & INFORMATION
TO HELP YOU
DO-IT-YOURSELF!

TRICKS OF THE TOOL TRADE

GOOD ADVICE & GREAT IDEAS...

Good Advice...

Penny-Wise, Pound-Foolish... While it's great to get a good bargain on the price of your tools, it's important to remember that even though most hand tools last a lifetime, it's well worth investing in good quality equipment. Even though it might cost more it will make difficult tasks simpler and save hours of frustration.

Your Toolbox... Here's a list of basic tools we suggest you keep in your toolbox:
- ~ Hammer with a curved-claw back for nail pulling
- ~ Multibit screwdriver
- ~ Tape measure, 10-foot retractable
- ~ Carpenter's level
- ~ $\frac{3}{8}$-inch electric drill, with accessories
- ~ Heavy canvas working gloves
- ~ Flashlight
- ~ Pliers
- ~ Putty knife
- ~ Electrical tape
- ~ Small handsaw
- ~ Adjustable wrench
- ~ Assorted nails and screws
- ~ Plunger
- ~ Pencils...you can never find one when you need it!

A "Closet" Workshop... If you don't have the space to dedicate a room as a workshop, here's a space-saving idea you can use:

~ First, clean out a seldom-used closet.

~ Line the back and side walls with Peg-Board, to hang lightweight tools and items on.

~ Build 2 or 3 strong shelves for heavier tools, etc. Fit some drawers under the shelves.

~ Make a workbench that is hinged to the inside of the closet door. Build it so that it has good, strong legs that you can fold out when you lower the bench.

~ Attach a length of eaves trough to the door above the workbench. Divide it with plywood partitions to make a great storage unit for nails and screws.

Rusty Tools... If you store hand tools in a damp basement, try putting a few mothballs in the toolbox or tool drawers to absorb the moisture.

♦ Rusty tools are easily cleaned by rubbing with a soap-filled steel-wool pad. Dip the pad in turpentine and rub vigorously.

♦ Prevent small garden tools from rusting by storing them in a bucket of dry sand.

♦ Self-polishing floor wax works wonders to protect household tools from rust. Simply coat the metal or cutting blade with wax and allow to dry.

File Care... To prevent your metal files from clogging up, rub some ordinary blackboard chalk on the file.

Free Advice!... Get to know your local hardware-store owner. They often know a lot about everything and can not only give you all sorts of free advice, but also provide you with the occasional "miracle tool" that makes an impossible job simple.

Great Ideas...

The Plastic Spatula Tool!... A plastic kitchen spatula may be added to your tool list as well. Here's why. To protect the surface when removing a nail, place the blade part of the spatula under the head of the clawhammer while you lever the nail out.

♦ You can also cut a small V in the bottom edge of the spatula's blade. When you're next driving a screw, simply slip the V around the base of the screw. This will protect the work surface, should the screwdriver blade slip.

Emergency Mallet... Cut a hole in a tennis ball and place it over your regular hammerhead.

Emergency Wire Stripper... Ordinary nail clippers work well if you don't have a wire stripper.

Emergency Screwdriver... In an emergency, a large nail will sometimes act as a Phillips screwdriver (star shape). Grip the nail with pliers.

Tough Screw?... If you find a screw is seized and you need some extra torque, try tightening an adjustable wrench onto the blade of the screwdriver. This will give you the extra leverage you need.

Wrenches... Cut some pieces of inner tube about the size of a quarter, make a slit in them and slide them onto your double-ended  wrenches. Now you can slide the rubber collar up to the end you're using and this will identify that end if you have to put the wrench down for a while.

♦ A box wrench is handy for keeping your fingers out of harm's way when using a cold chisel. Most cold chisels are hexagonal, so the wrench will fit perfectly while it holds the chisel in place.

♦ If you find a wrench isn't quite small enough, try slipping a thin piece of metal between the one jaw and the bolt head. This should give you a tight fit.

Chisel Storage... Cut a small slit in several tennis or rubber balls and insert your chisel blades into the slits. Your chisels will be protected against chipping and dulling.

Shear Genius... Attach the ends of a 2-foot length of garden hose to the handles of your cutting shears. The natural spring action created by the hose will move the handles up and down and make your cutting easier. In addition the rubber from the hose will cushion your hands from the shear handles.

Hot Water Tool Belt!... Take an old hot water bottle and cut across one side of the bottle about halfway up. Then cut up the two sides and across the top to create the pouch. Cut two vertical slits in the back to slip a belt through and you have a durable tool pouch.

At The End Of Your Rope?... Nylon rope that has been cut should have the raw end heated to prevent fraying. Ordinary rope can be dipped in shellac or varathane.

Ladder Catchall... The top wrung of your ladder, if you follow the cardinal rule of not standing on it, is normally obsolete. However, if you cut some leftover molding to size and nail it around the edge of the top wrung, this will create a handy carryall for your nails, screws, small tools, etc.

♦ Another idea is to partially open a large tin can. Bend the lid back to form a hook. Now you have a handy little tool container that you can hang over the rung of your ladder.

Rubber Bands... You can make good, strong rubber bands by cutting strips of car inner tube.

Easy Rubber Cutting... You should find it easier to cut rubber if you dip your scissors in water first.

WALLS, FLOORS, WINDOWS & DOORS

WALLS & FLOORS...

Walls...

Finding The Wall Stud... Wall studs (floor-to-ceiling lengths of 2 in. x 4 in. or 6 in.) are usually located 16 inches apart. If you start in the corner and measure 17 inches, you should hit the center of the first stud. Be careful: electrical wires often run through the center of the studs.

♦ Another way to locate a wall stud is to use a commercial stud finder. However, if you don't have one, you can substitute with a common compass, which works almost as well. Simply draw the compass across the wall and you will find the needle will be attracted to the drywall nails.

Avoid Cracking Plaster... Place a small piece of tape over the spot on the wall you plan to nail.

Repairing Plaster… When fixing small wall cracks, instead of mixing the plaster with water, use vinegar. Evidently, this makes a stronger fill.

No Plaster?… In a pinch, try some white carpenter's glue mixed into a paste with baking soda.

♦ Toothpaste also works great for filling small or wall nail holes.

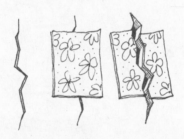

Cracking Up?… To determine if a crack in the wall is getting larger, simply glue a piece of wallpaper over the crack. If the crack widens it'll tear the wallpaper as it does so.

Steps To Protect Your Walls… Place old socks over the top ends of your ladder to protect the wall from being marked.

Wallpaper… Grease spots can be lightened and often removed by applying a mixture of cornstarch and water. Allow mixture to dry, then brush away. Repeat if necessary.

♦ To prevent grease spots on old wallpaper from soaking through to new paper, paint the spots with shellac before applying the new paper.

♦ Believe it or not, a piece of rye bread or an Artgum eraser rubbed over wallpaper in long vertical strokes will often remove soiled spots.

♦ When applying wallpaper in areas of the house where dampness or steam tends to occur, as in the bathroom or the kitchen, try this helpful tip. As soon as the wallpaper dries, paint some clear shellac over the joins and edges. You'll find that this will help prevent those areas of the paper from peeling back and looking unsightly.

♦ Peeling wallpaper can be reglued. Using wallpaper paste, smear some on a piece of writing paper with a kitchen knife. Blot excess. Working from the point closest to the intact wallpaper, rub the pasted paper against the underside of the unglued wallpaper. Hold paper against wallpaper for a moment. Then slide the writing paper out and press the wallpaper against the wall. Smooth away any air bubbles.

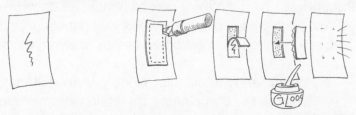

♦ To repair a rip or immovable mark, take some of the original paper and cut a piece an inch or two larger than the damaged area. Make sure the pattern matches. Hold the patch securely over the matching area and cut through both layers of paper with a sharp wallpaper knife. Ensure your cut lines are larger than the damaged section. Now, remove the old piece and glue the new piece into place. Invisible mending!

♦ When getting ready to wallpaper, start straight! Don't trust room corners. Suspend a chalked, weighted piece of string from a high point on the wall. When it comes to rest, pull it taut against the baseboard. Snap the string at the center. The mark it leaves will be a true vertical.

Measuring For Wallpaper... Here's a formula for determining how many rolls you'll need to cover any room in your house. Measure the height of the ceiling (floor-to-ceiling measurement). Measure the length of two walls and the width of two walls. Total the lengths and widths and multiply by the ceiling height. Divide this total by 25. Example: The room is 10 ft. x 12 ft. and the ceiling is 8 ft. high. The total lengths and widths is 10 + 10 + 12 + 12 = 44 ft. Multiply 44 ft. by the ceiling height of 8 ft. to arrive at 352. Divide 352 by 25 to get just over 14 single rolls. You can usually deduct 1 single roll for every 2 openings such as a door or window. However, after making all the calculations and deductions, add 1 single roll for safety.

Paneling... Even the most careful handyperson will find annoying white spaces between wall panels. Try spraying black paint on the backboard before applying the paneling.

♦ Water tends to discolor wood paneling. It may sound insane, but try covering the stain with mayonnaise at night. In many cases, by the morning, the stain will have disappeared!

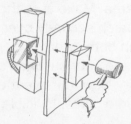

♦ When a switch box requires a cutout in the panel, place the panel in its normal position over the box. Lay a soft wood block over the approximate location of the switch box and tap the block soundly. The outlet box will make its imprint on the back of the paneling for easy and accurate cutting.

Finishing The Basement... Before application of paneling, check walls for excessive moisture. Failure to seal off moisture can cause molding, warping, separation and discoloration.

◆ To test for condensation on basement walls, place a small mirror against the wall. If droplets of moisture, or fog, appear on the mirror, you'll need to seal the wall. Allow walls to dry before applying paneling.

Floors...

Squeaky Floors... Oil everything that squeaks, except floors and complicated mechanisms like tumbler locks. Squeaky floorboards should be nailed at an angle with the nail heads just below the surface of the wood.

◆ If floors creak, sprinkle the area with talcum powder. Rub in lightly and sweep remaining powder away.

Floor First Aid... Gouges in resilient flooring can be repaired. Shave a little floor covering from a matching scrap or an inconspicuous tile. Mix scrapings with clear lacquer and apply with a putty knife.

◆ Remember to remove old nails and staples before applying tile to an old floor.

◆ To repair the chipped and cracked edges of your linoleum floor, try this. Cut a 12-inch strip off right around the perimeter, leaving the firmly glued linoleum intact. Then, place a border of 12-inch-square, self-stick floor tiles in its place. Saves the cost of laying a whole new floor!

WINDOWS & DOORS...

Windows...

Sticky Windows... Beeswax on the pulley stiles will make the window glide easily up and down.

Sweaty Windows... If sweating occurs on the inside window, the storm window is not properly sealed. If sweating occurs on the storm window, the inside window is leaking.

Window Locks... If you plan to install locks on your windows, make sure you screw right through the window frame into the wall studs to anchor the lock securely.

Doors...

Knobs And Hinges... Doorknobs that rattle are usually fixed easily by tightening the tiny setscrew just behind the handle. If this doesn't work, you may have to replace the spindle that goes through the hole in the door.

♦ It's also a good idea to dab a little clear nail varnish on the head of the setscrew once you've tightened it. This will keep it from loosening again.

♦ If hinges still squeak after oiling, remove and clean with steel wool. Remember to do one hinge at a time and avoid the awkward job of rehanging the door.

♦ Rusty door bolts are best lubricated with penetrating oil, but often liberal amounts of soda water will work.

Door Locks... Your locks are only as strong as what they are attached to. So if you have a hollow front or back door, it might be a good idea to replace it with a solid door, or even a metal one.

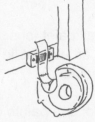

Demagnetizing Doors!... If the magnets on your cupboard doors are too strong, remove some of the magnets' strength by covering them with cellophane tape.

Recycled Doors... Don't throw out that old wooden door with the lovely recesses and ornate molding. Refinish it to your taste and mount it behind your bed as a headboard.

♦ It can also make interesting wainscotting!

THE PAINTER

GENERAL PAINTING DOS & DON'TS...

Do... paint a small piece of metal and dry it in the oven to make a quick comparison of a freshly mixed color. Wet paint appears to have a different color than dry paint.

Do... cut a piece of wire mesh to fit inside your old paint can. Old paint sometimes gets lumpy. The mesh will sink to the bottom carrying any lumps with it.

♦ Or strain the paint through panty hose. Also works to strain paint thinner for reuse!

Do... stir in a drop of black paint when painting with white paint. It should make the white paint whiter!

Don't... use the whole can when tackling small paint jobs. Pour paint into an old coffee mug. Or, use an old pot lid (with a handle) to hold small amounts of paint.

Don't... drink alcohol while painting. Even odorless paints can produce fumes that can be dangerous to your health. This is compounded when you have alcohol in your system. Save the celebration until after you've finished painting!

Don't... be a drip! If you have ever had paint drip from the handle of a brush and down your arm, try sticking the handle of the brush through the center of a paper plate, or half a tennis ball. Or, you could slip a rubber glove on your painting hand and turn the cuff up.

 **Don't...** allow those messy runs on the side of your paint can. Stretch a rubber band vertically over the can so that it runs across the open mouth of the can. You can now wipe your brush on the rubber band and the excess paint will fall neatly back into the can.

♦ You can also try punching small holes through the lip of the paint can. The paint drains right back into the can.

And What's More... For a handy way to fill those tiny holes and cracks when painting woodwork, mix a little flour with some of the paint you're using. It hardens well and blends with the paint perfectly.

♦ To get the paint to adhere to your rollers and paintbrushes better, soak them in paint thinner first. Then brush or roll out the thinner onto an absorbent cloth until the brush or roller is completely dry to the touch. This will also make cleanup a lot easier.

♦ For those awkward corners or delicate touch-up jobs, you might want to use a Q-tip instead of a brush.

♦ Another tip for fiddly paint jobs is to recycle your used shoe-polish applicators. Wash out the sponge and the container and simply fill with paint.

♦ You know you've saved those glass aspirin and jam jars, etc. for something. Use them for leftover paint and quick touch-ups.

WHEN PAINTING...

Radiators... Make sure you use heat-resistant paint when painting radiators. Also, ensure the rad is warm when you apply the paint. It tends to "bake" the enamel, giving a longer-lasting finish.

Knobs... To paint knobs, remove them from the drawer or cupboard first. Next, replace each screw back into the knob. Then place the knob, screw first, in the neck of a pop bottle. Now you can gently paint them or spray them with no mess.

Windows... Rub soft bar soap around window edges to avoid glass cleanup.

♦ Strips of writing paper soaked in warm water and placed snugly around the edges of the glass will stay in place long enough for you to paint the window frame. If you don't have writing paper, newspaper will work just as well. However, it may take a little window cleanup to remove any residual ink print marks.

♦ Or try applying a film of ordinary petroleum jelly on the window. It will rub off easily once the paint is dry.

♦ Make sure you clean all the dirt out of difficult-to-reach corners and edges before painting. Try using an artist's long-handled paintbrush to sweep it out.

♦ Save hours touching up new putty around your windows by mixing in paint with the putty—the same color as your window frames—before installing.

No Masking Tape?... Should you run out of masking tape when preparing to paint, dry strippable wallpaper cut into strips will work well.

Steps... Instead of painting all the steps at once, paint every other step. Wait for them to dry, then paint the remaining unpainted steps.

♦ To prevent serious accidents from slipping on painted steps, add a little sand to the paint when painting the steps. This will give a better foothold.

♦ To keep paint from peeling off concrete steps, apply a thin coat of vinegar before applying the paint.

Fences... When painting the bottom of fences and fence posts, to prevent your brush or roller picking up dirt or grass, use an old dustpan to shield it from the ground.

Houses... It's a good idea to paint your house every 3 to 5 years.

♦ Paint the north and west sides in the morning and the south and east sides in the afternoon. This avoids painting in direct sunlight, which can cause uneven drying.

♦ Choose your season when painting your house. You may want to consider spring or fall. Both months have fairly mild temperatures.

To Disperse Paint Odor... Leave a pail of water inside a freshly painted room and the odor should diminish considerably.

♦ It's also said that if you add some vanilla or peppermint extract to your paint, in the ratio of 2 teaspoons to 1 gallon, it should help cut down on paint odor.

♦ Some say that a plate of sliced apples placed in the room you are painting will help cut down on paint odor.

EASY CLEANUP...

Brushes... Even the best planners sometimes find themselves with a half-finished job at midnight. If it's too late, or you don't have time to thoroughly clean paintbrushes, try storing them in plastic sandwich bags overnight in the freezer. Secure with a rubber band around the handle.

♦ Don't throw away old hardened brushes. They can often be salvaged by soaking them in hot vinegar. Finally, comb the brush with an old fork.

♦ Paint thinner is reusable. Allow the container you've
   used to clean your brushes to sit for a few days. After
   the paint has settled to the bottom, carefully pour the
   thinner into a clean container.

♦ Another way to conserve your paint thinner when
   cleaning your brushes is to use a tall narrow container
   instead of a short flat one. This way you maximize
   the amount of thinner that will reach the bristles,
   creating less waste.

♦ Once you've cleaned and washed your brush, place a
   wide elastic band around the bristles. This will help
   them keep their shape while drying.

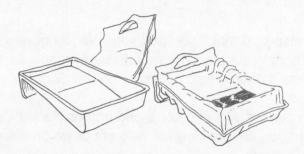

Rollers... If you're using a roller, slip a plastic shopping or
   garbage bag over the paint tray before pouring in the paint,
   to form a liner. Cleanup time will be reduced considerably.
   Simply invert the bag as you remove it and discard.
   No mess!

♦ To clean your roller easily, take one of those long
   containers you buy tennis balls in and pop your
   roller into it. Fill the container with solvent, enough to
   cover the roller, close the lid tightly and give it a good
   "cocktail" shake. Let it sit for a couple of hours, give it
   a last shake and your roller should be ready for that
   final soap and water treatment!

Paint Cans... When you've finished painting, mark the level of paint remaining in the can on the outside before cleaning your brush. Next time, you'll know how much is in the can without having to open it. You'll also know the color!

♦ When replacing the lid on old paint or shellac cans, you'll want a tight fit. Before hammering the lid shut, place an old rag over the can to catch excess paint that has accumulated in the groove around the lip of the can.

♦ To avoid some of the cleanup from dripping paint cans, glue a paper or foam plate under the paint can to catch the drips.

Hardware... Apply petroleum jelly on brass hinges, doorknobs and any other hardware you don't want painted.

Yourself!... Cooking oil will remove most paint from skin without the irritation caused by some commercial products.

♦ It might also be a good idea to rub petroleum jelly on the back of your hands and face before painting, to make washing up a simpler matter.

Paint Stains... Turpentine will work on paint stains. Just soak and scrape with an old putty knife or razor blade.

♦ Vinegar and water will remove newly dried paint from glass surfaces.

♦ Apply nail-polish remover to old paint splatters on windows. Wait a few minutes and wash off.

THE PLUMBER

JUST "PLUMB" EASY...

Frozen Pipes... If your pipes aren't frozen too badly, try turning the faucets upside down with a wrench, then pouring a gallon of boiling, salted water down the faucet.

♦ Frozen pipes can sometimes be rescued by applying steady heat with a hair-dryer. If you put your vacuum-cleaner hose in the exhaust outlet, sometimes the warm air blowing from your vacuum cleaner will be enough to thaw the pipes.

♦ Alternatively, try wrapping the frozen pipes with hot cloths or towels.

♦ Always start near an open valve or faucet when heating a frozen pipe. This allows steam to escape harmlessly. Never let the pipe get too hot to touch with your hands.

Leaking Pipes... Know where the main valve that brings water to your house is and know how to shut it off. In the event of a broken water pipe, this will be your first action. Finding and correcting the leak can then proceed. If the leak is in the hot-water system, turn off the electricity to the hot-water heater and, if your house is heated by water, the boiler.

♦ If you must tighten exposed plumbing pipes, wrap them first with 2 or 3 layers of plastic electrical tape to protect them from the wrench's metal teeth.

♦ If you have a leak in your sink drainpipe this may be because of a loose nut above the U-shaped section of the drain. Try tightening this nut with a large wrench. If the drainpipe continues to leak the problem could be the threads have been stripped on the nut; if so, try replacing the nut.

Soldering Pipes... When soldering copper or gluing plastic waterpipes, keep them dry by stuffing a piece of bread into the pipe in either side of where you're working. The bread will soak up any water before it can reach your work area. When finished, turn the water on and the bread plugs will be washed away.

Cutting Pipes... When cutting round metal pipes, it's often hard to get a cut started accurately, because the saw teeth move around on the hard surface. If you use a three-corner file first to start the cut, you'll find you'll be far more accurate. The file mark will guide the saw blade. Tape the file onto the back of your hacksaw frame to have it on hand at all times.

Faucets...Nobody Likes A Drip!... Solve your problem with these easy steps:
1) Turn off water under sink, or at source.
2) Open faucet to drain water.

3) Unscrew faucet handle.
4) Unscrew nut that holds faucet stem in place with an adjustable wrench.
5) Pull out faucet stem.
6) Remove screw at bottom which holds washer.
7) Remove washer and replace with same size new washer.
8) Repeat above steps in reverse order.

♦ If a leaking faucet keeps you awake at night, try tying a piece of cotton string or cording to the tap so that the water will run the length of the cord right into the drain. Make a mental note to fix it tomorrow and get a good night's rest!

♦ When buying a replacement washer, buy 2 or 3 extra and tie them with a twist tie to your shutoff valve beneath the faucet. Next time you'll have the right size on hand!

When Your Toilet Won't Stop Running... Check the tank float by first removing the lid and simply lifting the float. If it stops the water, bend the rod connected to the float down slightly. Also check for a leak in the float. Unscrew it from the rod and shake. Replace if there is water inside.

Tile Cracks... Fix cracks around the bathtub by filling with tile cement. While it may not show, there could be water seepage into the ceiling of the floor below.

♦ When replacing caulking around your bathtub, fill the bath with water to just below the overflow first. Apply caulking and allow to dry before draining the water. This helps prevent later stretching and pulling away of the sealant you just applied.

♦ Two lines of masking tape on either side of a crack to be caulked will prevent messes and leave a finished line after the caulking has dried.

Chip Off The Old Tub!... Instead of using expensive porcelain paint to repair small chips on your bathtub or sink, ask your local auto body shop to give you a small amount of auto touch-up paint. Find one that matches your bathroom color.

THE ELECTRICIAN

PLUGGING BRIGHT IDEAS...

Fuses And Circuit Breakers... Fuses protect your electrical system from overloading. One too many appliances drawing electricity can cause the wires to heat and, without fuses or a circuit breaker, can start a fire inside the walls. Replace blown fuses with fuses of the correct amperage and, if necessary, unplug one or more appliances on that circuit.

♦ Always test an electrical circuit before beginning work. A voltage tester is simply two wires with a little bulb between them. Make sure you periodically check your voltage tester in a circuit that does work so that you are sure it's operating.

♦ An inexpensive pencil flashlight clipped to the panel or fuse box will save time in the event of a power failure.

◆ Know what's where! Here's a good rainy-day activity. Turn on several electrical appliances and lamps in the house. Go to the fuse box and remove one fuse. Note which appliance stops working or which light goes out. Repeat with each and every fuse and keep a record in the fuse box for future reference. If you have

circuit breakers instead of fuses, you simply switch off each breaker and note which appliance or light goes off. Write the appliance or circuit on a small label and stick it next to the corresponding breaker.

◆ If you get tired of buying fuses, you can buy individual "circuit breaker" fuses. They are more expensive than regular fuses but they save the inconvenience of running out of fuses. Make sure you still use the right size fuse for that circuit.

◆ Large appliances often have their own cartridge fuse. Be sure to remove these only with a fuse puller and preferably with the main power switched off.

Cords And Cables... When storing an appliance, instead of knotting the cord to hold it in place, glue a magnet to the plug and magnetically attach the plug to the appliance.

◆ Thin wire in a long extension cord drains electrical power. It can significantly reduce power to an electric heater and even your electric drill will turn more slowly if it's at the end of a long extension cord. It also can damage the appliance if used continuously.

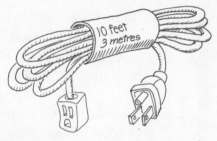

♦ Electrical extension cords can be kept tangle free by winding the cord and inserting it into a cardboard roll (from a toilet roll or paper-towel roll). Write the length of the cord on the outside of the tube.

♦ When cutting electric cable, be sure to add 20% to your straight-line measurement. Cable does not bend easily or lay perfectly flat.

♦ If you're attaching plastic-sheathed cables with staples, be careful not to drive the staple too far or you may cause a short in the cable.

Fluorescent Lights… All fluorescent lights generate a hum. They are rated from low noise level A to a high, annoying level B. Be sure to check the noise level before buying.

Christmas Lights… When draping Christmas lights on the tree, as you go, attach the wire adjacent to each light to the branch with an ordinary bread tag. It has just the right size hole to fit around the branches. You can even paint them different colors and decorate them!

Replacing Lightbulbs… To replace lightbulbs in ceiling fixtures, here's a handy gadget you can make. Take a long cardboard mailing tube and cut 2 slits a few inches long, lengthwise down one end. Then slide 2 elastic bands around the end. The slits will allow the tube to expand enough to cover the bulb and the rubber bands will provide enough tension to grip the bulb.

♦ To remove a lightbulb that has broken in a ceiling fixture try this. First, turn off the power supply to that outlet. Then, using a piece of cork, carefully push the cork into the broken bulb and remove.

Lamp Wires... When inserting a new lamp cord into your old lamp base, simply tape the new wire to the old wire. By pulling the old wire out, you'll be pulling the new wire in!

Toasters... It is possible for old toast crumbs in a toaster to conduct electricity from the heating wire to the metal casing. Remember to clean the toaster and never poke anything in the toaster while it is plugged in.

Teakettle... To keep it running efficiently, remember to remove any sediment buildup in the bottom. You'll find that the water will boil much faster, using less power.

Small Motors... Small appliances often have fan blades to force air past the motor. Heat can destroy motors, so make sure adequate ventilation is available.

THE CARPENTER

WORKING WITH WOOD...

Carpenter's Golden Rule... Measure twice, cut once.

Wood Tips... Even newly purchased lumber is rarely squared. Always check corners before measuring.

♦ If you need small odds and ends of wood to complete a minor repair, ask your local lumber dealer if you can look through his "scrap box."

♦ Top and bottom surfaces of plywood are graded as either A, B or C, depending on the appearance of the wood. A/A finish would have smooth, well-finished wood on both sides. A/C would have one smooth surface and one coarse surface, and of course would cost less.

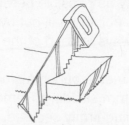 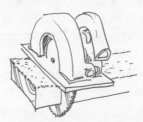

Sawing... Remember, when using a handsaw, always saw from the finished side, and when using a power saw, saw from the unfinished side.

♦ Prevent splitting plywood by starting the cut with a fine-toothed saw.

♦ Keep a large paper clamp in your workshop. The next time you cut a large piece of plywood or paneling, as soon as you've cut about 6 inches, clip the paper clamp over the cut so that it holds both cut edges at the same level. This will help prevent the saw from binding.

 Hammering... When hammering a nail into wood, to prevent the wood from splitting, first cut the tip of the nail off with a pair of sharp wire cutters.

♦ When driving in small nails or tacks, first place the nail between the teeth of a comb. Now you can hit the nail with your hammer while your fingers are out of harm's way.

♦ Another way of protecting your fingers is making sure the head of your hammer doesn't slip off the head of the nail. Rough up the face every so often by rubbing it over some coarse sandpaper.

Nail Removing… If you find the head of the nail you are trying to remove comes off (or was headless in the first place), grip the nail as tightly as possible between the claws of the hammer. Then, pull the nail out by moving the handle of the hammer sideways instead of the usual way.

Drilling… Whether in wood or metal, punch a small hole in the surface to prevent drill from skidding. Remember to have the object you are drilling firmly secured.

♦ To drill straight holes with an electric drill, employ the use of a child's wooden building block. Align the drill bit vertically with the corner of the block.

Mr. Sandman… When sanding wood, to check the smoothness, slip the foot of a pair of panty hose over your hand, like a mitt. Run your hand over the wood, and wherever the panty hose snags, is where you need more sanding.

♦ Sanding large, flat areas is easier and more even if you wrap the sandpaper around a block of wood that fits easily into your hand.

♦ Don't throw that piece of sandpaper away just because if feels smooth. Sandpaper often becomes clogged, but can easily be cleared by a fine-bristle shoe brush.

♦ Multileveled cardboard storage containers are commonly available at office-supply stores. They are excellent for organizing the various grades of sandpaper you keep in the workshop.

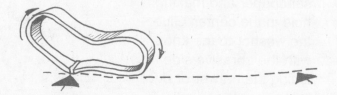

Measuring... To easily measure the length of a motor belt or band-saw blade, try this. Make a mark on the floor and a mark on the blade. Align the two marks and then roll the belt until the mark reaches the floor again. Mark this point and measure the distance between the two marks on the floor.

Gluing... If you should lose the screw top to your glue container (or caulking tube), you can easily replace it with a plastic wire nut, the kind you use to connect electrical wiring. They fit well and screw on tight.

REPAIRING & REFINISHING FURNITURE...

Repairing...

♦ If you are rebuilding old furniture, loosen glued joints by applying nail-polish remover from a small oil can.

♦ Wobbly furniture drawers can be reinforced with small triangular wood blocks glued and nailed into the corners.

◆ Don't force sticky drawers. Rub the edges with hard soap or wax. If that doesn't work, try sanding the drawer edges lightly.

◆ To fix wobbly knobs, create a sandpaper washer by cutting a small circle of sandpaper and making a hole in the center. Glue the washer to the knob with the abrasive side facing the drawer or door and screw the handle in. It'll grip a lot better.

◆ Wax sticks are terrific for repairing minor furniture scratches, but keeping trace of them can be a problem. Try taping the wax stick that matches your table to the underside so that it's there when you need it.

◆ Large gouges in furniture can be repaired by sanding an inconspicuous surface of the piece to be repaired. Mix the sawdust with white glue and apply the paste to the damaged area.

◆ Here's a handy tip you can use if you find a tabletop or any large flat wood surface is badly warped. First, remove the top from the base, then place the item warped-side (concave-side) down on a dampened lawn. Leave in the sun for a few hours or until the warping has been remedied.

Refinishing...

◆ When painting or refinishing anything with legs, hammer a small nail or tack in the bottom of each leg and avoid sticky paper residue.

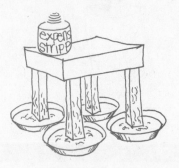

♦ When stripping, place aluminum pie plates under the legs of tables and chairs to catch drippings. Saves on cleanup time, prevents potential damage to working surface and economizes on expensive stripper.

♦ When stripping old furniture, they say it's a good idea to cover the area immediately with a sheet of tinfoil after applying paint stripper. This evidently prevents dissipation of the volatile chemicals and makes it more efficient.

♦ Lighten spots or stains in old furniture by using laundry bleach. Bleach the spot bit by bit with multiple applications.

♦ Keep some vinegar handy when applying bleach to furniture. You can stop the action of bleach with it as soon as the wood reaches the correct tone.

♦ Many stains are very thin and unless you have very large brushes, you'll be working for hours on those large, flat surfaces. Try using a sponge instead, but be sure to wear rubber gloves.

♦ Try a homemade stain for furniture—strong tea!

♦ To prevent stain from being absorbed and overdarkening the end grain, first apply a little shellac to the exposed ends. Let it dry for a couple of hours and continue staining. Wood glue works well too!

THE ENERGY SAVER

CONSERVATION & INSULATION...

Conservation...

No One Home?... Invest in a "clock thermostat." There's no need to heat the entire house while you're at work, and the device will turn the furnace on at the time you desire.

♦ Going away for the weekend? Turn the hot water heater off and lower your thermostat to 60 degrees.

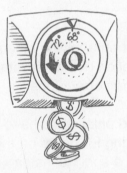

A Matter Of Degree... Dropping the temperature from 72 degrees to 68 degrees can save you as much as 15% on your heating bill. Drop it one degree each week to acclimatize yourself to the new temperature.

Using Your Fan... Conserve heating energy in the winter and cooling energy in the summer by adjusting your ceiling-fan rotation accordingly. In the summer, have it rotate clockwise to draw the hot air up, allowing cooler air to replace it. In the winter, have it rotate counterclockwise to push the hot air down.

Illuminating Lightbulb Tips... It's hard to believe, but a 25-watt fluorescent tube gives as much light as a 100-watt bulb.

♦ Also, one 100-watt bulb gives off 50% more light than four 25-watt bulbs yet draws the same amount of current.

♦ Dusty bulbs can reduce the efficiency of your lighting fixture by as much as 75%.

Switch On To Switching Off... Install a controlling switch at the entrance to your room. This saves you having to turn each individual lamp off, which means you're more likely to switch off more often.

♦ Or save your bulbs by installing dimmer switches. three-way switches also save energy, giving you the convenience of switching on at one entrance and off at another.

♦ Actually, they now have bulbs on the market that turn on and off automatically each time you exit or enter a room.

Water Conservation... Shower instead of taking a bath. The average bath uses 20–30 gallons of water while the average shower uses only 10 gallons. Install a hand shower in a showerless tub and save on water-heating bills.

♦ Did you know that if you don't let the water run while you're brushing your teeth, you can save about 2 gallons every time you brush!

Dishwasher... Instead of using the drying cycle, allow your dishes to dry naturally with the door open.

Clothes Dryer... Place your dryer where it gets clean, dry air. A humid area causes moisture inside the dryer which lengthens the drying time, and thus wastes energy.

Gas Appliances... In order to operate at maximum efficiency, pilot lights on gas appliances should be regulated until the flame is blue with just a touch of yellow at the tip.

Chimneys... A soot-lined chimney is a fire hazard. Have it cleaned once a year and improve the efficiency of your fireplace or woodstove.

Insulation...

Attic Insulation... Icicles may look very attractive hanging from your roof, but they're a sure sign of heat loss and pose a danger to those who walk under them. Have your attic insulated to keep the valuable heat inside.

Basement Insulation... Insulate your basement ceiling and stop those annoying draughts from chilling your toes.

Hot Water Tank And Pipe Insulation... More hot water for less! Insulate your hot water tank and pipes. For the tank, wrap some batts of ordinary household insulation around it and fasten it on with strong duct tape or good twine. If you own a gas water heater, don't insulate right down to the floor. The heater needs air to breathe at the bottom. For your pipes, simply wrap them in ordinary household aluminum foil, with the shiny side in.

Window Insulation... Draw drapes or pull down window shades at dusk and leave them down until morning. The air pocket between the window and the drape forms an insulation layer.

Economical Weather Stripping… Save your old rubber garden hose and attach a length of it as weather stripping along the bottom of your garage door.

Radiators… A reflecting shield between the radiator and the wall will prevent the wall from absorbing heat that you want circulating within the room.

Refrigerator… Close the refrigerator door on a strip of paper. If you can remove it easily, you're wasting electricity and should replace the door stripping.

THE JACK-OF-ALL TRADES

GENERAL DO-IT-YOURSELF TIPS AROUND THE HOME…

Loose Screws?… Remove screw and fill hole with wood putty. Allow putty to harden overnight; then replace screw.

♦ If small screws in doorknobs and appliances keep coming unscrewed, try a touch of shellac on the head just before tightening.

♦ Almost anything screws in clockwise and unscrews counterclockwise.

Tight Screws?... To remove a stubborn screw, hold the tip of a hot soldering iron against the head of the screw for about 15 seconds. The heat should expand it enough to make it easier to remove with your screwdriver.

♦ Or place the blade of the screwdriver in the head of the screw and tap the handle of the screwdriver with a hammer while exerting counterclockwise pressure.

Awkward Screws... When you have to place a screw in an area where you can't get your other hand it to guide it, try this clever idea. Cut a narrow strip of cardboard and push the screw through the one end of it. Now you can insert your cardboard holder into the tight spot. And this does a great job of keeping the screw in place while you're tightening it.

Straightening Wire...
To straighten bent wire, take a length of wood and screw 5 screws into it in a straight line. Make sure the screws are in about halfway and are set about  3 inches apart. Grasp the end of the wire with pliers and draw the wire through the line of screws, alternating to the left and right of each consecutive screw, like a slalom skier! Make several passes, turning the wire each time.

Mirror Image... If your mirror is a little worn around the edges, try this. Get a glazier to cut 4 1-inch-wide strips of mirror to match the perimeter of your old mirror. Now you can disguise those worn edges by gluing the new strips on in the form of a frame!

♦ To hide worn spots on your mirror, tape pieces of tinfoil on the back of the mirror where the marks are.

♦ To get rid of scratches on the surface of the mirror, apply a little metal polish onto the scratch and buff with a soft rag. This also works well on glass windows and tabletops.

Hung Up On A Picture Frame... When measuring to hang pictures, take into account how many inches the wire sags under the weight of the picture.

♦ You can easily mark the spot for the nail with a wet fingerprint!

Reducing Noise Pollution... Place major appliances that vibrate like washing machines, dryers and refrigerators on resilient pads. This also works when moving appliances.

Ladder Safety... For every 4 feet up, your ladder should be at least 1 foot away from the wall.

♦ Extend your ladder at least two rungs higher than the place at which you are working.

♦ Always keep your hips within the ladder rails.

♦ Never use a ladder in its horizontal position for scaffolding. That's not what it was designed for. It could buckle, resulting in injury.

♦ When carrying a ladder upright (especially aluminum) keep an eye out for overhead obstacles and powerlines.

♦ Never rest your ladder on the eaves trough. It could cause the eaves trough to sag and create a low spot. Come winter, you could have ice formation you don't need!

Up On The Roof... Clogged downspouts may fill with ice and burst. Try inserting wire mesh to prevent leaves and other debris from returning.

♦ When using tools on the roof, to prevent them sliding off, place a large piece of foam rubber next to you and put the tools on that.

Hatchet Handles... You can extend the life of your hatchet or ax handle by tightly winding some thin wire around the handle for about two fingers' width below the blade head.

Check Your Chainsaw Chips!... A good way to determine when your chainsaw blade needs honing is to take note of the size of the wood chips. If they appear to be almost like sawdust, then it's a sign of a dull blade.

Garage Cleanups... Remove oil drippings from concrete by placing several newspapers over the oil stain. Soak with water and allow to dry.

♦ Or if you have wood shavings, sprinkle them to absorb the oil stain.

♦ Spread sand over the oil spill. Sweep up when sand has absorbed the oil. Kitty litter works as well!

♦ For stubborn oil stains on pavement, soak the area in mineral spirits and scrub vigorously. Soak up moisture with newspaper and allow to dry. Wash with a mixture of detergent, bleach and cold water.

♦ Often oil spills can be soaked up from your garage floor with this method. Ask your hairdresser or pet groomer for their thrown-out hair. Place the hair in legs of panty hose and apply to the oil spill.

Moisture-Free Storage... A handy way to keep your lumber, paneling, etc. dry when storing is to lay the sheets of lumber on several old car tires. The tires provide an excellent insulation against ground moisture. They also will support the lumber evenly, and discourage warping.

— ♦ —

THE APPLIANCE TROUBLESHOOTER

Checklist...
What to look for when one of your appliances acts up.

APPLIANCE	PROBLEM	POSSIBLE SOLUTION
Food mixers and blenders	Will not run	Could be a dirty or defective speed control. Clean or replace.
Automatic clothes washer	Lacks power on all settings	Could be a defective control switch. Try replacing the switch.
	Tub does not fill	The water hoses could be disconnected or blocked. Check for kinks or pinching in hoses.
	Tub does not drain	The drain hose may be blocked. Check for blockage and clean hose.
	No spin cycle	The drive belt may be loose or broken. Tighten the belt or replace if broken.
	Washer vibrates	Could be small or uneven load distribution. Rearrange garments and add a few towels if necessary.

APPLIANCE	PROBLEM	POSSIBLE SOLUTION
Coffeemaker	Lukewarm water, but doesn't perk	Check thermostat and replace if defective—the circular unit located in the base.
Refrigerator	Interior not cold enough	Could be inadequate ventilation around the vents. Be sure refrigerator is well away from back wall so that air can circulate.
Automatic dishwasher	Dishes not clean	Water may not be hot enough to thoroughly clean. Check domestic water temperature.
Electric clothes dryer	Does not start	The door interlock switch may be defective. Replace if necessary.
	Does not heat	May be defective heating element. Disassemble and check element; replace if necessary.
	Does not rotate	It may be that the drive belt is broken or the drum is sticking. Check for small articles that may cause drum to stick and/or replace drive belt if necessary.
Can opener	Slow running	The cutting edge may be dull or chipped. Sharpen or replace.
	Noisy	The gears may be defective. Try lubricating or replacing.

APPLIANCE	PROBLEM	POSSIBLE SOLUTION
Portable fan	Fan erratic or slow	It may be the motor armature binding. Clean and lubricate the motor bearings.
	Fan vibrates	The blades may be unbalanced. Clean all accumulated dirt. If blades are bent, realign.
Vacuum cleaner	Little suction, motor sounds normal	The exhaust outlet may be blocked. Clean or replace filter.
Sewing machine	Slow and noisy	Lubrication may be required. Follow manufacturer's instructions.
Waffle iron	Too much or too little heat	Check thermostat. Clean or replace if necessary.
	Waffles stick to grill	Grill not seasoned. Brush grill with cooking oil and heat for 30 minutes.
Toaster	Toast won't pop up	Bread may be caught in wires. Unplug toaster, remove bread and shake out crumbs.
	Toast is too light or too dark	Linkage from color control to release mechanism may be broken or loose. Check that sliding parts are properly connected and replace if necessary.

CHAPTER 8

PET PARADE

TIPS YOUR PETS
WILL LOVE YOU FOR!

GROOMING, RAISING & PICKING UP AFTER

THE WELL-GROOMED PET...

Dry Shampoo... Give your pet an occasional dry shampoo. Rub in baking soda and brush his coat until the soda has been swept away along with the dirt. This is an especially safe way of keeping him clean during the cold winter months.

Something Smells... Animals dislike the smell of perfume odors on their coats. Use only odorless "animal" shampoos or soaps when bathing your pet.

Bathtime Tip... After you've bathed your dog, he'll want to shake his dog-scented spray all over the bathroom. Before he can do this, get him into the shower stall and let him shake there. It will make cleanup a lot easier.

Staying Dry... Employ the use of that old shower curtain or plastic tablecloth to stay dry when washing Fido. Simply cut slits for your head and arms and wash away.

Skunked Again... Get out the tomato juice and douse your pet thoroughly. Shampoo and add a few drops of lemon juice to the rinse water. Be sure to rinse well.

Removing Burrs... Using work gloves, work baby oil into coat areas tangled with burrs. This should loosen the grip enough to free the burrs. Cornstarch works well too!

Fleas... To prevent these pests from pestering your dog, keep sachets of chamomile leaves in the doghouse to help drive fleas away. If you don't have loose chamomile leaves handy, you can also use the regular chamomile tea bags you find in your local supermarket.

♦ They also say that if you put garlic in your dog's food, it'll stop fleas bothering him.

♦ Try brewer's yeast! Just add a little to your pet's food.

♦ When giving your dog a flea bath, lather well around the neck area. Fleas tend to migrate toward the head.

A Third Hand!... To keep your cat still while applying flea powder, try this. Take an old fishing net and gently place it over the cat. Put your foot on the handle and you'll now have both hands free. One to apply the powder and the other to cover his face and eyes.

A Shiny Coat... If you have any leftover egg yolks, give them to your dog. It's said to make their coat nice and shiny.

THE WELL-RAISED PET...

I Want My Mother... Little puppies and kittens need motherly love and warmth. Place a warm hot water bottle securely under his blanket along with a ticking clock for those first few nights.

Indoor Kitty Lawn... Place a layer of potting soil in a tray and plant some grass seeds. Your cat will love chewing on the grass.

Beware Of Driver!... Paint an inexpensive dog tag with iridescent paint and attach to your pet's collar. This will enable drivers to see him at night.

♦ Or put a hole in a small plastic bicycle reflector and attach to his collar.

♦ Cut small pieces of reflector tape and apply to both sides of a dog tag. Affix to collar with other tags.

The Irresistible Electrical Cord... Discourage your dog or cat from the dangerous habit of chewing on your electrical cords by rubbing the cords with a bar of laundry soap. Pets dislike the taste.

The Irresistible Couch... Discourage your cat from sharpening his claws on your furniture by spraying a little perfume on the couches, etc. They hate the smell.

Medicine... If you have difficulty getting your cat to take it's medicine, try wiping the dose on the top of it's paw. The cat will be quick to lick it off. If the medicine is in pill form, just crush it, mix it with a little milk and smear the paste on the cat's paw.

CLEANING UP AFTER YOUR PET...

Oops, Another Accident!... Soda water will remove the odor from accidents caused by untrained pups. Gently rub the area with a cloth dampened with soda water. This is especially good on fabrics.

Fur Balls... To cut down on your cat ejecting fur balls onto your carpet, try feeding him sardines in oil once a month. They say it helps smooth the passageways, allowing the hair a speedy transit, thus preventing the fur balls from forming.

♦ You could also try wiping a little bit of petroleum jelly on the bridge of your cat's nose. They'll simply lick it off.

Disposable Cat-Litter Box...
The next time you buy a case of 24 canned pop, remove the cans carefully without damaging the plastic wrap and the cardboard tray. They make great disposable kitty bathrooms!

Dog-Dish Mess... Stick a thin piece of rubber carpet underlay under your dog's dish. This will help keep it in its place while your dog devours his food and will prevent messy spills.

— ♦ —

CHAPTER 9

PEST PEEVES

GETTING RID OF
WHAT'S BUGGING YOU!

CONTROLLED PEST CONTROL

GETTING RID OF WHAT'S BUGGING YOU...

Ants... Sage or white pepper will repel ants. Sprinkle around affected areas in crevices and in cupboards.

♦ Or boil 1 pint of tar in 2 quarts of water. Set in an uncovered dish where ants gather.

♦ Leftover cucumber peelings? Sprinkle them with salt and place them where the ants are.

♦ Campers swear by mothballs. Just create a border around your site.

♦ This may sound strange, but draw a chalk line on the floor (or the wall) where ants march. According to some sources, ants won't cross a chalk line, so you can set up your own boundaries.

♦ Leave apple pieces, cores or peelings where ants enter. When brought back to the anthill, it's said the acid in the apple kills the queen and the colony.

♦ Or mix equal parts of honey and boric-acid powder and place the mixture on small pieces of paper in the problem areas. Evidently the ants carry the concoction back to their nests where the boric acid disrupts their digestive systems. However, some ants prefer grease to sweetness, so you may want to try substituting lard or butter for the honey.

Cockroaches... Boric acid is generally an effective way to eliminate cockroaches. It may take some time to be rid of them, but it will do the job. Sprinkle in cracks and trouble areas and leave the container open in the cupboard.

Crawling Bugs... They'll depart quickly when baseboards, walls and cracks are painted with a mixture of 3 quarts of boiled water with 2 tablespoons of alum.

Earwigs... To deter these "creepy" insects, sprinkle crushed bay leaves along the baseboards and along window- and doorsills.

♦ Epsom salts sprinkled in the same areas works too.

♦ For garden earwigs, cut a few 12-inch pieces of garden hose and place them where the earwigs congregate. Make sure the inside of the hose is dry. Leave overnight and in the morning it 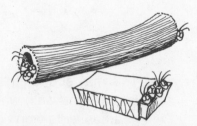 should be full of earwigs. Dispose of them in a can of kerosene. Slightly open matchboxes and pieces of corrugated cardboard work well too.

Flies... Leave a dish of molasses and black pepper where they congregate.

Small Flies... Try spreading some petroleum jelly on bristol board and place around the house.

Fruit Flies... Place a dish of apple-cider vinegar out. The flies will head straight for the vinegar and drown.

Flying Bugs... Flying bugs hate smoke, so light an incense stick or candle to drive them away.

Hornets And Bees... Use hair spray to stop bees or hornets in action. "Bee" careful though!

♦ Pour hot water down crevices and anywhere you suspect hornets are nesting.

♦ Place a glass jug with a small opening outside your door or where you suspect they congregate. Fill the jug halfway with water and smear honey or fruit juice along the rim and inside the opening. The bees will gather here and drown in the water.

♦ If the bee is inside the house, turn the lights off inside and turn the patio light on. The bee will generally fly to the light and out the window or door.

Wasps... To discourage wasps, mix tinned tuna with some powered cleanser and leave where the wasps gather.

Mealworms... Found in flour, spaghetti and other starchy items. Place some fresh mint leaves in any effected area. Dry leaves will do if they still have lots of scent. Alternatively, mint-flavored chewing gum often works!

Mosquitoes... It's said that mosquitoes also dislike the scent of oranges and onions. Rub over your exposed areas.

♦ Avoid wearing clothing that is damp or colored blue. They say mosquitoes love damp or blue clothing.

♦ When you see mosquitoes on your walls and windows at night, simply suck them up with a vacuum hose.

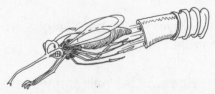

♦ Try planting the herb tansy, or basil, in sunny spots near your doors. Mosquitoes are repelled by the smell.

♦ To keep mosquitoes from breeding in your rain barrel, pour a little cooking oil on the surface of the water.

Moths... Darken the room and leave a bright light burning outside. They'll fly to the light.

♦ Hang sachets of cedarwood chips in the closet to keep moths away.

♦ Wrap some cloves in pieces of cheesecloth and suspend them from your closet rod or tuck them into clothes' pockets.

Slugs And Snails... Bait a trap for slugs and snails by laying out, every evening, lettuce or cabbage leaves. Slices of turnip, potato or inverted grapefruit rinds will also do the trick. Wait until they are snacking away and remove them.

Spiders... Leave a cotton wad dampened with oil of pennyroyal where spiders reside. They'll flee quickly!

Tent Caterpillars... Wait until nightfall, when their tent is full. Take a squirt oil can of motor oil and shoot some oil into the tent. This should eliminate them!

FUR & FEATHER FIENDS...

Garbage Raiders... Keep a spray bottle filled with turpentine or ammonia and spray garbage bags and pails lightly. This will repel animals like raccoons from raiding your garbage and leaving you with a mess to clean up. Or soak an old sock with turpentine or ammonia and tie to the pail lid.

Mice... Still the most popular form of mice control is of course the mousetrap. But, instead of using the old cheese standby as bait, you might want to try a gumdrop instead. It lasts longer, and doesn't go moldy!

♦ You can also try baiting with a cotton ball. Just tie it with thread to the trigger, and the mouse will do the rest. Evidently they like to use the batten for their nests.

♦ On a more humane level, you could try leaving containers of peppermint extract wherever you suspect the mice from entering; this should keep them away.

♦ Mothballs are said to work well too!

Squirrels... To keep squirrels away from your new plants, sprinkle blood meal in the hole when planting your bulbs. Also spread a little around on the surface of the soil.

Pigeons... If you have trouble with pigeons on your balcony, try this trick. Smear some petroleum jelly or powdered chalk on the top of the railing where they land. You'll find they hate the feeling and will land elsewhere.

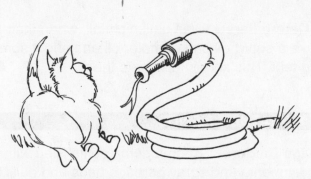

Cats!... If you're ever troubled by unwanted cats in your yard, place some short lengths of black garden hose around the garden. The hose resembles snakes and scares the cats away!

Deer... If you hang car air fresheners in your trees, it will discourage their unwanted nibbling!

— ◆ —

CHAPTER 10

THE CAR MECHANIC

ALL YOU WANT TO KNOW
ABOUT CARS
BUT WERE AFRAID TO ASK!

PREVENTIVE MAINTENANCE

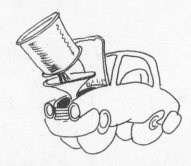

UNDER THE HOOD...

Radiator... The temperature of burning gasoline (4,000°F) is hard on your engine. Keep it cool. If your car is standing in traffic the water in the radiator doesn't circulate around the engine. The car will overheat and stall. Simply allow the car to sit for 15 or 20 minutes with the engine disengaged.

♦ Antifreeze will prevent the water in your radiator from freezing and can be saved from season to season. Have the radiator flushed clean twice each year when changing to and from summer coolant.

♦ The operating temperature of your engine is influenced by the environment. Many people install a winter thermostat in the fall to keep the engine temperature consistent with outside conditions. A regular thermostat is then installed in the spring.

Air Filters... Your car engine requires clean air to efficiently burn gasoline. Have the air filter checked every three months. Dust and grime can be washed from  many filters with warm water and detergent; however, filters should be replaced periodically.

Gasoline Filters... Before gasoline is pumped from your gas tank into the engine, it travels through a filter, usually made of wire mesh, to remove suspended particles. Periodic inspection and cleaning will help to ensure a longer life for a host of moving engine parts.

Oil Filters... Oil is continually circulating and recirculating through your engine, picking up small bits of carbon and other residue resulting from the combustion of gasoline. In order to act as an effective lubricant between moving metal surfaces, the residue must be removed from the oil by a filter. Eventually the filter will become clogged and must be replaced. Exactly when depends on how much driving you do and how efficiently your car burns gas. As a measure, if oil has changed in color from a light amber to black, it's a sign to change the oil and the filter.

Motor Oil... Check your car's level regularly and while you're at it, check the color. Few things are more important to the proper maintenance of your engine than an adequate supply of a good quality oil. Many modern oils are advertised to last thousands of miles, but driving conditions, individual driving methods and the condition of your car can make a tremendous difference in its longevity.

♦ If you have difficulty remembering when to change the oil in your car, or how long it has been since it was last lubricated, etc., try clipping a small card to the underside of the sun visor and record all service details and dates on the card at the time of servicing. It's also a good idea to note mileage and gas consumption on the card.

Other Lubricants... Older cars should have parts checked and be lubricated more often than newer cars with self-lubricating systems.

Battery... Heavy cables connect your car's starter to the battery posts. The battery posts and the terminal on the cable may become badly corroded. Clean thoroughly with a solution of baking soda and water. To prevent corrosion, cover terminals with petroleum jelly, making sure the connection between the battery and the terminal is clean and secure.

♦ Most batteries nowadays do not require maintenance, but older batteries should be checked periodically. Each chamber in the battery has a plastic cap and distilled water should be added to keep the fluid level ½-inch above the top of the battery plates.

Distributor... The distributor takes an electrical charge from the battery and distributes it to each spark plug. It also contains moving parts which must be replaced periodically. It's a good idea to have it checked twice each year.

Spark Plugs... Spark plugs receive an electric charge from the battery and send a spark across a gap only thousandths of an inch wide to ignite gas in the engine. This gap or space must be maintained exactly as specified in your owner's manual in order for your car to run efficiently. Have spark plugs checked twice a year and replaced if necessary.

Quick-Clean Spark Plugs!... For a fast and easy way to clean dirty spark plugs, place the tips in some oven cleaner for about two hours. If the plugs are badly caked, you might need to use a piece of sandpaper or even an emery board.

Generator/Alternator... Most older cars have a generator, while newer ones have an alternator. Both are responsible for producing all of the electricity your car needs for starting, radio, lighter, power windows, etc. Both contain moving parts and should be checked twice a year.

UNDER THE CAR...

Tire Pressure... The air pressure in each tire should be checked four times a year to be certain it matches manufacturer's specifications. You'll save on both tire wear and gas consumption.

Tire Balancing... If your car seems to shake or shimmy at certain speeds, the wheels may need to be balanced. Unbalanced or misaligned wheels can reduce tire life by one-half. Have tires checked for balance every three months.

Tire Rotating... All tires eventually wear out, but each tire on your car wears in a different spot. At least twice each year move each tire (including the spare) in a clockwise direction to the next wheel.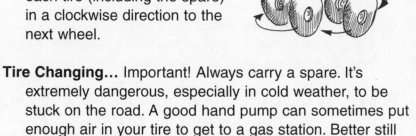

Tire Changing... Important! Always carry a spare. It's extremely dangerous, especially in cold weather, to be stuck on the road. A good hand pump can sometimes put enough air in your tire to get to a gas station. Better still are some commercial products which inflate your tire temporarily from a pressurized can.

♦ You'll need a car jack and preferably a relatively flat surface (to be remembered when you pull off to the side of the road). You'll also need a prying tool to remove the hubcap and a good wrench to remove the nuts which hold the wheel on. Those are the same nuts originally installed at the factory using a powerful electronic tool. It's a good idea to periodically check to see that none of the nuts have loosened.

♦ Tires are tough, but striking curbs, holes, rocks or any hard object will severely shorten tire life. Check tires often for major defects.

Underbody Rinse... Once winter is over, try this quick way to remove corrosive salt buildup under your car. Place a lawn sprinkler under the car and turn it on for a half hour or so. The most suitable sprinkler is the type that traverses back and forth through 180 degrees.

Steel Belted Or Glass?... Tires surrounded by a glass or steel belt covered with several plys, usually a synthetic material, are generally warranted to last longer than regular tires. Some belted tires are advertised as year-round; however, in snow, nothing beats two good snow tires for traction.

Brakes... The most important thing about a smoothly running automobile is that it is able to STOP as smoothly. At the first sound of squeaking brakes, have them checked.

Homemade Creeper... Take an old padded ironing board and remove the legs. Attach 4 swivel castors underneath and you have an inexpensive garage creeper!

EXTERIOR & INTERIOR...

Exterior...

Locks... If the lock sticks, try blowing powdered graphite into the keyhole. The graphite is usually sold in containers which facilitate such an application. Alternatively, rub your key with the point of a soft lead pencil. Oil in locks tends to collect grime and therefore impedes smooth operation.

Body Rust... Remove small rust stains from bumpers and other chrome surfaces by scrubbing with fine steel wool soaked in kerosene.

♦ A ball of aluminum foil dipped in water often works too!

♦ Rust prevention techniques have improved dramatically in the last decade and a variety of treatments are now on the market. Most new cars have a rust perforation warranty or guarantee, which means that you must have a hole caused by rust from the interior to the exterior before you can make a claim against the warranty.

Body Dents... Sometimes dents can be taken out by placing a bathroom plunger over the area. Pump the plunger and pull.

Polishing Your Car... After you apply polish to your car, sprinkle 2 teaspoons of cornstarch onto your buffing cloth. You'll find that when you buff, it'll give you that extra shine. The cornstarch evidently helps remove any polish buildup.

Exterior Windows... To remove pressure-sensitive stickers from the exterior of the car window, rub with nail-polish remover or lighter fluid. Gently scrape with a razor blade.

♦ For stubborn stickers, try saturating with salad oil before you begin scraping.

♦ Plastic net bags (cooking onions are usually wrapped in them) will remove insects from the windshield without harming the glass. Some commercially available nylon pot scrubbers will do a good job too.

♦ Baking soda on a damp rag will easily clean dust and grime from glass and chrome surfaces. Be sure to rinse with clean water and dry with a soft cloth.

♦ Tired of scraping ice off your windshield? Store a box of fine-grain salt in the trunk and rub on built-up ice.

♦ Replace windshield-wiper blades at least once a year. Driving with dirty or streaked windows is not only hard on your eyes and nerves, but is definitely dangerous.

♦ Tar can be removed from the exterior by soaking the area in linseed oil. Allow a few minutes for the tar to soften, then wipe with a clean cloth sprinkled with linseed oil.

♦ Windshield wash is expensive. Try making your own with 2 quarts rubbing alcohol, 1 cup of water and 1 teaspoon of detergent. It should not freeze, even at −30°F.

Interior...

Interior Windows... If you're tired of wiping the inside windows of your car while waiting for the defroster to take effect, try using a chalkboard eraser. It cleans windows quickly and without streaking, and can be kept in the glove compartment.

♦ Very often you can prevent the inside of your car windshield (or car window) from fogging with foamy shaving cream. Apply the shaving cream to the windshield with a damp sponge and then buff clear with a paper towel. Repeat when necessary or after cleaning.

Carpets... Remove stubborn salt residue from carpeting by scrubbing with a mixture of one part vinegar to two parts water.

Eau Du Auto... Keep some potpourri in the ashtray of your car. It works better than many air fresheners.

♦ Or simply place one or two fabric-softener sheets in a side pocket or under the seat.

Ashtray Candy... For those of you who don't smoke and to discourage your passengers who do, place some individually wrapped candies in your car ashtray. Wrapped chewing-gum sticks are also a good idea.

Smoldering Cigarettes... Prevent this by placing an inch or two of sand or baking soda in the ashtray.

DRIVING, PARKING & ALL THE REST!

DRIVING...

Mountains And Hills... The safest way to descend steep hills is in low gear. Brakes, when used, should be applied intermittently to avoid burning out. If brakes feel low, stop and let them cool. Never coast with the clutch disengaged or in neutral. Also remember that on high mountain roads, engines might only develop 50% of their expected horsepower, which means less power for accelerating and passing.

Speeding... Keep speed moderate. High speeds consume more gas than slower speeds. Accelerate evenly and maintain a steady pace. Pedal pumping reduces efficient burning of gas.

Smoothing It Out... Avoid jumping starts and sudden stops. It's hard on gas, hard on the car and hard on your nerves!

Staying Alert... You'll increase your driving alertness on a long trip if you take a short rest break every so often. But did you know that whether you rest for an hour or 15 minutes, there's no noticeable difference in driving ability.

♦ It's said that if you have a snack on your rest break, it will increase your alertness.

Driving With A Trailer... Note that acceleration is more sluggish. You will need more room to pass and stop. When turning, drive further into the intersection  before starting the turn to avoid striking curbs. Remember, when backing a trailer, the steering wheel is turned in the opposite direction from which you want the trailer to go.

Emergency Chewing Gum... Keep a pack of chewing gum in your glove compartment. It could come in handy in an emergency, like if you develop a leak in your fuel tank.

PARKING & THE REST...

Parking Lot(tery)... Having trouble locating your car in a large parking lot? Try this clever hint. Tie a bright piece of ribbon on your car antenna. Simple and effective!

Parking Garage... Avoid front-fender bumps when parking in your garage by hanging a brightly colored ball level with the center of your car's windshield. Also locate it 12 inches farther from the distance between the center of your windshield and your front fender.

Sap Buster... If you park under a tree, a rag dipped in turpentine should remove most varieties of tree sap from your car's surface. Wash well!

Avoiding The Hot Seat!... If you've almost had third-degree burns on the back of your leg from sitting on a hot car seat, you'll like this tip. Next time you park your car in hot sun, leave an open umbrella on your car seat.

Avoiding Theft... By etching your vehicle identification number into all the windows of your car, you're forcing any thief to replace all the windows to avoid getting caught. Most won't want the inconvenience!

Avoiding Loss... It's a good idea to scratch your name and phone number on the inside of your hubcaps. If you accidentally lose them, they might find their way back to you this way.

Avoiding Finger Loss!... If you break down and are working under the hood, be careful. Many cars have electric fans that are temperature controlled. Even with the engine turned off, an increase in heat could activate it. Make sure you keep your hands well away from the fan area.

HOT TIPS FOR THE COLD

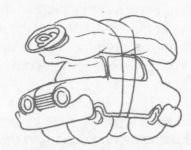

WINTER SMARTS...

Starting Up... Racing a cold engine greatly increases wear. Allow your car to warm up before driving. Plan ahead during the winter months. Not only will your engine have a chance to warm up, but the passenger compartment will warm up as well.

♦ In extremely cold weather you may want to remove an old battery at night and reinstall it in the morning. But be careful. The fluid in a battery is very corrosive and will turn your clothes into swiss cheese. Never smoke or bring a flame close to a battery or it may explode.

♦ Just in case, on very cold evenings and if you aren't 100% sure about the battery, try backing the car into the garage. This way the battery is easily accessible for jumper cables.

Ignition Timing... Have your ignition timing checked in the Spring and the Fall. If the spark plugs are sparking after the gasoline has entered the engine and not at exactly the same time, you will waste gas, lose power and the car will not run smoothly.

Stuck In The Snow: Stage 1... First try gently "rocking" the car. Don't race the engine and don't spin the wheels. Drive slowly forward, then stop. Drive slowly in reverse, then stop. Repeat 10–12 times. If you're still stuck, proceed to Stage 2.

Stuck In The Snow: Stage 2... If the wheels of your car are spinning in the snow or mud, put something under them which will regain traction. Suggestions include salt, sand, ashes, boards, branches, floor mats and canvas.

- It sometimes helps to let a little air out of the drive tires to get more traction. Works in mud too!

- Here are two reasons to keep coffee cans filled with salt and gravel in your trunk. First, they'll get you out of an icy situation. Second, you can put some reflector tape around them and use them to place behind your car in case of a breakdown.

- Keep 2 or 3 asphalt roof shingles in the trunk for winter traction. It's less messy than sand.

- Don't throw away your old rubber bathroom mat. Cut it in two lengthwise and leave in your trunk. They'll come in handy when you need increased traction.

Icy Windshield... Save yourself some time and trouble on cold winter mornings. If you are leaving your car outside at night, place the floor mats on the front windshield and secure underneath the wipers. This should effectively eliminate the formation of ice on the glass.

♦ Plastic garbage bags will also do the trick. Sew or tape two together and fasten them tightly in place by closing a front door over each end.

No Ice Scraper?... A strong plastic egg lifter will substitute in an emergency. If the frost is on the inside, a plastic pot scourer will remove it.

♦ It's also a handy idea to keep an expired credit card in your glove compartment for scraping frost off the inside of your car windows.

Frozen Out?... If you find in the morning your door locks are frozen stiff, try this: First (never apply excessive force) try inserting the key, then put a match to a twist of paper and hold close to the lock for 20 seconds. Be careful of that new paint finish though.

♦ Perhaps a safer way is to try warming the key with a lighted match and reinserting it in the frozen keyhole. Make sure you're wearing gloves, or you may thaw your fingers too!

♦ Or if you have any heat liniment, try squirting some of it into the keyhole. It will often loosen it up.

♦ Place some thin, flat refrigerator magnets over the car door locks. It should prevent the frost from getting in.

Avoiding Winter Rusting... One of the best rust-prevention techniques is simply regular washing and waxing, especially during winter months when salt builds up quickly on the exterior surfaces. Especially the underside of your vehicle.

— ◆ —

CHAPTER 11

GARDENING WITH
A GREEN THUMB

WONDERFUL WAYS
TO IMPROVE A GARDEN…
BOTH INDOORS & OUT!

SEEING TO YOUR SOIL

SERIOUS SOIL CARE...

Save Your Soot... It makes excellent fertilizer for your garden and potted plants.

Save Your Sawdust... If you own a workshop, you have a perfect supply of good mulch for your garden soil. They say sawdust, especially from pine lumber, when mulched in with your garden soil will not only help hold moisture but will provide much needed nutrition. Avoid sawdust from lumber that has been treated with chemical additives.

Homemade Fertilizer... A crystalline compound called "Urea" is available at drug stores and makes an inexpensive fertilizer. One teaspoon to a gallon of water.

Fern Goodness' Sake... Try this homemade fertilizer on your ferns. Four raw oysters, finely chopped and worked into the soil. What a treat!

Headline Mulch... Want a handy mulch for the soil in your new garden? Simply lay some newspapers down whole and secure them with a few large rocks. Cover the newspaper with a few inches of soil, and you'll have a mulch that will help retain the moisture in your soil. Use only newspaper. Dyes and colorings in other products may not be water based.

Compost Corner... Here are some inexpensive composters you can use instead of the store-bought variety. Substitute with a strip of snow fencing or small-meshed wire formed into a roll. Even old garbage cans with holes poked in the sides work well.

♦ Compost should be moist, not wet. Place your composter where there is good drainage or where it is sunny.

♦ To avoid turning your compost every 2 weeks, place a whole bunch of live worms inside your composter. They'll do the work of aerating it for you. They say that sow bugs are good little workers too.

♦ Because compost material decays faster if it's in small pieces, you might want to pop your kitchen scraps into your food processor first.

♦ For a pick-me-up for your houseplants, make some compost "tea." Simply throw some of your compost soil into a watering can of water, let it "steep" for a while and then water your plants with it.

Lawn Aerating... Next time you want to aerate your lawn, don your golf spikes and walk up and down on it!

A "Clover" Idea!... Place a clove of garlic in plant soil to eliminate bugs. The garlic keeps the nasty bugs away and will also grow along with your plant.

 Warding Off Worms... Stick several matches into the soil so that the sulfur tip is covered. It's said that this will definitely ward off worms.

- ◆ When planting vegetables, such as radishes, carrots, onions, etc., try sprinkling some ground coffee in the soil first and then plant your seeds. This should discourage worms.

- ◆ To foil cutworms from dining out on your cucumber plants, try planting a popsicle stick about 2 inches into the ground next to the cucumber plant. Evidently this prevents the cutworm from curling around the cucumber stem and killing the plant.

- ◆ To prevent root worms from attacking vegetable roots, try this. Place slices of raw potato in the bottom of the holes when planting. The worms should feed on the potato instead of your vegetable roots.

BRANCHING OUT TO LEAVES & STEMS

TAKING CARE OF YOUR FINICKY FOLIAGE...

Dust Is A Nasty Word... And can filter as much as 50% of the sunlight that your plant needs to be healthy. Use a feather duster for quick, gentle cleaning.

Leaves Leaves Shining... Use a few drops of glycerin on a soft cloth to put a sheen on plant leaves.

- ◆ The inside of a banana peel gently wiped on your plant leaves will not only remove dust, but will shine them as well. As does a rub with beer!

◆ Or mix equal parts milk and water and rub plants.

◆ Another method for cleaning houseplant leaves is to give them a rub with a cotton ball dipped in egg white.

My Plant Is Bugged!... Wash leaves with a very mild detergent solution to remove many common bugs.

Withering Foliage... Give your plant a boost by adding a tablespoon of castor oil mixed with its regular water.

Stem Gems... Chopsticks make terrific splints for leaning stems.

◆ A popsicle stick taped to a weakened or broken stem might save that little plant.

◆ To mend a broken limb on your houseplant, take a small layer of onion skin and wrap it around the damaged area. Secure it well with some thin twine or thread and leave it for a few days.

THE WATERING HOLE

LIQUID REFRESHMENT FOR YOUR PLANTS...

What's On Tap?... If you use tap water, let it stand in a bucket for a few days before watering your plants. This will allow the water to warm to room temperature and most of the harmful chemicals will settle to the bottom of the bucket.

Rain, Rain, Don't Go Away!... The best water for plants is rainwater. It's naturally the right temperature and does not contain chlorine. Keep a "rain barrel" outside in summer and treat your plants to nature's bounty. In winter, collect a bucket of clean snow and let it melt.

Starch Your Plants?... Plants love starch. So when you're boiling spaghetti or potatoes, save the water, allow this leftover water to cool and sprinkle it over your plants.

Teatime For Falling Ferns... Spruce up an ailing fern by  substituting diluted tea instead of its normal water solution. This procedure should only be repeated once each month until the fern returns to normal.

Get Crackin'... Rejuvenate ailing plants by watering with a mixture of egg shells and water. Allow the shells to sit in the water for 24 hours prior to watering the plants, but be sure not to leave it any longer.

 **Plant-Sitters...** They're harder to find than a good baby-sitter. If you're going away for a week and want to treat your plants kindly, try this hint: Use a length of cloth cording long enough to bury several inches into the soil and to reach a large container of water set slightly above the plant. This is particularly useful for large plants that are difficult to move.

♦ Or fill the bathtub with several inches of water (make sure the faucet isn't left dripping). Set plants on bricks inside the tub but don't sit directly in water. Check to be sure that all pots have drainage holes, and have a carefree vacation!

♦ A washable blanket placed in the tub with an inch or two of water will hold enough moisture to keep plants from drying out. Sit plants directly on top of the blanket.

♦ For smaller plants, try constructing a miniature greenhouse. First water the plants and then cover with a plastic bag. Secure at one end with an elastic band or twist tie and move away from direct sunlight.

♦ For your outdoor plants, take a large plastic soft drink bottle and cut the bottom off. Punch a small hole in the metal cap and screw it on. Now bury the bottle, cap-side down, about two inches into the soil near the plants. Fill the bottle with water and you have an instant watering system while you're away.

♦ For your outdoor hanging plants, attach the planter to either your wall bracket or eaves trough with a bungee (elasticized) cord. Place a small mark on the wall in line with the bottom of the basket when the soil is dry. Water the plant thoroughly. The weight of the water will cause the planter to hang lower. Place another mark on the wall at the lower level. When you see your planter rise to the higher "dry" level, you'll know it's time to rewater.

Hanging-Plant Watering... Place a small funnel in the pot with the spout inserted in the soil. You'll find it easier to pour the water into the funnel mouth. Allow the plant to grow around the funnel.

Oops! I Forgot To Water The Plants... If the soil has crusted, most of the water you pour will run directly out of the pot. This calls for immediate attention. Loosen the soil as much as possible with a fork without damaging the roots. Work some peat moss or vermiculite into the top layer of soil, and finally give the plant a good soaking in the sink.

Help, We're Drowning!... Overwatering is as dangerous as underwatering, and depending on the humidity and placement of a plant, it may require a different watering schedule than its offshoot across the room. As a general rule of thumb, sink your finger into the soil to test for moisture. If it feels dry, water, if not, pass by and test again in a few days.

Hose Hints... Guide your garden hose through croquet hoops strategically placed on the lawn around your flower beds. This does a great job of keeping your hose off the plants while watering.

♦ To stop your garden hose from leaking through small holes and cracks, take a hot soldering iron and hold it against the offending area. The heat will seal the hole or crack.

♦ Here's how to keep track of the spray nozzle for your garden hose. When you take it off the hose to put on the sprinkler head, pop it into a spring broom clamp that you have attached to the wall right beside your outdoor tap.

♦ To discourage hose thieves, disguise your perfect hose for an imperfect one. Put fake patches on it and wrap bands of black tape around it at regular intervals.

PERFECT POTTING

POTTED-PLANT POINTERS...

New Plants... Keep newly purchased plants, or plants you

bring in from the garden, away from the rest of your collection until you are sure the new addition is healthy and bug free.

Potting Materials... Plants in clay pots require more frequent watering than those in plastic pots, due to the porous nature of the clay.

♦ Collect materials such as stones, walnut or peanut shells, fruit pits, even children's marbles. Place in the bottom of each pot to allow adequate drainage.

♦ Don't throw out that broken clay pot. Hammer it several times and save the pieces to provide drainage when repotting.

When To Transplant... Transplant when root-bound or when growth has stopped, but never to a pot more than 2 inches larger than the present container.

When Sunlight Hurts... Leave a newly transplanted plant out of direct sunlight for a few days to allow roots to grow again. Snip away tiny budding leaves to promote root growth.

♦ Even if you are just moving the plant from one place in the house to another, the shock may give it a temporary setback. So take care when rearranging.

Removing The Root-Ball From The Pot... Never pull a plant out by the stem. Tap several times on the bottom of the pot. Using a spoon, gently loosen surrounding soil and lift the entire root and stem with one motion. Shake gently and place in the new container.

Hawaiian Delight... An exotic plant will grow from the top of a pineapple planted in a jar of water.

Vine Line... Sweet potatoes planted in sandy soil will produce an attractive hanging vine with dark green leaves.

Pots, Pans And Other Plant Holders... Place some miniature geraniums in an old basket lined with aluminum foil.

♦ Save the plastic base of your solid air freshener. Clean thoroughly and place a miniature African violet in it.

♦ An unused copper teapot makes a lovely container for "baby tears." Line the inside of the teapot with a good layer of petroleum jelly and place the pot of little darlings inside. They'll grow to cover the entire pot.

♦ An old wooden salad bowl makes an interesting container for your cactus garden. Place several layers of foil in the bottom and fill with 2 inches of coarse gravel. Add a sandy mixture and arrange your desert garden.

♦ Do the same with a chipped or lidless fancy sugar bowl. But this time place a few clay pieces in the bottom and fill with soil. Now you'll have a matching centerpiece for your table settings.

♦ Glue five fancy bathroom tiles together with epoxy— one for the bottom and four for the sides—to make an attractive plantholder for the kitchen or bathroom.

♦ Make a decorative hanging planter by weaving ribbon through the top slots of several plastic strawberry containers, placed inside one another. Tie colored cord to each corner and knot at the top.

CUT FLOWERS

CARING FOR YOUR FLORAL SHOWPIECES...

Beautiful Bouquets... If the stems are dark tipped, snip half an inch and place in deep, cool water.

♦ Place a few layers of colorful stones in the bottom of a vase if the flower stems are too short.

♦ To keep long-stemmed flowers upright in the vase, place thin pieces of tape across the mouth of the vase to form a crisscross pattern.

♦ To make a stem longer, fit the stem into a plastic straw.

♦ When cutting stems, use a sharp knife or scissors and cut while holding under cold water. This prevents air from forming tiny pockets in the lower stem.

♦ Splice the ends of large stems to allow greatest absorption of water.

Sweet Smell Of Success... Always remove leaves below the waterline to avoid contaminating the water.

♦ Add a spoon of sugar plus a few drops of lemon juice to vase water. This helps keep flowers fresher and avoids unpleasant odors.

♦ Change water daily to help flowers last longer.

Wilted Flowers... Wilted flowers will perk up if you place the stems in hot water for 20 minutes. Replace in regular vase water.

♦ To revive wilted flowers you can also pop them in a plastic bag together with a slice or two of apple.

♦ Spray cut flowers with hair spray the day before they wilt to enjoy several extra days of pleasure from them and to prevent petals from dropping off. Spray from beneath the vase in an upward direction.

Open "Sez Me"... To get the buds of your cut flowers to open, replace the cold water with warm water.

Tulips And Roses... They say tulips last longer if you put a few pennies in the bottom of the vase.

♦ To prevent your fresh-cut tulips and roses from drooping, try putting a pinhole through the stems just below the blooms. This should keep them perky for a while longer.

Clever Centerpiece... To enhance a bowl of flowers, place a decorative mirror under it. It'll make your centerpiece twice as clever!

♦ The next time the head of one of your roses breaks away from the stem, first cut the stem off totally. Then take a shallow glass bowl, fill it with water and add a little sugar. Let the rose float on the surface and it makes a wonderful centerpiece. You might want to ask your florist to save their broken-stemmed flowers for you!

Miniature Centerpieces... For special floral accents around your home here's a clever way to use those small spice shaker jars. The plastic shaker-top holes are ideal for holding small-stemmed cut flowers from your garden. You can even decorate the little jars with a ribbon or some lace.

Drying Flowers... Prepare a mixture of 30% borax and 70% white cornmeal. Cover flowers entirely with mixture and leave for several weeks.

THE BEST VEGGIE CROP IN TOWN

PLANNING, PREPARING, PLANTING & PROTECTING...

Planning...

Choosing The Right Location... The best of sites receive sun all day, but at least six hours of midday sun is required.

♦ Avoid low-lying areas that collect water and promote root rot.

♦ Be careful not to plant too close to buildings or trees that cast shade. Tree roots also soak up essential nutrients.

Planning The Garden... Perennials such as rhubarb and asparagus should be kept at the outer edge of the garden, or in a separate area, to avoid damage when plowing the rest of the garden.

♦ Rows should run north to south so plants won't shade each other. Keep corn at the north end, or separately, to avoid shading smaller crops.

♦ Instead of planting lettuce all at once, plan several small plantings so you'll have a steady growth all summer.

♦ Keep a diagram and notebook for your garden, jotting down planting dates and maturity dates. You'll also want to keep track of ideas you have for next year's garden.

Picture Perfect... It's a good idea each spring to take a photo of your flower garden. This will assist you next year when you begin planning changes and additions to your garden—e.g., color, size, style, etc.

Preparing...

Getting Ready... Before digging the soil, test for dampness. Soil should be fairly dry and should crumble when rubbed between your fingers.

♦ Lift soil in chunks, then turn and shatter with spade or pitchfork.

♦ Follow manufacturer's instructions on fertilizers, remembering less is better.

♦ After fertilizing, rake surface smooth.

Seeding Indoors... Save egg cartons, milk cartons and shallow aluminum trays for starting seeds.

♦ Use a good planting medium and fill containers. Vermiculite and an equal amount of milled sphagnum moss is ideal. Dampen mixture.

♦ Scatter seeds over surface and press firmly into soil. Cover with about ¼ inch of potting soil.

♦ Cover container with damp newspaper or dark green plastic and store in a warm damp place. Check daily.

♦ The secret of successful indoor seeding is warmth (70–80°F) and dampness.

♦ Once seeds have sprouted, remove plastic or paper covering and place in an area with 12 hours of light a day, preferably a bright light. If you haven't a spot that's sunny, ordinary fluorescent lighting will do, as long as the seedlings are kept about 3 inches from the light (a fluorescent desk lamp has a double use here).

♦ Temperature can be lowered to 55–60°F once seeds have reached this stage. Water when soil is dry to the touch.

♦ Allow a second pair of leaves to form before transplanting. Thin seedlings if necessary, to allow room for growth.

Bad Seeds?... To sort good seeds from bad seeds, drop all the seeds into a tray of water. Leave overnight and in  the morning the good germinating seeds will have sunk to the bottom. Skim the problem floating seeds and discard.

Planting...

Seeing Sowed Seeds... Sometimes it is difficult to see the seeds against the soil when you sow them. Next time, mix some ordinary cake flour with the seed and you'll be able to see exactly where it's going!

Transplanting Seedlings... Transplanting will help the growth of strong roots. Use a mixture of equal parts potting soil, sphagnum moss and perlite.

♦ Gently uproot by lifting with a spoon, taking care not to disturb roots or surrounding soil too dramatically.

♦ Place in the new mixture and 3 inches apart, forming a small hole in the soil first. Pour water in the hole, and fill the remainder of the hole with the mixture, making sure roots are firmly planted. Allow to rest in the shade for several hours.

♦ Keep a close check on seedlings, making sure there is sufficient air circulation (no crowding, please) and sunlight. Check soil dampness daily and water when it feels dry to touch. Indoor-plant fertilizer can be added to watering solution one week after transplanting or when second pair of leaves are well developed.

♦ To cut down on the trauma experienced by trans-planted perennials, first mix ⅓ cup of hydrogen peroxide in a gallon of water and then pour about ¾ cup of the liquid into the transplant hole.

Planting Your Garden... Cut intersecting lines in plant containers using a sharp knife. Do not remove from container, simply sever joining roots in preparation for outdoors. Allow two weeks before transferring to garden for strong root-balls to form. Allow containers to sit outside for several hours a day in part shade to prepare for the outdoors. Reduce watering for the week preceding planting.

♦ Dig small holes in garden soil and remove seedling from container. Place in hole and fill with loose soil. Water and press firmly in place.

♦ Make sure the stem is planted up to the second pair of leaves. If stakes will be required later, drive them in now in order to avoid damaging a well-formed root later.

♦ If strong winds or rain occurs within a few days of planting outdoors, protect seedlings by covering with inverted buckets or containers.

Tomato Tips... They say you can improve the size of your tomato crop by using the following method. Make the planting holes a little deeper than normal and drop in 2 teaspoons of Epsom salts into each hole. Sprinkle a little dirt into the hole and then add your seedling.

Protecting...

Protecting Seeds... Make a simple "scarecrow" by stapling a foam cup, with the bottom cut out, onto a long stick and plant it in the ground. Cut several long, 1-inch-wide strips from a plastic garbage bag and staple them to the mouth of the cup.

Companion Planting... Companion plants are those that tend to get along extremely well when planted next to each other. Each one discourages the bugs that usually feed on the other.

♦ To keep bugs from roses, plant onion and garlic alongside.

♦ Morning glories require corn or melons next to them.

♦ Petunias seem to keep bugs away from beans.

◆ Parsley can be planted near asparagus, celery or leeks.

◆ Dill does nicely with cabbage.

◆ Peas and tomatoes tend to do
better when planted next to
each other.

◆ To keep worms and flies from
your tomato plants, plant basil near them.

◆ Oregano works for pretty well all garden crops.

◆ Marigolds keep virtually everything away.

GENERAL GARDEN TIPS

HINTS BY THE YARD...

Got A New Golf Bag?... What are you going to do with the old one? It'd be a pity to turn it out to pasture. Why not use it to store all your gardening tools, like hoes, rakes, garden brooms, shovels, etc. Not only will this keep them neat and together, but the golf bag makes a handy carryall for toting around the garden.

Unwanted Pests?... To keep garden pests like mosquitoes and black flies at arm's length while you garden, spray your garden tools with a good outdoor pest repellent.

Unwanted Moles?... If you stick a few of those plastic windmills in your lawn, it should discourage moles.

♦ Or bury some small plastic bottles in the ground with about an inch of the open bottle neck protruding above the ground. The sound of the wind blowing over the bottle scares the moles away.

Cleaning Eaves Troughs Or Guttering... To avoid a messy cleanup on your lawn, place a leg of panty hose over the end of each downspout and secure it with a strong rubber band so as to leave about 18 inches or so  hanging. When you hose the eaves troughs, the leaves will now get caught in the panty hose as they get washed down the downspout.

♦ An old fan belt is an excellent tool for cleaning out your eaves trough. Because it's so flexible, it can take the exact shape of the gutter, and because it's tough, it can lift out whatever is in the eaves trough.

Pine Needles... To pick up pine needles around your patio and lawn, make use of your wet/dry vacuum cleaner. But first place a leg of panty hose over the wand, allowing about 18 inches to hang off the end. When you turn on the vacuum, it will suck the leg up inside the wand. This forms an ideal catchall for those prickly pine needles. But remember not to try this when the lawn is damp or wet.

Bagging Leaves... To make a handy leaf-bagging receptacle, recycle the leg part of that old TV tray. Simply place a garbage bag over the legs and throw the leaves in!

♦ To cut down on the amount of bags you use, try this clever tip. First, place some of the leaves into a large sturdy garbage can to about the halfway mark. Next, take your grass/weed trimmer and reduce the leaves to less than half the size they were, which will take up considerably less bag space. Continue this way until all your leaves have been bagged. Care and caution should be exercised and protective clothes and eyewear should be worn when using this method.

Canned Plants... If you live in a windy area, or your garden is plagued by animals, take a large tin can and cut off both ends. Place it around the plant and push it down an inch or so into the soil. This will protect your plants and also work as a water well, feeding the plant directly without allowing the water to spread into the garden.

Down On Your Knees!... To create nifty knee pads for gardening, save your foam meat trays. Simply attach them to your knees with a rubber band and they'll protect your knees from pebbles and damp ground, etc.

♦ Another idea for a knee pad, is to take an old hot water bottle and stuff it with your old panty hose. Soft and insulating!

♦ Or take one of your kitchen aprons and sew a 6-inch hem in the bottom of it. Stuff the hem with old rags or any soft padding material. This will cushion your knees perfectly.

♦ Use a kid's skateboard to sit on while gardening. You can move up and down the garden with out getting up!

Unwanted Growth?... To discourage weed or grass growth in your stone patio or walkway, heat a gallon of water with a pound of salt. Stir well and pour between the stones.

Economical Trellis... Recycle your old baby gate by opening it out and hanging it on your house or garden wall. It's much stronger than ordinary trellis so it'll last longer.

Economical Plant Supports... The wire frames from old lampshades make ideal plant supports for tomatoes, etc.

Wobbly Wheelbarrow?... Take an old set of bicycle training wheels and bolt them onto the wheel of your wheelbarrow. It'll tip sideways less easily this way.

 **Patio Umbrella...** Store your patio umbrella in panty hose for the winter. Stretch one leg over the umbrella and tie the other leg around the handle to hold it in place. Your umbrella will breathe, which will discourage mildew and rot. It also prevents bugs and spiders from nesting.

Tree First Aid... Give your trees and shrubs a little TLC. After pruning or if damaged, treat the cut areas of the branches with this solution: 1 cup mineral oil and 1 cup zinc oxide.

♦ When cutting grass close to the tree bark with a rotary nylon clipper, protect any cut marks by slicing a large plastic pot open, remove the bottom and wrap around the tree bark.

CHAPTER 12

ROUGHING IT...THE EASY WAY

TIPS WHEN CAMPING, PICNICKING
OR ENTERTAINING IN THE BACKYARD!

CAMPING & PICNIC TIPS

CAMPING & PICNICKING MADE EASY...

Wet Kindling?... Start your fire with those wet twigs by making a sort of tepee out of the twigs, and set a burning candle in the middle. By the time the candle has burned down, it'll have dried the twigs and your fire should be well on its way.

Pinecone Kindling... Collect some pinecones for great campfire kindling. They burn well and hot.

Position Your Kindling... When starting a fire, always place the kindling on the windward side. This way any wind will direct the kindling's flame into the rest of the fire, instead of away from it.

Free Fire Starter... Don't throw away the grease from your camp cooking. Soak it up in paper towels and store the towels in a plastic bag. The next time you start your campfire, you'll have some effective fire starters.

Waterproofing Your Matches... Melt a candle into a small bowl and dip about half the length of the match into the melted wax. Or leave the matches in the open matchbox and pour the melted wax over all the matches.

Cool Around The Campfire?... To make your campfire more efficient, you might want to put up a makeshift heat deflector. A light-colored tarp or tablecloth is ideal. Place it upwind and for safety, not too close to the fire.

Camp Cooking?... Not enough burners to go around?

Try taking along a couple of old double boilers. This way you'll be able to warm up your stew in the top boiler while your potatoes are boiling away in the bottom boiler...with only one burner being used!

Camp-Cooking Cleanup... To make pot cleanup easier on an open fire, try this handy tip. Just before using the pot, rub the outside with a bar of soap or soap paste.

No Egg Cups?... Take the cardboard center of a toilet roll and cut 2-inch pieces. They make great egg holders!

Efficient Cooling... For compact cooler ice blocks, fill wax milk cartons with water, freeze them and place upright in your cooler. Long lasting and waterproof. Later, the cartons will come in handy as campfire kindling.

Leaky Cooler Is No Picnic... Simply melt some candle wax and work it into the crack or hole.

Ant Catchers... To discourage ants from joining you and your food at the picnic or camping table, fill some empty tuna cans ¾ full of water and set each table leg in one.

No Flies On You!... They say that if you place a stick of mint-flavored chewing gum on the side of your paper plate while eating, flies will avoid you and your food!

Tent Tips… To reduce the risk of having your tent blow down on you, try using a piece of inner tube as a link in your guy lines. The elasticity will give your lines more shock absorption.

♦ If you find you're short a tent peg or two, you can use a metal meat skewer in a pinch.

♦ For best results, drive the tent pegs 12 inches into the ground.

♦ It's a good idea to color your tent pegs with luminous paint. This way you're less likely to trip over them at night, or in the day for that matter!

♦ Tent pegs are sharp and can damage your tent fabric when stored unprotected with your tent. Always place your tent pegs in a sturdy bag first.

♦ If your tent or sleeping-bag zipper breaks, replace it with a strip of Velcro. Either sewn or self adhesive.

Sleeping-Bag Smarts… To maintain smooth operation and prevent sleeping-bag zippers from corroding, simply apply some petroleum jelly to the zipper at the start of each season.

♦ To discourage odors, before putting your sleeping bags away each season, give them a good outdoor airing first. Then sprinkle some baking soda inside the bags and roll them up. Next season, simply give them a good shake before using.

♦ Add a few drops of nail-polish remover to thickened nail polish and shake. Results in a smoother finish.

Quick-Drying Nail Polish... Plunge freshly polished nails into ice-cold water. Be careful when drying your hands.

Hard-As-Nails Nail Polish... Brush baby oil on just-polished nails to prevent nicks and chipping.

Long-Lasting Nail Polish... Prior to applying your nail polish, apply a little vinegar to each nail with a cotton swab.

Nail-Polish Remover... Remove existing nail polish by rubbing with fresh nail polish.

Nail-Polish Bottles... If you want to prevent the cap on your nail-polish bottle setting as hard as a rock, here's a tip to try. Rub a little petroleum jelly onto the threads of the bottle.

Filing Nails... Always file nails when perfectly dry from sides to tip. Never back and forth, as it will split and roughen edges.

Perfume... Keep opened perfume in plastic containers in the refrigerator to prevent them from turning rancid.

♦ Apply a little petroleum jelly wherever you dab on perfume. The scent will last longer.

Lipsticks... Lipsticks can be used right to the very bottom. Try creating your own color by saving old tubes until you have a few. Using a toothpick, scrape the remains into a small butter melter and melt over a low heat. Pour into one of the tubes and refrigerate. You might be surprised at the new color, intended just for you!

♦ Or invest in a good lipstick brush. It gets down deep into the lipstick tube and removes all the hard-to-get-at lipstick. In addition, the lipstick brush will give you a better-defined lip line.

Eyebrow Pencils & Lip Liners... To prolong the life of your cosmetic pencils, and to keep them from breaking too easily, store them in the freezer for a few minutes prior to use.

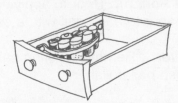

Stop Those Rolling Tubes... Tack a length of elastic to the inside of your cosmetic drawer to keep small tubes from sliding and tipping over.

YOUR WARDROBE

CARING FOR YOUR CLOTHES...

Hats...

Cleaning Felt Hats... Cleaning felt hats is simple if you follow these two easy steps: hold the hat over a steaming kettle then brush with a soft brush, in the direction of the nap.

♦ Some say that you can clean your felt hat by rubbing with a heel of bread!

Washing And Drying Berets... After washing your favorite beret, place a dinner plate inside of it, so it will dry to the right size.

♦ A Frisbee works well too!

Sprucing Up Straw Hats... A quick shot of hair spray on your dull straw hat will renew its gloss!

Windy Hats!... To help keep your hat on, take 2 or 3 small hair combs and sew them onto the sweatband inside your hat. Place one on either side and maybe one at the back.

♦ Another method is to cut a piece of elastic the size of your head and sew that onto the inside of the sweatband, where it's hidden.

Scarves...

Storing Scarves... Save the cardboard rolls from paper towels and toilet tissue and tuck your folded scarves into these. Line them up neatly in your drawer.

Winter Organizer... Ask your local liquor store for one of those boxes they ship bottles in. The type with all those neat dividers. Keep it on its side in your closet or by the front door and store your woolen hats, mitts and scarves in the little compartments.

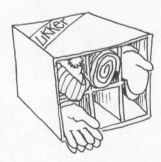

Sweaters...

No-Shed Angora Sweaters... The next time you plan to wear your angora sweater, stick it in the refrigerator for about 12 hours before using. It should prevent your angora from shedding for up to 24 hours.

Unfuzzing Fuzzy Sweaters... Sweaters that have pilled can be restored by gently shaving the surface with a clean razor.

Coats...

Storing Fur Coats... Friction will age your expensive fur coat more quickly than any other common cause. Try to avoid repeated friction whenever possible and don't let it rub against other objects in the closet.

Caring For Wet Coats... Never hang a wet coat near heat. Hang on a wooden coat hanger in the center of a well-ventilated room. Brush with a soft brush when dry.

Cleaning Coats With A Nap... If you own winter coats with a fabric nap, use the "fabric" attachment to your vacuum cleaner and gently clean the coat by running the vacuum in the direction of the nap.

Repairing Raincoats... Rubber raincoats that have torn are quickly repaired by applying adhesive tape to the inside of the garment along the tear line.

Hosiery...

Nylons That Run... The old favorite, clear nail polish, is still the handiest way to stop a run from running.

♦ Or try rubbing a bar of soap over the torn stocking.

Stretching The Life Of Panty Hose... When one leg has a run, but the other is still good, cut away the unwanted "leg" at the very top and save the rest. When another matching pair has a run in it, do the same. You will then have two matching "legs." All you do is wear both at the same time! Remember too that the discarded legs make great fillers for stuffed pillows and toys.

♦ Store your panty hose in the freezer. They'll last longer.

♦ Extend the life of your panty hose and knee-highs. Try applying some ordinary hair spray to the toe area. A quick spray after each wash will prevent the toe area from wearing through.

Belts And Zippers...

Belt Care... Cloth belts with synthetic backing should not be sent to the cleaners. Solvents used in cleaning will weaken the backing and leave the belt limp.

Zippers That Won't Zip... Sticky zippers come unstuck when sprayed heavily with starch or when they are rubbed with a candle.

♦ Two other zipper-lubricating tools are paraffin wax or a lead pencil. Be careful with the pencil though, you don't want to get it on the fabric.

FOOTWEAR FACTS...

What You Should Know About Shoes... Shoes that are allowed to "air" for a day between wearing will last a lot longer. Accumulated perspiration tends to destroy linings, so keep this in mind if you tend to overwear your favorite pair.

Cleaning Canvas Shoes... Use fabric protector or spray starch on new canvas shoes to keep them in great shape. They'll be easier to clean.

♦ White canvas shoes should be cleaned with soap and water. Then add a little lemon juice to the rinse water. It'll brighten and deodorize at the same time!

♦ Clean rope espadrilles by brushing with a small, stiff brush that has been dipped in rug shampoo.

♦ Use nail-polish remover to rid white canvas shoes of tar or grease.

Cleaning Leather Shoes... To clean scuff marks off your  light-colored leather shoes, apply some toothpaste with a soft cloth and then buff. If the marks are really persistent, you could try applying some metal polish the same way. Follow up with clear shoe polish.

Patent-Leather Maintenance... Did you know that petroleum jelly helps prevent cracking and splitting of patent leathers? Try it.

Cleaning Patent Leather... Clean patent leather with a little milk wiped on with a soft cloth. Buff with a dry, soft cloth, or a nylon stocking.

Repairing Scuffs On Your Favorite Kid-Leather Shoes... Gently lift the torn leather and place a small dot of rubber cement on its underside. Wait a moment and press back into place. Allow to dry and rub away any excess glue with your fingers.

Suede-Shoe First Aid... To repair scuff marks on suede shoes, sand very carefully with very fine sandpaper.

Slippery Shoes... Avoid slipping on newly purchased shoes by sanding the soles slightly or scraping two or three times on pavement.

Heels That Ruin... With new shoes, the sharp edges on the heels sometimes tend to catch on your trouser cuffs when you put your trousers on or take them off. To prevent this, take a wood file or coarse sandpaper and bevel the edges a little. Or take your shoes off first!

Heels That Have Worn... Have worn heels replaced as soon as possible to prevent destroying the shape of the shoe.

♦ You can often touch up the heels on your high-heel shoes with auto touch-up paint.

Shoe-Polish Substitutes... If you've run out of shoe polish, try using paste floor wax. It's a great substitute and its neutral color works well on light or dark leather.

♦ Furniture polish will shine leather shoes in a jiffy.

♦ After polishing your shoes, rub them with a sheet of wax paper. Not only will it give your shoes a nice shine, but it will leave a light, protective wax coat.

♦ Raise a good shine on your shoes by rubbing with the inside of a banana peel. Then buff with a clean, dry rag.

♦ A dab of hand cream, rubbed in and buffed, will also work.

Panty Hose Buffer... Raise a great shine by buffing your shoes with panty hose!

Spit 'N Polish... For a patent-leather look, try this army tip. Apply shoe polish with a duster stretched over your forefinger. Rub the polish in with small circular movements of the finger tip. Every so often dip the duster in clean water and continue with the same rubbing motion. Finally, buff it with a clean duster. Never use a brush.

Silencing Squeaks... Silence those squeaking shoes by piercing the sole with a darning needle four or five times at the ball of the foot.

♦ If the squeak persists, try this. Place shoes in a solution of salt water at room temperature. Ensure just the soles are covered. Soak for 15 minutes, dry off and place the soles in boiled linseed oil overnight. The next morning, remove the shoes and dry them well, and your finicky footwear should be completely silenced!

Buying Shoes... They say you should never buy a pair of shoes first thing in the morning. At that time of day your feet tend to be a little smaller than later in the day when you've been on them for a while.

♦ When you buy rubber rain boots, buy them a half to one size larger. Worn with a thick pair of socks, you have an inexpensive pair of winter snow boots. In the summer you can wear them with an insole if you need to.

Shoe Storage... Save all your shoe boxes and cut one end out of each box. Place your shoes in the boxes and stack them neatly, open end out, on the shelf or floor of your clothes closet.

Shoelaces... If you wear white shoes, to prevent black marks forming on the laces near the eyelets, coat the eyelets with clear nail varnish. It creates a barrier.

When Boots Go Into Hibernation... Clean boots thoroughly with leather cleaner and allow to dry. (It's a good time to apply water repellent for next year's use). Stuff the insides with old newspaper, or, if available, stiff cardboard. Store standing up.

Wet Boots?... Nothing can feel quite so chilling as having to step into damp winter boots. If time permits, use your hair dryer by placing the nozzle in at the top of each boot. Set at high and hold in position for five minutes or so. Make sure all zippers or laces are undone for better air circulation.

Boot Care... Keep a cloth coated with petroleum jelly in a sealed container at your front and back door. Everytime you go in or out, give your boots a light rub with the cloth. You'll banish salt marks and preserve the leather.

♦ To prevent the tops of your boots becoming creased, try this. Bind three cardboard tubes (paper-towel tubes) together and shove them into each boot. This keeps them upright and crease free during summer storage.

Free Innersoles!... Don't throw away those foam super-market trays. Cut them to the shape of your shoes or boots for innersoles. They not only cushion your feet but they insulate them from cold or damp ground.

GENERAL WARDROBE WISDOM...

Fragrant Storage... Make your own fragrance sachet by taking your favorite spiced tea bag and wrapping it in a piece of nylon netting or a lace doily. Tie it with a pretty ribbon and leave it in your drawer.

Hanger Hang-Ups!... If your pants or skirt hanger has lost its grip, don't throw it away. Simply place your garment in the hanger as normal, and wrap a strong rubber band around each end. This will keep it tightly closed.

♦ To create a padded coat hanger from a wire coat hanger, poke a hole in the crotch of an old pair of panty hose and thread the hook of the hanger through the hole. Wrap the legs loosely over each side of the hanger, and then pull the waistband down over the hanger. The elastic will hold it all in place.

♦ Instead of panty hose, you can also use those old neckties you were going to throw out.

♦ To avoid having to search for empty hangers, every time you take an item off a hanger, discipline yourself to hang the empty hanger at the end of your closet rod. Now you'll know where to find one!

Unclinging Static Cling... It's said that a piece of wire will draw some of the static electricity if you run it along the garment.

♦ Next time you're plagued with static cling, spray a little hair spray next to your skin, or under the clinging clothing.

♦ If you develop static cling while wearing panty hose, rub some hand cream or moisturizer over your stockinged legs.

Cleaning Vinyl Purses And Luggage... To clean vinyl items, pour a drop of lemon extract on a clean cloth and simply wipe the item with it.

Packing Clothes... When packing clothes in a suitcase, don't lay them flat, roll them instead. They'll take up less space and should unfold with less wrinkles.

JEWELRY GEMS

VALUABLES ADVICE!...

Fixing...

Broken Bead Necklaces... Use dental floss to restring bead or pearl necklaces.

♦ To facilitate threading the beads, line them up on an old washboard, or on a piece of grooved wallboard.

Gold Chains... If your gold chain breaks at the connector ring, you can replace it with the little round end of a brass safety pin. Simply cut it off with wire cutters.

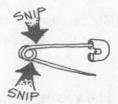

Storing...

A Jewel Of An Idea... Keep fine gold and silver chains from knotting in your jewelry box by cutting a plastic straw to measure half the length of the chain less ¼-inch. Slip the chain through the straw and fasten the catch.

Jewelry Organizer... Glue some cork tile to a child's chalkboard. Press your stud earrings into the cork, while pushpins will support other earrings, rings, necklaces, etc. Butterfly earring backs can be placed on the chalk rail at the bottom, or slipped into a small envelope and pinned onto the jewelry board.

Cleaning...

Sparkling Diamonds!... Place your diamonds in a tea strainer and dip them into a pot of boiling water containing several drops of ammonia and a spoonful of soap flakes. Hold for a few seconds, then remove and rinse in cold water. Soak for 5 minutes in alcohol, and finally rinse and pat dry.

Old-Fashioned Diamond-Jewelry Cleaner... A tried and true formula:

1 oz. dry borax
½ oz. washing soda
½ oz. mild soap shavings
2½ oz. liquid ammonia
1 pint water

Mix first three ingredients in the water and boil until dissolved. Partly cool, and stir in liquid ammonia. Add enough water to make 2 quarts. When ready, place jewelry in an enamel pan, cover with the solution and bring to a boil. Using a soft toothbrush or mascara brush, rub jewelry gently and rinse in hot water. Pat dry.

Cleaning Silver Jewelry... To clean tarnished silver jewelry, make a paste of lemon juice and baking soda. Brush it onto your jewelry with a toothbrush and allow to dry. Finally, brush it off and then polish it gently with a soft cloth.

Cleaning Costume Jewelry... Take your costume jewelry and pop it into a small container. Pour in a little rubbing alcohol over the item and allow it to soak for three or four minutes. Remove it and wipe dry with a soft cloth.

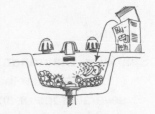

♦ Fill your bathroom sink with hot water and pop in two denture tablets. Drop your costume jewelry in and leave for a while.

♦ Another handy way to clean jewelry is to apply some toothpaste with an old toothbrush, brushing gently. Then rinse well in cold water.

Cleaning Pearls... A quick way to give those pearls a cleaning is to first dampen a soft cloth with olive oil. Then rub each pearl with the oiled cloth.

In General...

Ring Reaction... If you develop a bad reaction to a brass or copper ring, try applying some clear nail polish on the inside of the ring. It'll insulate your skin from the metal. Reapply as necessary.

Ring Removal... If your fingers have swelled, making it difficult to get your ring off, try this trick. Take some thin string and wind it 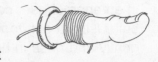 evenly around your finger above the ring so that it covers and compresses your knuckle. Run the end of the string under the ring and slowly pull through the ring. This serves to unwind the string, at the same time easing the ring off your finger.

Costume Jewelry... To extend the life of your costume jewelry, try giving it a light coating of clear nail polish. This creates a barrier between the jewelry and exterior elements like soap, water and your own body oils. When necessary just reapply the clear nail polish.

— ♦ —

CHAPTER 16

HINT GRAB BAG

A HOST OF HELPFUL HINTS
FOR EVERY OCCASION!

HANDY HINTS FROM A TO Z

~ A ~

Animal Doorstop... Want a cute idea for a doorstop? Cut a hole in the bottom of a stuffed animal your kid doesn't use anymore. Remove half the stuffing, replace it with dry sand or marbles and sew the hole closed.

~ B ~

Bad Breath... A quick way to check for bad breath is to lick the back of your hand and smell the saliva. If it smells bad, chew a little fresh parsley!

Bike-Basket Bin!... Take an old bicycle basket, paint or decorate it and hang it on the outside wall next to your front door. When you return home with your arms full, you can set your parcels in the basket until you've found your keys and unlocked your door.

Books And Bindings... Try to keep books in a cool, dry atmosphere. However, if they do get damp and moldy, sprinkle some baby powder in between the pages.

♦ Don't jam books too tightly on the shelf or bindings may break from the pressure.

♦ Books should be stored in an upright position, never leaning to one side. If the book is too small for the shelf, lay it flat. Use bookends to hold the books completely upright.

Bookmarks... Here are a few handy bookmark ideas to prevent dog-eared pages:

~ Cut the corner off an envelope and fit it over the page corner.

~ Stretch a thin rubber band over both the pages and the cover.

~ Slip a loose paper clip over the page.

~ A bobby pin works well too!

~ And those plastic sticks you get with your garden flowers also make great markers.

Book Page Repairs... If you have a tear in one of the pages of your favorite old book, you can repair it as follows: Take a raw egg and separate the white from the yolk. Using a small paintbrush, apply the egg white carefully over the tear. Leave the page to dry with the book open.

♦ To remove spots from book pages, rub them very, very gently with some extrafine sandpaper.

♦ To remove grease spots, however, try rubbing the area with a rubber eraser or an old piece of dry bread.

♦ For waterlogged books, place paper towels on either side of each wet page. Then close the book and weight it down overnight.

~ C ~

Candles... Keep spare candles in the refrigerator or freezer. They'll burn slowly and evenly if cold.

♦ It's a good idea to store your candles in cardboard tubes like the ones you get in paper towels. This will prevent them breaking in the freezer.

♦ In an emergency, a quick, portable, nontipping candlestick is as close as your nearest juice or coffee tin. Hold the taper candle against the tin and slip an elastic band around both to secure them together.

♦ If you have no candles, in an emergency, you can dip a cotton swab in some petroleum jelly and light it. The jar of jelly will also act as a convenient holder for the swab.

♦ Sometimes decorative candles can split when you stick them onto a spiked base. To prevent this, using pliers, heat an ordinary nail, slightly thinner than the spike, and poke a hole in the bottom of the candle with it. It should now fit snugly over the spike without splitting.

♦ Make your own decorative candles by recycling all those small, different colored pieces of used candle. Melt them together in a pot and pour the wax carefully into an old tennis-ball container. Don't forget to hold a length of string in place while you pour. This will serve as the wick.

♦ Prevent an accident from occurring. If your candleholder is too large for the candle you have, melt some wax and fill the socket. Before it hardens, insert the too-small candle.

Cushion Stuffing... For an economical way to fill those sagging cushions and pillows, save your old panty hose and use them as stuffing.

~ D ~

Dirt-Free Fingernails... Here's a neat way to avoid dirty fingernails when gardening or working in a dirty environment. Before you start working, simply dig your nails into a bar of soft soap. It'll make later cleanup a lot easier.

~ E ~

Eyeglass Fog?... Try applying a little shaving cream to your eyeglasses. Wipe clean with a soft cloth. This will help prevent your glasses from misting up when you come inside from the cold.

~ F ~

Fireplace... Impress your guests by removing the fire grate from your fireplace and arranging several candles in its place. Light the candles just before your guests arrive and replace the fire screen.

♦ Replace long matches with a length of raw spaghetti when lighting a deep candle or fireplace. The spaghetti should burn evenly and slowly giving you lots of time to light the fire.

♦ Instead of regular kindling, try saving all your orange and lemon peels. Dry them and use them for kindling. They last a lot longer than newspaper because of the flammable oils they contain.

♦ To make your own fireplace logs out of newspaper, roll the newspaper up fairly loosely into a 2- to 3-inch-thick "log." Secure with thin wire.

~ G ~

Getting Your Shoes On Easier...
If you don't have a shoehorn, a large spoon will do the trick.

~ H ~

Homegrown Polish... To preserve the shine on your newly polished ornamental copper, just give it a light coating of hair spray!

Homemade Postcards... Cut the back page off your old greeting cards. Draw a line down the center of the blank side for the address and message. You now have a handy, inexpensive postcard.

♦ You can personalize your postcards by utilizing leftover photos from double prints. Save the cardboard inserts from your panty hose packages and trim them to the size of your photograph. Glue the cardboard to the back of the photograph, draw a line down the center and you have an inexpensive, memorable greeting card.

~ I ~

Ice Cream Storage... To make your ice cream last longer in the freezer, try covering the ice cream tub first with aluminum foil.

~ J ~

Jeans Too Stiff?... They say you can make new blue jeans more pliable by leaving them for 12 hours in a bath of cold water, to which you've added a cup of table salt.

~ K ~

Key-Ring String... Take a piece of elastic and tie one end to your key ring and the other end to the zipper on your purse. The stretchy elastic will allow you to pull the keys out when you need them, and you will always know where to find them. A tug on the zipper and your keys appear.

~ L ~

Labels... After writing the address on a label, stick the label on the parcel. Instead of using your fingers to smooth the label on, simply roll a pencil over the label. It will apply just the right pressure, but won't smudge the ink.

Leveling Furniture... A great way to level the legs on tables and chairs is to stick a small piece of adhesive carpet tile under the offending leg.

~ M ~

Modeling Knives... To sharpen your modeling knives, use the striking strip on a matchbox. It has just the right abrasiveness.

Moving Furniture... When moving heavy furniture across the floor, to make it slide better and to save the floor from getting scratched, flatten some wax milk cartons and put one under each leg.

~ N ~

No Birds In Your Birdbath?... Try sprinkling a little birdseed on the surface of the water. That should attract them.

~ O ~

Odors... In order to absorb the odors from dirty dishes that sit in the dishwasher all day, try pouring a cupful of baking soda in the bottom of the dishwasher.

~ P ~

Photographs... You can often rejuvenate old black-and-white photographs by a applying a thin layer of clear shoe polish to the surface. Buff with a soft cloth or flannel rag.

♦ Don't leave your snapshots in a shoe box. The weight of the top photographs will damage the bottom ones. Constant shuffling will allow dust particles to rub the surfaces and cause fading and scratching.

♦ When framing a photograph, keep the photo from touching the glass by using an acid-free matte of cardboard or paper. This helps prevent dampness which could destroy the finish.

♦ Don't throw away those corrugated cardboard lightbulb covers. Fold the cover flat and slip your photographs inside it when you send them by mail. This way they should arrive intact!

~ Q ~

Quick-Clean Coffee Grinder... Grind ½ cup of uncooked rice through your coffee grinder for a quick clean.

Quick Shop... Instead of spending valuable time shopping in stores for basic clothing, like socks, underwear, T-shirts, etc., buy them through a reputable mail-order company. Generally speaking, size range and quality are good.

~ R ~

Rubber-Glove Removal... Run cold water over stubborn rubber gloves. They'll slide off easier.

Rug Hooking... Use panty hose! It dyes well and doesn't shrink!

Rust On Your Cutlery?... Often small amounts of rust can be removed from knives and forks, etc., by rubbing the item with a cut onion. Leave the onion juice on for an hour or so, then rinse and dry well.

~ S ~

Snoring Problem?... They say that people will snore less if they don't sleep on their backs. To discourage this practice, you might want to try attaching a small plastic baggie with a pebble inside to the back of your pajama top. Positioned in the center, it should encourage you to roll over on your side during the night.

Stuck Stopper?... If the glass stopper of your glass decanter is stuck, don't try to force it. Take a piece of thick string and wind it once around the neck of the bottle in line with the stopper. Have someone hold the bottle tight while you  draw the string quickly back and forth. This should generate enough heat to expand the glass neck and release the stopper.

~ T ~

Television-Reception Tip... It's a good idea not to place electrical items on the top of your color TV. They sometimes can affect the color on your TV.

~ U ~

Umbrella Tips... When buying an umbrella, hold it up to the light. If a lot of light comes through, rain will too!

♦ The greater the number of ribs, the stronger the umbrella. The greater the number of tacks holding the fabric to the ribs, the less likely to tear.

♦ Automatic-opening umbrellas are generally weaker, and tend to turn inside out more easily.

♦ Before you throw away your old umbrella, save the tips from the rib ends for future repairs on your new umbrella.

♦ To repair a broken rib, attach a splint of coathanger wire with a piece of masking tape.

♦ To attach a loose cover from the rib, it is best to use dental floss threaded on a large needle. It will last longer.

♦ To prevent your new umbrella from rusting, and to help it open and close easily, rub a little petroleum jelly onto the hinges.

~ V ~

Videotape Storage... It's said that you should always store your videotapes vertically, not lying down.

Venetian-Blind Surprise!... Using washable colored markers, write your surprise message on a white venetian blind that has been set in the flat, closed position. Allow to dry and restore to the open position. When the guest of honor arrives, turn the venetian blind to the closed position and reveal the message! Afterward, simply clean with soap and water.

~ W ~

Window-Screen Damage...
Here's an emergency solution if you should develop a hole or tear in your window or door screen. Simply take two pieces of plastic cling wrap and place one piece on either side of the screen over the damage. The wrap will cling together and cover any rips.

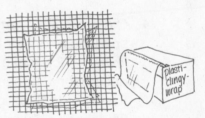

~ X ~

Xmas-Present Tips... If you're sending a Christmas parcel in the mail and want to ensure the string won't come undone, wet the string before you tie the package. As it dries, it shrinks, which gives you a tight, secure parcel.

♦ Collect odd dinner plates from yard sales, flea markets and auctions throughout the year. At Christmas, bake cookies and candies, and place them on these plates covered with cellophane and tied with a bright bow. They make appealing, inexpensive Christmas gifts.

Xmas Decorations... Save your plastic scoops from your laundry-detergent containers. Create little Christmas or Nativity scenes inside the scoop using old craft supplies that you have around the house. Paint the outside a Christmas color, drill a hole through the handle and thread a bright ribbon through the hole for hanging on the tree.

♦ Have the kids cut out circles from old Christmas cards to the size of small plastic-container lids. They can then glue the cutouts to the lids. Finally, decorate with sparkles, then cut a hole and hang it on the tree with a colorful ribbon.

♦ Old lightbulbs, spray painted and decorated with sparkles and various oddments of old necklaces and jewelry, etc., make inexpensive, colorful Christmas decorations. Experiment with different sized bulbs, from flashlight to floodlight and hang them from the tree with Christmas ribbons or string.

Xmas Leftovers... Save those leftover candy canes from Christmas. On cold winter days, the kids can use them as flavorful peppermint stir sticks for their hot chocolate. Yummy!

~ Y ~

Yellowing Blind Tapes?... A quick and effective way to spruce up the tapes that hold your white venetian-blind slats together is to simply rub them with white canvas-shoe polish!

~ Z ~

Zippers Rusting?... To prevent the zippers on your camping sleeping bags from rusting due to dampness, try coating the zippers first with a little petroleum jelly.

THE LAST WORD

The Best Hint of All... Be good to yourself! Give yourself regular vacations. Here are a few tips to help you fly away.

♦ Request the emergency-exit row or bulkhead seats for greater leg room.

♦ Arrange meal requirements at the same time you book.

♦ Check several travel agencies; some have better connections than others. Or surf the Web.

♦ Wear comfortable lace-up shoes. They can be loosened.

♦ Use a baggage tag that covers the address portion, revealing only your name.

♦ Remember, no caffeine or alcohol. Drink a glass of water every hour for dehydration.

♦ Pack valuables, medication, swimsuit and coverup in your carry-on. If your luggage is delayed, you can still start your holiday!

— ♦ —

CHAPTER 17

INFORMATION AT A GLANCE

USEFUL CHARTS ON
MEASUREMENTS,
METRIC & SUBSTITUTES!

MEASUREMENTS... IN OTHER WORDS

Metric Mathematics... If you can multiply and divide by 10, you think in metric. Changing from one multiple or submultiple of a unit to another is done by simply moving the decimal point (e.g., 100 cm = 1 m).

Thinking Metric... If you can associate specific metric measurements with a visual experience or activity (e.g., a meter is the length of a long step; normal room temperature is 21°C), it's easy! And there are only 7 base units compared to 53 in the imperial system!

AREA (SQUARE MEASURE)

1 sq. centimeter	= 100 sq. millimeters	= 0.15 sq. inches
1 sq. meter	= 100 sq. centimeters	= 10.8 sq. feet
1 sq. dekameter	= 100 sq. meters	= 120 sq. yards
1 sq. hectometer (hectare)	= 10,000 sq. meters	= 2.5 acres
10 hectares	= 1 sq. kilometer	= 0.4 sq. miles

Knowing:	Multiply by:	To obtain:
square inches	6.5	square centimeters
square feet	0.009	square meter
square yards	0.8	square meters
square miles	2.6	square kilometers
acres	0.4	hectares
square centimeters	0.16	square inches
square meters	1.2	square yards
square kilometers	0.4	square miles
hectares (10,000 m^2)	2.5	acres

LENGTHS

1 centimeter (cm)	= 10 millimeters (mm)	= 0.3937 inches
1 decimeter (dm)	= 10 centimeters	= 3.937 inches
1 meter (m)	= 10 decimeters	= 3.3 feet
1 dekameter (dk)	= 10 meters	= 11 yards
1 hectometer (hm)	= 10 dekameters	= 110 yards
1 kilometer (km)	= 10 hectometers	= 1100 yards

Quick Conversions... If you know a length and need to convert to either metric or standard, simply multiply by the number given.

Knowing:	Multiply by:	To obtain:
millimeters	0.04	inches
centimeters	0.40	inches
meters	3.30	feet
meters	1.10	yards
kilometers	0.60	miles
inches	2.50	centimeters
feet	30.00	centimeters
yards	0.90	meters
miles	1.60	kilometers

♦ Add a few drops of nail-polish remover to thickened nail polish and shake. Results in a smoother finish.

Quick-Drying Nail Polish... Plunge freshly polished nails into ice-cold water. Be careful when drying your hands.

Hard-As-Nails Nail Polish... Brush baby oil on just-polished nails to prevent nicks and chipping.

Long-Lasting Nail Polish... Prior to applying your nail polish, apply a little vinegar to each nail with a cotton swab.

Nail-Polish Remover... Remove existing nail polish by rubbing with fresh nail polish.

Nail-Polish Bottles... If you want to prevent the cap on your nail-polish bottle setting as hard as a rock, here's a tip to try. Rub a little petroleum jelly onto the threads of the bottle.

Filing Nails... Always file nails when perfectly dry from sides to tip. Never back and forth, as it will split and roughen edges.

Perfume... Keep opened perfume in plastic containers in the refrigerator to prevent them from turning rancid.

♦ Apply a little petroleum jelly wherever you dab on perfume. The scent will last longer.

Lipsticks... Lipsticks can be used right to the very bottom. Try creating your own color by saving old tubes until you have a few. Using a toothpick, scrape the remains into a small butter melter and melt over a low heat. Pour into one of the tubes and refrigerate. You might be surprised at the new color, intended just for you!

♦ Or invest in a good lipstick brush. It gets down deep into the lipstick tube and removes all the hard-to-get-at lipstick. In addition, the lipstick brush will give you a better-defined lip line.

Eyebrow Pencils & Lip Liners... To prolong the life of your cosmetic pencils, and to keep them from breaking too easily, store them in the freezer for a few minutes prior to use.

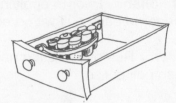

Stop Those Rolling Tubes... Tack a length of elastic to the inside of your cosmetic drawer to keep small tubes from sliding and tipping over.

YOUR WARDROBE

CARING FOR YOUR CLOTHES...

Hats...

Cleaning Felt Hats... Cleaning felt hats is simple if you follow these two easy steps: hold the hat over a steaming kettle then brush with a soft brush, in the direction of the nap.

♦ Some say that you can clean your felt hat by rubbing with a heel of bread!

Washing And Drying Berets... After washing your favorite beret, place a dinner plate inside of it, so it will dry to the right size.

♦ A Frisbee works well too!

Sprucing Up Straw Hats... A quick shot of hair spray on your dull straw hat will renew its gloss!

Windy Hats!... To help keep your hat on, take 2 or 3 small hair combs and sew them onto the sweatband inside your hat. Place one on either side and maybe one at the back.

♦ Another method is to cut a piece of elastic the size of your head and sew that onto the inside of the sweatband, where it's hidden.

Scarves...

Storing Scarves... Save the cardboard rolls from paper towels and toilet tissue and tuck your folded scarves into these. Line them up neatly in your drawer.

Winter Organizer... Ask your local liquor store for one of those boxes they ship bottles in. The type with all those neat dividers. Keep it on its side in your closet or by the front door and store your woolen hats, mitts and scarves in the little compartments.

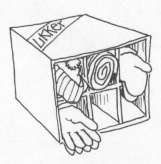

Sweaters...

No-Shed Angora Sweaters... The next time you plan to wear your angora sweater, stick it in the refrigerator for about 12 hours before using. It should prevent your angora from shedding for up to 24 hours.

Unfuzzing Fuzzy Sweaters... Sweaters that have pilled can be restored by gently shaving the surface with a clean razor.

Coats...

Storing Fur Coats... Friction will age your expensive fur coat more quickly than any other common cause. Try to avoid repeated friction whenever possible and don't let it rub against other objects in the closet.

Caring For Wet Coats... Never hang a wet coat near heat. Hang on a wooden coat hanger in the center of a well-ventilated room. Brush with a soft brush when dry.

Cleaning Coats With A Nap... If you own winter coats with a fabric nap, use the "fabric" attachment to your vacuum cleaner and gently clean the coat by running the vacuum in the direction of the nap.

Repairing Raincoats... Rubber raincoats that have torn are quickly repaired by applying adhesive tape to the inside of the garment along the tear line.

Hosiery...

Nylons That Run... The old favorite, clear nail polish, is still the handiest way to stop a run from running.

♦ Or try rubbing a bar of soap over the torn stocking.

Stretching The Life Of Panty Hose... When one leg has a run, but the other is still good, cut away the unwanted "leg" at the very top and save the rest. When another matching pair has a run in it, do the same. You will then have two matching

"legs." All you do is wear both at the same time! Remember too that the discarded legs make great fillers for stuffed pillows and toys.

♦ Store your panty hose in the freezer. They'll last longer.

♦ Extend the life of your panty hose and knee-highs. Try applying some ordinary hair spray to the toe area. A quick spray after each wash will prevent the toe area from wearing through.

Belts And Zippers...

Belt Care... Cloth belts with synthetic backing should not be sent to the cleaners. Solvents used in cleaning will weaken the backing and leave the belt limp.

Zippers That Won't Zip... Sticky zippers come unstuck when sprayed heavily with starch or when they are rubbed with a candle.

♦ Two other zipper-lubricating tools are paraffin wax or a lead pencil. Be careful with the pencil though, you don't want to get it on the fabric.

FOOTWEAR FACTS...

What You Should Know About Shoes... Shoes that are allowed to "air" for a day between wearing will last a lot longer. Accumulated perspiration tends to destroy linings, so keep this in mind if you tend to overwear your favorite pair.

Cleaning Canvas Shoes... Use fabric protector or spray starch on new canvas shoes to keep them in great shape. They'll be easier to clean.

♦ White canvas shoes should be cleaned with soap and water. Then add a little lemon juice to the rinse water. It'll brighten and deodorize at the same time!

♦ Clean rope espadrilles by brushing with a small, stiff brush that has been dipped in rug shampoo.

♦ Use nail-polish remover to rid white canvas shoes of tar or grease.

Cleaning Leather Shoes... To clean scuff marks off your  light-colored leather shoes, apply some toothpaste with a soft cloth and then buff. If the marks are really persistent, you could try applying some metal polish the same way. Follow up with clear shoe polish.

Patent-Leather Maintenance... Did you know that petroleum jelly helps prevent cracking and splitting of patent leathers? Try it.

Cleaning Patent Leather... Clean patent leather with a little milk wiped on with a soft cloth. Buff with a dry, soft cloth, or a nylon stocking.

Repairing Scuffs On Your Favorite Kid-Leather Shoes... Gently lift the torn leather and place a small dot of rubber cement on its underside. Wait a moment and press back into place. Allow to dry and rub away any excess glue with your fingers.

Suede-Shoe First Aid... To repair scuff marks on suede shoes, sand very carefully with very fine sandpaper.

Slippery Shoes... Avoid slipping on newly purchased shoes by sanding the soles slightly or scraping two or three times on pavement.

Heels That Ruin... With new shoes, the sharp edges on the heels sometimes tend to catch on your trouser cuffs when you put your trousers on or take them off. To prevent this, take a wood file or coarse sandpaper and bevel the edges a little. Or take your shoes off first!

Heels That Have Worn... Have worn heels replaced as soon as possible to prevent destroying the shape of the shoe.

♦ You can often touch up the heels on your high-heel shoes with auto touch-up paint.

Shoe-Polish Substitutes... If you've run out of shoe polish, try using paste floor wax. It's a great substitute and its neutral color works well on light or dark leather.

♦ Furniture polish will shine leather shoes in a jiffy.

♦ After polishing your shoes, rub them with a sheet of wax paper. Not only will it give your shoes a nice shine, but it will leave a light, protective wax coat.

♦ Raise a good shine on your shoes by rubbing with the inside of a banana peel. Then buff with a clean, dry rag.

♦ A dab of hand cream, rubbed in and buffed, will also work.

Panty Hose Buffer... Raise a great shine by buffing your shoes with panty hose!

Spit 'N Polish... For a patent-leather look, try this army tip. Apply shoe polish with a duster stretched over your forefinger. Rub the polish in with small circular movements of the finger tip. Every so often dip the duster in clean water and continue with the same rubbing motion. Finally, buff it with a clean duster. Never use a brush.

Silencing Squeaks... Silence those squeaking shoes by piercing the sole with a darning needle four or five times at the ball of the foot.

♦ If the squeak persists, try this. Place shoes in a solution of salt water at room temperature. Ensure just the soles are covered. Soak for 15 minutes, dry off and place the soles in boiled linseed oil overnight. The next morning, remove the shoes and dry them well, and your finicky footwear should be completely silenced!

Buying Shoes... They say you should never buy a pair of shoes first thing in the morning. At that time of day your feet tend to be a little smaller than later in the day when you've been on them for a while.

♦ When you buy rubber rain boots, buy them a half to one size larger. Worn with a thick pair of socks, you have an inexpensive pair of winter snow boots. In the summer you can wear them with an insole if you need to.

Shoe Storage... Save all your shoe boxes and cut one end out of each box. Place your shoes in the boxes and stack them neatly, open end out, on the shelf or floor of your clothes closet.

Shoelaces... If you wear white shoes, to prevent black marks forming on the laces near the eyelets, coat the eyelets with clear nail varnish. It creates a barrier.

When Boots Go Into Hibernation... Clean boots thoroughly with leather cleaner and allow to dry. (It's a good time to apply water repellent for next year's use). Stuff the insides with old newspaper, or, if available, stiff cardboard. Store standing up.

Wet Boots?... Nothing can feel quite so chilling as having to step into damp winter boots. If time permits, use your hair dryer by placing the nozzle in at the top of each boot. Set at high and hold in position for five minutes or so. Make sure all zippers or laces are undone for better air circulation.

Boot Care... Keep a cloth coated with petroleum jelly in a sealed container at your front and back door. Everytime you go in or out, give your boots a light rub with the cloth. You'll banish salt marks and preserve the leather.

◆ To prevent the tops of your boots becoming creased, try this. Bind three cardboard tubes (paper-towel tubes) together and shove them into each boot. This keeps them upright and crease free during summer storage.

Free Innersoles!... Don't throw away those foam super-market trays. Cut them to the shape of your shoes or boots for innersoles. They not only cushion your feet but they insulate them from cold or damp ground.

GENERAL WARDROBE WISDOM...

Fragrant Storage... Make your own fragrance sachet by taking your favorite spiced tea bag and wrapping it in a piece of nylon netting or a lace doily. Tie it with a pretty ribbon and leave it in your drawer.

Hanger Hang-Ups!... If your pants or skirt hanger has lost its grip, don't throw it away. Simply place your garment in the hanger as normal, and wrap a strong rubber band around each end. This will keep it tightly closed.

◆ To create a padded coat hanger from a wire coat hanger, poke a hole in the crotch of an old pair of panty hose and thread the hook of the hanger through the hole. Wrap the legs loosely over each side of the hanger, and then pull the waistband down over the hanger. The elastic will hold it all in place.

♦ Instead of panty hose, you can also use those old neckties you were going to throw out.

♦ To avoid having to search for empty hangers, every time you take an item off a hanger, discipline yourself to hang the empty hanger at the end of your closet rod. Now you'll know where to find one!

Unclinging Static Cling... It's said that a piece of wire will draw some of the static electricity if you run it along the garment.

♦ Next time you're plagued with static cling, spray a little hair spray next to your skin, or under the clinging clothing.

♦ If you develop static cling while wearing panty hose, rub some hand cream or moisturizer over your stockinged legs.

Cleaning Vinyl Purses And Luggage... To clean vinyl items, pour a drop of lemon extract on a clean cloth and simply wipe the item with it.

Packing Clothes... When packing clothes in a suitcase, don't lay them flat, roll them instead. They'll take up less space and should unfold with less wrinkles.

JEWELRY GEMS

VALUABLES ADVICE!...

Fixing...

Broken Bead Necklaces... Use dental floss to restring bead or pearl necklaces.

♦ To facilitate threading the beads, line them up on an old washboard, or on a piece of grooved wallboard.

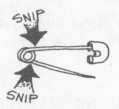

Gold Chains... If your gold chain breaks at the connector ring, you can replace it with the little round end of a brass safety pin. Simply cut it off with wire cutters.

Storing...

A Jewel Of An Idea... Keep fine gold and silver chains from knotting in your jewelry box by cutting a plastic straw to measure half the length of the chain less ¼-inch. Slip the chain through the straw and fasten the catch.

Jewelry Organizer... Glue some cork tile to a child's chalkboard. Press your stud earrings into the cork, while pushpins will support other earrings, rings, necklaces, etc. Butterfly earring backs can be placed on the chalk rail at the bottom, or slipped into a small envelope and pinned onto the jewelry board.

Cleaning...

Sparkling Diamonds!... Place your diamonds in a tea
strainer and dip them into a pot of boiling water containing
several drops of ammonia and a spoonful of soap flakes.
Hold for a few seconds, then remove and rinse in cold
water. Soak for 5 minutes in alcohol, and finally rinse and
pat dry.

Old-Fashioned Diamond-Jewelry Cleaner... A tried and
true formula:

1 oz. dry borax
½ oz. washing soda
½ oz. mild soap shavings
2½ oz. liquid ammonia
1 pint water

Mix first three ingredients in the water and boil until
dissolved. Partly cool, and stir in liquid ammonia. Add
enough water to make 2 quarts. When ready, place jewelry
in an enamel pan, cover with the solution and bring to a
boil. Using a soft toothbrush or mascara brush, rub jewelry
gently and rinse in hot water. Pat dry.

Cleaning Silver Jewelry... To clean tarnished silver jewelry,
make a paste of lemon juice and baking soda. Brush
it onto your jewelry with a toothbrush and allow to dry.
Finally, brush it off and then polish it gently with a
soft cloth.

Cleaning Costume Jewelry... Take your costume jewelry
and pop it into a small container. Pour in a little rubbing
alcohol over the item and allow it to soak for three or four
minutes. Remove it and wipe dry with a soft cloth.

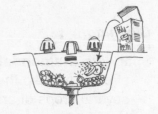

♦ Fill your bathroom sink with hot water and pop in two denture tablets. Drop your costume jewelry in and leave for a while.

♦ Another handy way to clean jewelry is to apply some toothpaste with an old toothbrush, brushing gently. Then rinse well in cold water.

Cleaning Pearls... A quick way to give those pearls a cleaning is to first dampen a soft cloth with olive oil. Then rub each pearl with the oiled cloth.

In General...

Ring Reaction... If you develop a bad reaction to a brass or copper ring, try applying some clear nail polish on the inside of the ring. It'll insulate your skin from the metal. Reapply as necessary.

Ring Removal... If your fingers have swelled, making it difficult to get your ring off, try this trick. Take some thin string and wind it evenly around your finger above the ring so that it covers and compresses your knuckle. Run the end of the string under the ring and slowly pull through the ring. This serves to unwind the string, at the same time easing the ring off your finger.

Costume Jewelry... To extend the life of your costume jewelry, try giving it a light coating of clear nail polish. This creates a barrier between the jewelry and exterior elements like soap, water and your own body oils. When necessary just reapply the clear nail polish.

— ♦ —

CHAPTER 16

HINT GRAB BAG

A HOST OF HELPFUL HINTS
FOR EVERY OCCASION!

HANDY HINTS FROM A TO Z

~ A ~

Animal Doorstop... Want a cute idea for a doorstop? Cut a hole in the bottom of a stuffed animal your kid doesn't use anymore. Remove half the stuffing, replace it with dry sand or marbles and sew the hole closed.

~ B ~

Bad Breath... A quick way to check for bad breath is to lick the back of your hand and smell the saliva. If it smells bad, chew a little fresh parsley!

Bike-Basket Bin!... Take an old bicycle basket, paint or decorate it and hang it on the outside wall next to your front door. When you return home with your arms full, you can set your parcels in the basket until you've found your keys and unlocked your door.

Books And Bindings... Try to keep books in a cool, dry atmosphere. However, if they do get damp and moldy, sprinkle some baby powder in between the pages.

♦ Don't jam books too tightly on the shelf or bindings may break from the pressure.

♦ Books should be stored in an upright position, never leaning to one side. If the book is too small for the shelf, lay it flat. Use bookends to hold the books completely upright.

Bookmarks... Here are a few handy bookmark ideas to prevent dog-eared pages:

~ Cut the corner off an envelope and fit it over the page corner.

~ Stretch a thin rubber band over both the pages and the cover.

~ Slip a loose paper clip over the page.

~ A bobby pin works well too!

~ And those plastic sticks you get with your garden flowers also make great markers.

Book Page Repairs... If you have a tear in one of the pages of your favorite old book, you can repair it as follows: Take a raw egg and separate the white from the yolk. Using a small paintbrush, apply the egg white carefully over the tear. Leave the page to dry with the book open.

♦ To remove spots from book pages, rub them very, very gently with some extrafine sandpaper.

♦ To remove grease spots, however, try rubbing the area with a rubber eraser or an old piece of dry bread.

♦ For waterlogged books, place paper towels on either side of each wet page. Then close the book and weight it down overnight.

~ C ~

Candles... Keep spare candles in the refrigerator or freezer. They'll burn slowly and evenly if cold.

♦ It's a good idea to store your candles in cardboard tubes like the ones you get in paper towels. This will prevent them breaking in the freezer.

♦ In an emergency, a quick, portable, nontipping candlestick is as close as your nearest juice or coffee tin. Hold the taper candle against the tin and slip an elastic band around both to secure them together.

♦ If you have no candles, in an emergency, you can dip a cotton swab in some petroleum jelly and light it. The jar of jelly will also act as a convenient holder for the swab.

♦ Sometimes decorative candles can split when you stick them onto a spiked base. To prevent this, using pliers, heat an ordinary nail, slightly thinner than the spike, and poke a hole in the bottom of the candle with it. It should now fit snugly over the spike without splitting.

♦ Make your own decorative candles by recycling all those small, different colored pieces of used candle. Melt them together in a pot and pour the wax carefully into an old tennis-ball container. Don't forget to hold a length of string in place while you pour. This will serve as the wick.

♦ Prevent an accident from occurring. If your candleholder is too large for the candle you have, melt some wax and fill the socket. Before it hardens, insert the too-small candle.

Cushion Stuffing... For an economical way to fill those sagging cushions and pillows, save your old panty hose and use them as stuffing.

~ D ~

Dirt-Free Fingernails... Here's a neat way to avoid dirty fingernails when gardening or working in a dirty environment. Before you start working, simply dig your nails into a bar of soft soap. It'll make later cleanup a lot easier.

~ E ~

Eyeglass Fog?... Try applying a little shaving cream to your eyeglasses. Wipe clean with a soft cloth. This will help prevent your glasses from misting up when you come inside from the cold.

~ F ~

Fireplace... Impress your guests by removing the fire grate from your fireplace and arranging several candles in its place. Light the candles just before your guests arrive and replace the fire screen.

♦ Replace long matches with a length of raw spaghetti when lighting a deep candle or fireplace. The spaghetti should burn evenly and slowly giving you lots of time to light the fire.

♦ Instead of regular kindling, try saving all your orange and lemon peels. Dry them and use them for kindling. They last a lot longer than newspaper because of the flammable oils they contain.

♦ To make your own fireplace logs out of newspaper, roll the newspaper up fairly loosely into a 2- to 3-inch-thick "log." Secure with thin wire.

~ G ~

Getting Your Shoes On Easier...
If you don't have a shoehorn, a large spoon will do the trick.

~ H ~

Homegrown Polish... To preserve the shine on your newly polished ornamental copper, just give it a light coating of hair spray!

Homemade Postcards... Cut the back page off your old greeting cards. Draw a line down the center of the blank side for the address and message. You now have a handy, inexpensive postcard.

♦ You can personalize your postcards by utilizing leftover photos from double prints. Save the cardboard inserts from your panty hose packages and trim them to the size of your photograph. Glue the cardboard to the back of the photograph, draw a line down the center and you have an inexpensive, memorable greeting card.

~ I ~

Ice Cream Storage... To make your ice cream last longer in the freezer, try covering the ice cream tub first with aluminum foil.

~ J ~

Jeans Too Stiff?... They say you can make new blue jeans more pliable by leaving them for 12 hours in a bath of cold water, to which you've added a cup of table salt.

~ K ~

Key-Ring String... Take a piece of elastic and tie one end to your key ring and the other end to the zipper on your purse. The stretchy elastic will allow you to pull the keys out when you need them, and you will always know where to find them. A tug on the zipper and your keys appear.

~ L ~

Labels... After writing the address on a label, stick the label on the parcel. Instead of using your fingers to smooth the label on, simply roll a pencil over the label. It will apply just the right pressure, but won't smudge the ink.

Leveling Furniture... A great way to level the legs on tables and chairs is to stick a small piece of adhesive carpet tile under the offending leg.

~ M ~

Modeling Knives... To sharpen your modeling knives, use the striking strip on a matchbox. It has just the right abrasiveness.

Moving Furniture... When moving heavy furniture across the floor, to make it slide better and to save the floor from getting scratched, flatten some wax milk cartons and put one under each leg.

~ N ~

No Birds In Your Birdbath?... Try sprinkling a little birdseed on the surface of the water. That should attract them.

~ O ~

Odors... In order to absorb the odors from dirty dishes that sit in the dishwasher all day, try pouring a cupful of baking soda in the bottom of the dishwasher.

~ P ~

Photographs... You can often rejuvenate old black-and-white photographs by a applying a thin layer of clear shoe polish to the surface. Buff with a soft cloth or flannel rag.

◆ Don't leave your snapshots in a shoe box. The weight of the top photographs will damage the bottom ones. Constant shuffling will allow dust particles to rub the surfaces and cause fading and scratching.

◆ When framing a photograph, keep the photo from touching the glass by using an acid-free matte of cardboard or paper. This helps prevent dampness which could destroy the finish.

◆ Don't throw away those corrugated cardboard lightbulb covers. Fold the cover flat and slip your photographs inside it when you send them by mail. This way they should arrive intact!

~ Q ~

Quick-Clean Coffee Grinder... Grind ½ cup of uncooked rice through your coffee grinder for a quick clean.

Quick Shop... Instead of spending valuable time shopping in stores for basic clothing, like socks, underwear, T-shirts, etc., buy them through a reputable mail-order company. Generally speaking, size range and quality are good.

~ R ~

Rubber-Glove Removal... Run cold water over stubborn rubber gloves. They'll slide off easier.

Rug Hooking... Use panty hose! It dyes well and doesn't shrink!

Rust On Your Cutlery?... Often small amounts of rust can be removed from knives and forks, etc., by rubbing the item with a cut onion. Leave the onion juice on for an hour or so, then rinse and dry well.

~ S ~

Snoring Problem?... They say that people will snore less if they don't sleep on their backs. To discourage this practice, you might want to try attaching a small plastic baggie with a pebble inside to the back of your pajama top. Positioned in the center, it should encourage you to roll over on your side during the night.

Stuck Stopper?... If the glass stopper of your glass decanter is stuck, don't try to force it. Take a piece of thick string and wind it once around the neck of the bottle in line with the stopper. Have someone hold the bottle tight while you draw the string quickly back and forth. This should generate enough heat to expand the glass neck and release the stopper.

~ T ~

Television-Reception Tip... It's a good idea not to place electrical items on the top of your color TV. They sometimes can affect the color on your TV.

~ U ~

Umbrella Tips... When buying an umbrella, hold it up to the light. If a lot of light comes through, rain will too!

♦ The greater the number of ribs, the stronger the umbrella. The greater the number of tacks holding the fabric to the ribs, the less likely to tear.

♦ Automatic-opening umbrellas are generally weaker, and tend to turn inside out more easily.

♦ Before you throw away your old umbrella, save the tips from the rib ends for future repairs on your new umbrella.

♦ To repair a broken rib, attach a splint of coathanger wire with a piece of masking tape.

♦ To attach a loose cover from the rib, it is best to use dental floss threaded on a large needle. It will last longer.

♦ To prevent your new umbrella from rusting, and to help it open and close easily, rub a little petroleum jelly onto the hinges.

~ V ~

Videotape Storage... It's said that you should always store your videotapes vertically, not lying down.

Venetian-Blind Surprise!... Using washable colored markers, write your surprise message on a white venetian blind that has been set in the flat, closed position. Allow to dry and restore to the open position. When the guest of honor arrives, turn the venetian blind to the closed position and reveal the message! Afterward, simply clean with soap and water.

~ W ~

Window-Screen Damage...
Here's an emergency solution if you should develop a hole or tear in your window or door screen. Simply take two pieces of plastic cling wrap and place one piece on either side of the screen over the damage. The wrap will cling together and cover any rips.

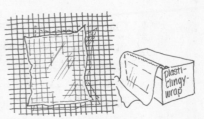

~ X ~

Xmas-Present Tips... If you're sending a Christmas parcel in the mail and want to ensure the string won't come undone, wet the string before you tie the package. As it dries, it shrinks, which gives you a tight, secure parcel.

♦ Collect odd dinner plates from yard sales, flea markets and auctions throughout the year. At Christmas, bake cookies and candies, and place them on these plates covered with cellophane and tied with a bright bow. They make appealing, inexpensive Christmas gifts.

Xmas Decorations... Save your plastic scoops from your laundry-detergent containers. Create little Christmas or Nativity scenes inside the scoop using old craft supplies that you have around the house. Paint the outside a Christmas color, drill a hole through the handle and thread a bright ribbon through the hole for hanging on the tree.

♦ Have the kids cut out circles from old Christmas cards to the size of small plastic-container lids. They can then glue the cutouts to the lids. Finally, decorate with sparkles, then cut a hole and hang it on the tree with a colorful ribbon.

♦ Old lightbulbs, spray painted and decorated with sparkles and various oddments of old necklaces and jewelry, etc., make inexpensive, colorful Christmas decorations. Experiment with different sized bulbs, from flashlight to floodlight and hang them from the tree with Christmas ribbons or string.

Xmas Leftovers... Save those leftover candy canes from Christmas. On cold winter days, the kids can use them as flavorful peppermint stir sticks for their hot chocolate. Yummy!

~ Y ~

Yellowing Blind Tapes?... A quick and effective way to spruce up the tapes that hold your white venetian-blind slats together is to simply rub them with white canvas-shoe polish!

~ Z ~

Zippers Rusting?... To prevent the zippers on your camping sleeping bags from rusting due to dampness, try coating the zippers first with a little petroleum jelly.

THE LAST WORD

The Best Hint of All... Be good to yourself! Give yourself regular vacations. Here are a few tips to help you fly away.

♦ Request the emergency-exit row or bulkhead seats for greater leg room.

♦ Arrange meal requirements at the same time you book.

♦ Check several travel agencies; some have better connections than others. Or surf the Web.

♦ Wear comfortable lace-up shoes. They can be loosened.

♦ Use a baggage tag that covers the address portion, revealing only your name.

♦ Remember, no caffeine or alcohol. Drink a glass of water every hour for dehydration.

♦ Pack valuables, medication, swimsuit and coverup in your carry-on. If your luggage is delayed, you can still start your holiday!

— ♦ —

CHAPTER 17

INFORMATION AT A GLANCE

USEFUL CHARTS ON
MEASUREMENTS,
METRIC & SUBSTITUTES!

MEASUREMENTS... IN OTHER WORDS

Metric Mathematics... If you can multiply and divide by 10, you think in metric. Changing from one multiple or submultiple of a unit to another is done by simply moving the decimal point (e.g., 100 cm = 1 m).

Thinking Metric... If you can associate specific metric measurements with a visual experience or activity (e.g., a meter is the length of a long step; normal room temperature is 21°C), it's easy! And there are only 7 base units compared to 53 in the imperial system!

AREA (SQUARE MEASURE)

1 sq. centimeter	= 100 sq. millimeters	=	0.15 sq. inches
1 sq. meter	= 100 sq. centimeters	=	10.8 sq. feet
1 sq. dekameter	= 100 sq. meters	=	120 sq. yards
1 sq. hectometer (hectare)	= 10,000 sq. meters	=	2.5 acres
10 hectares	= 1 sq. kilometer	=	0.4 sq. miles

Knowing:	Multiply by:	To obtain:
square inches	6.5	square centimeters
square feet	0.009	square meter
square yards	0.8	square meters
square miles	2.6	square kilometers
acres	0.4	hectares
square centimeters	0.16	square inches
square meters	1.2	square yards
square kilometers	0.4	square miles
hectares (10,000 m^2)	2.5	acres

LENGTHS

1 centimeter (cm)	=	10 millimeters (mm)	=	0.3937 inches
1 decimeter (dm)	=	10 centimeters	=	3.937 inches
1 meter (m)	=	10 decimeters	=	3.3 feet
1 dekameter (dk)	=	10 meters	=	11 yards
1 hectometer (hm)	=	10 dekameters	=	110 yards
1 kilometer (km)	=	10 hectometers	=	1100 yards

Quick Conversions… If you know a length and need to convert to either metric or standard, simply multiply by the number given.

Knowing:	Multiply by:	To obtain:
millimeters	0.04	inches
centimeters	0.40	inches
meters	3.30	feet
meters	1.10	yards
kilometers	0.60	miles
inches	2.50	centimeters
feet	30.00	centimeters
yards	0.90	meters
miles	1.60	kilometers

Even Quicker... We're giving you charts for at-a-glance conversions.

Inches	=	Centimeters
1 in.	=	2.5 cm
6 in.	=	15 cm
8 in.	=	20 cm
10 in.	=	25 cm
12 in. (1 ft.)	=	30 cm
14 in.	=	35 cm
36 in. (1 yd.)	=	90 cm
40 in.	=	100 cm (1 m)
4 ft.	=	1.2 m
5 ft.	=	1.5 m
6 ft.	=	1.8 m
7 ft.	=	2.0 m

TRAVELING LENGTHS

Mileage To Kilometers... When converting miles to kilometres, take the number of 10s in the mileage figure and multiple by 6. Add this number to the number of miles to arrive at total kilometers. Example: 90 miles = 9 x 6 = 54 + 90 = 144 kilometer.

Kilometers To Miles (Rough Estimate)... Divide the number of kilometres by 3 and multiply by 2. Example: 96 kilometer divided by 3 = 32 x 2 = 64 miles.

Miles	=	Kilometers
1 mil.	=	1.6 km
5	=	8
10	=	16
30	=	48
50	=	80
75	=	120
100	=	161

Determining Gas Consumption... Have your gas tank filled and make a notation of the odometer reading. On the next fill-up, divide the number of liters of gasoline it took to fill the car into the number of kilometers traveled since the last fill-up, arriving at the number of kilometers traveled per liter of gas consumption.

♦ If you are still thinking in terms of miles per gallon, use this handy reference to measure the fuel efficiency of your car.

10.65 km per liter is equivalent to 30 miles per gallon
8.88 km per liter is equivalent to 25 miles per gallon
7.11 km per liter is equivalent to 20 miles per gallon
5.33 km per liter is equivalent to 15 miles per gallon
3.55 km per liter is equivalent to 10 miles per gallon

TEMPERATURE

Knowing:	Multiply by:	To obtain:
Degrees Celsius	1.8 (then add 32)	Fahrenheit temperature.
Degrees Fahrenheit	.56 (after subtracting 32)	Celsius temperature.

0°C (32°F)…	is the freezing point of water
10°C (50°F)…	is the temperature of a warm winter day
20°C (68°F)…	is the temperature of a mild spring day and the recommended central-heating living-room temperature
30°C (86°F)…	is the temperature of a hot summer day
37°C (98°F)…	is normal body temperature
40°C (104°F)…	is heatwave hot
43°C (110°F)…	is hot bath temperature
49°C (119°F)…	is hand-hot water temperature
100°C (212°F)…	is the boiling point of water

Oven Temperature… For the range of temperatures used for cooking, the number of degrees Fahrenheit is roughly twice the number of degrees Celsius.

MEAT PROBE

Meat	Degree of Doneness	Internal Temperature
Beef	Rare	60˚C
	Medium	65˚C
	Well-done	75˚C
Veal	Well-done	80˚C
Lamb	Rare	60˚C
	Medium	70˚C
	Well-done	75˚C
Pork	Fresh	80˚C
Ham	Cured	55˚C
	Ready to serve	70˚C
Poultry		85˚C

Fresh Fish... For each 3-cm thickness, bake 10 min. at 230˚C.

Frozen Fish... For each 3-cm thickness, bake 20 min. at 230˚C.

Tip... When baking in ovenproof glassware, reduce oven temperature by 10˚C.

VOLUME

1 centiliter	=	10 milliliters
1 deciliter	=	10 centiliters
1 liter	=	10 deciliters
1 decaliter	=	10 liters
1 hectoliter	=	10 decaliters
1 kiloliter	=	10 hectoliters

Common Conversions... When converting your recipes to metric, round either upward or downward, but be consistent with all measurements.

5 milliliters (ml)	=	1 teaspoon
10 milliliters (ml)	=	1 tablespoon
50 milliliters (ml)	=	¼ cup (60 ml, to be exact)
100 milliliters (ml)	=	½ cup (120 ml, to be exact)
200 milliliters (ml)	=	¾ cup (180 ml, to be exact)
250 milliliters (ml)	=	1 cup (240 ml, to be exact)

Knowing:	Multiply by:	To obtain:
teaspoons	5	milliliters
tablespoons	15	milliliters
fluid ounces	30	milliliters
cups	0.24	liters
pints	0.56	liters
quarts	1.1	liters
gallons	4.5	liters
cubic feet	0.03	cubic meters
cubic yards	0.76	cubic meters
milliliters	0.03	fluid ounces
liters	1.75	pints
liters	0.87	quarts
liters	0.22	gallons
cubic meters	35	cubic feet
cubic meters	1.3	cubic yards

WEIGHTS

1 centigram	=	10 milligrams
1 decigram	=	10 centigrams
1 gram	=	10 decigrams
1 decagram	=	10 grams
1 hectogram	=	10 decagrams
1 kilogram	=	10 hectograms
1,000 grams	=	2.2 pounds
25 grams	=	just under 1 ounce.
100 grams	=	3.6 ounces.
400 grams	=	just under 1 pound.

Pounds to Kilograms… Divide by 2 and subtract 10%.
Example: 140 lbs. divided by 2 = 70 − 10% or 7 = 63 kg.

Knowing:	Multiply by:	To obtain:
ounces	28	grams
pounds	0.45	kilograms
short tons (2000 lbs.)	0.9	tons

Kilograms to Pounds… Multiply by 2 and add 10%.
Example: 110 kg x 2 = 220 + 10% or 11 = 231 lbs.

Knowing:	Multiply by:	To obtain:
grams	0.035	ounces
kilograms	2.2	pounds
tons (1000 kg)	1.1	short tons

SHOPPERS' GUIDE

Food	Supermarket Unit	Yield
Meats:		
Boneless ground meat	500 g	4 servings
Medium bone: roasts, chops, steaks	800 g	4 servings
Bony cuts: spareribs	1.5 kg	4–5 servings
Bacon, sliced	500 g	22–24 slices
Poultry:		
Chicken breasts & legs	1 kg	4 servings
Chicken wings	1 kg	3 servings
Turkey	4 kg	8–10 servings
Fish & Seafood:		
Fillets	500 g	3–4 servings
Steaks	500 g	3 servings
Scallops, shrimps, lobster	500 g	4 servings
Dairy Products:		
Milk	1 L	5 glasses (200 ml ea.)
Milk powder	100 g	1 L fluid milk
Cottage cheese	500 g	4 servings (125 ml ea.)
Butter or margarine	500 g	530 ml
Produce:		
Apples, peaches, pears	500 g	3–4 medium
Bananas	500 g	4 small
Onions	500 g	4–5 medium
Potatoes	500 g	4 medium
Tomatoes	500 g	3–4 medium

EMERGENCY SUBSTITUTES

For	Substitute
250 ml cake & pastry flour	220 ml all-purpose flour
15 ml cornstarch	30 ml flour
5 ml baking powder	2 ml baking soda plus 3 ml cream of tartar
250 ml milk	125 ml evaporated milk plus 125 ml water
250 ml skim milk	45 ml skim-milk powder plus 250 ml water
250 ml sour milk or buttermilk	15 ml lemon juice or vinegar plus milk
250 ml table cream (18%)	225 ml milk plus 45 ml butter
1 whole egg	2 egg yolks
1 square unsweetened chocolate	50 ml cocoa plus 15 ml fat
250 ml honey	175 ml sugar plus 50 ml liquid
1 clove garlic	0.5 ml garlic powder
1 small onion	15 ml onion flakes

CHAPTER 18

EASY-FIND INDEX

THE MOST IMPORTANT PART OF
THE BOOK! FIND THE EXACT
HINT YOU WANT INSTANTLY!

A

Acrylic Paint
stains 145
Air Filters
for car 248
Alarms, Smoke 127
Allspice
substitute for 13
Almonds
nutritional equivalent 23
Alternator
of car 251
Antiques
cleaning 102
deodorizing 102, 103
Ants
around the home 241, 242
when camping 287
Apples
baked 58, 60
green tomatoes, to ripen 43
nonbrowning 32
saltiness, to eliminate 52
stuffed with marshmallow 59
Appliances
gas
efficiency 226
large
cleaning 80–83
mechanical 232–234
noise reduction 229
small
cleaning 83–84
mechanical 218, 232–234
storage of cords 216–217
to whiten 83
Apricots
as face scrub 311
Arthritis
easy cutlery 188–189
easy-grip coins 189
light switch made easy 189
limb warmer 189

Artificial Plants/Flowers
to clean 122
Artwork
to preserve children's 170
Ashtray
in car 255
to clean 122
Asparagus
wilted 45
Astringents 312–313
Attic
insulation 226
Avocado
as beauty mask 311
Ax
extend life 230

B

Baby
bedtime stories 166
bottles 165
diaper rash 167
diapers 166
extending sleeper life 167
from crib to bed 166
liquid medicine 181
new-baby present 180
noisemaker 166
powdering 167
sleeping bag, homemade 167
spit-ups 167
teething 166
thank-you notes 167
toys 165–166
when bathing 165–166
wipes, inexpensive 166
Baby Powder
as dry shampoo 315
Baby-Sitting
at bath time 188
calming tape 168
Backaches
relief 303

Backyard Entertaining . .291–294

Bacon
cooking 48
drippings 48
leftovers . . . .*See* Leftovers
prevent curling 47
when used as substitute 48

Baking Dishes
burned food, to remove 89
ovenproof 73

Baking Powder
substitute for 13

Baking Soda
for odors 82, 90, 343
boot odors 290
frying pans, to clean 84
ovens, to clean 81, 82
sunburn relief 182
whiten appliances 83

Ball-Point Ink
stains 141

Banana Peel
to shine houseplants 266
to shine shoes 328

Bananas
as popsicles 59
baking 60
how to buy 33
too ripe 33
to ripen 33
to tenderize meat 46

Band-Aid
removal of 180

Bandsaw Blade Or Drive Belt
measurement 221

Barbecues
cleaning and care 293, 294
cooking sausages 292
hot-dog cooking 292
preparing charcoal 294
preparing hamburgers 292

Baseball
bat grip 297
glove care 297

Basement
finishing 203
insulation 226
wall condensation 203

Bath
for feet 317
for pets 236
powder 320
sachets 318
to relax 318
using herbal
tea bags 318

Bathroom
chrome, to clean 98, 99
hard-to-reach cleaning 99
mat mildew 99
mirror defogging 99
shampoo leftovers 99
shower
curtain cleaning 96
door cleaning 96
drain cleaning 97
head cleaning 96
track cleaning 96
wall cleaning 96
sink maintenance 95
soap-dish maintenance 96
tile
cleaning grout 98
to clean 98
toilet
condensation 97
paper storage 98
ring removal 97
running 214
towel rack 99
towel tidiness 99
wastebaskets 100

Bathtub
caulking replacing 214–215
grip sides 188
mold, to remove 95
porcelain repair 215
removing decals 95
stain removal 94
tile-crack repair 214–215

Batteries
smoke alarm 127
Battery
car .250
Beach Blanket
homemade 155
Beach-Toy Holder 289
Beans
cutting 36
how to buy 36
rust spot, to remove 36
storing 36
Beer
to prevent flat 292
Bees
to discourage 243
to relieve sting 182
Belts
care for 325
Beret
care of 323
Beverages 60–62
Bicycle
to identify if stolen 300
Birdbath
to attract birds 343
Birdfeeder
homemade 171
Blackheads
treatment 310, 311
Black Lacquer
to clean 102
Bleach
for furniture stains 223
for hand odor 41
remove dishwasher film 80
to whiten appliances 83
Blemishes
to treat skin . . .183, 310, 313–314
Blender
cleaning 83
mechanical problems 232
prevent "foot" marks 75

Blood
stains 109, 139, 140
Boating
duck decoys as floats 299
Bookmarks
various types 337
Books
binding, to preserve 337
care & storage 337
grease spots, to remove 338
if wet 338
page repair 337
page spots, to remove 338
Boots
care of 329–330
hiking 290, 330
how to buy rain boots 329
to dry 329
to put on easily 190
to store 126, 330
winter storing 329
Bottles
baby, to clean 165
checking contents 75
hard to open 74, 75
Brakes
for car 252
Brass
to clean 123
Bread
bread-bag crumbs, uses for . . .26
cooling 24
crumbs
for leftover potatoes 64
for oysters 51
hamburger stretcher 47
in bread bag 26
other uses for 23
to make 24
for burned rice 44
making croutons 24
oil paintings, to clean 121
rejuvenating 25
rising 24

Bread . . . .(cont'd)
  slicing 24
  stale 23, 24, 166
  storage 24
  tag substitutes 70
Breakers & Fuses 215, 216
Breath
  bad 336
  garlic 39
Broccoli
  eliminating cooking odor 37
  how to buy 36
  nutritional value 37
  storing 37
Broom
  cleaning 114, 115
  maintaining shape 115
  storage 115
  sweeping tips 114, 115
Brown Sugar . . . .*See* Sugar
Brushes
  for kid's painting 176
  to clean hairbrushes 315
  to clean paintbrushes . . .209, 210
Brussels Sprouts
  eliminating cooking odor 37
  how to buy 37
Bulletin Board
  homemade for office 306
Buns . . . . .See Rolls
Burn
  removing from carpet 112
  removing from wood 103
Burned
  food odors 125
  food on pans 85
Burrs, Removing
  pets 237
Butter
  balling 28
  extending 28
  homemade 171
  measuring when hard 22
  storage 28

  substitute for 13
  to prevent creamer drips 74
  to soften 28
Buttermilk
  substitute for 13
  to soften cheese 29
Buttonholes
  when sewing 161
Buttons
  when sewing 161

C

Cabbage
  coring 38
  eliminating cooking odors 37
  freezing 67
Cables & Cords, Electric 216–217
Cakes
  cooling 18
  cutting and slicing 16, 17
  freezing 68
  frosting 20–22, 68
  keeping moist once cut 17
  nonstick 17
  to make light 17
  to make moist 17
  using coffee 69
Camping
  ants, to discourage 287
  beach blanket 289
  beach-toy holder 289
  campfire tips 286
  change room, outdoor 289
  cooking tips 287
  cooler repair, leaky 287
  cooler, to keep cool 287
  egg-cup substitute 287
  fireproof matches 286
  flies, to discourage 287
  hiking boots 290
  kindling, wet 286
  outhouse tips 289
  panty hose, uses for 290
  pests, to discourage 290

Camping . . . .(cont'd)
sleeping-bag care 288
tar, to remove from feet 289
tent tips 288
weather forecasting 290

Candleholders
to clean 121

Candles
emergency substitute 338
make your own 339
outside use 292
splitting, to prevent 339
storage of 338

Candle Wax
on carpets 110, 111
on clothing 140
remove from holders 121
remove from wood 103
remove from woodwork 116

Cane & Wicker
care and cleaning 104, 105

Canker Sores
to relieve 181

Can Opener
as a shrimp deveiner 71
cleaning 83
mechanical problems 233
to clean 90
to open cartons 72

Cantaloupe
how to buy 33

Cardboard Cartons
to open easily 72

Cards, Playing
easy grip 189
to clean 123

Car In Winter 259–262
ice scraper 261
ignition timing 260
locks frozen 261
parking 259
starting 259
stuck in snow 260
windshield, icy 260, 261

Car Maintenance 248–255
air filters 248
alternator 251
ashtray 255
battery 250
body dents, to repair 253
brakes 252
car creeper 252
distributor 250
gas consumption 354
gas filters 249
generator 251
glass & chrome, to clean 253, 254
locks that stick 253
lubricants, other 250
motor oil 249
oil changes 249
oil filters 249
polishing car 253
radiator 248
rust, to remove 253
salt on carpets, to clean 255
spark plugs 250
stickers, to remove 254
tar, to remove 254
tires 251–252
washing 251, 252
windshield-blade replacement 254
windshield wash, homemade .254
windows, to clean 254–255

Car Parking 257–258

See Parking

Carpentry
general 218–223

Carpets
candle-wax removal 110, 111, 140
car cleaning, salt 255
cigarette burns 112
cleaning 108–11
curling 112
drying outside 111
fraying 112
gum removal 111
homemade shampoo 108
mud stains 109

nonslip 112, 113
pet stains 110, 238
raising pile 112
removing glue 111
soot removal 111
stain remover 109, 110
static 111
vomit 110
Carpet Sweepers 113
Carrots
leftover 64
planting 266
wilted 45
Car Safety
discouraging theft 258
driving alert 256, 257
keeping seat shaded 258
smoldering cigarette 255
Cast-Iron Pans 85
Caterpillars, Tent 245
Cats . . . .*See also* Pet Care
disposable litter box 239
furball treatment 238, 239
furniture clawing 238
unwanted in garden 246
Cauliflower
eliminating cooking odor 37
how to buy 38
to keep white 38
Caulking Tube
missing top 221
Ceiling Fans
to conserve home energy 224
Celery
for cooking a roast 46
substitute for 13
wilted 45
Centerpieces 273, 275
Cereal-Box Liners
recycling 73
Chains
gold, to store 332

Chainsaw
check blade sharpness 230
Chamois
softening 118
Chandeliers
to clean 124
Chapped Lips Or Hands
to relieve 182
Charcoal
barbecue 294
for odors 82
recycling 294
Cheese
drying out, to prevent 29
freezing 68
grater 75, 76
moldy 29
storing 29
to soften 29
when dried 29
Cherries
how to buy 33
Chewing Gum
removal from hair 140
to discourage flies 287
to remove from carpet 111
to remove from clothing 140
Chicken . . . .*See* Poultry
Children . . . . .*See also* Kids, Baby
back to school 179
bath toys, to organize 165
bedtime stories 166
birthday cakes 180
bitter-tasting medicine 181
bottle cleaning 165
Christmas tips 179
clothing, laundering 138
ideas & tips 177–180
infant bathing 166
invitations in balloons 180
shoes 175, 176
teething 166
wrapping paper 179, 180

Chimney
cleaning warning 121
safety & efficiency 226
to clean 120

China
care of 88
cracks 88
scratches 88
stains 87
to buy 88
to store 88

Chintz
ironing 151

Chisel
storage 197

Chocolate
fondue 59
frosting, substitute for 14
instant mousse 59
melting 59
stains 109, 144
substitute for 13

Christmas
decorations homemade 348
ideas with children 179
leftovers 348
lights 217
present, homemade 347
present, mailing 347
present, protection 179

Chrome
to clean 98, 99, 124
to clean on car 253, 254

Cigarette
burns on carpet 112
burns on wood 103
reduce smoking 183

Clams . . . .*See* Shellfish

Cleaning
antiques 102, 103
artificial plants/flowers 122
ashtrays 122
baby bottles 165
bathroom 94–96

black lacquer 102
brass 123
candle wax 121
cane & wicker 104, 105
carpets 108–111
cars 253–255
chimney 120
chrome 124
compact discs 121
copper 85, 86
crystal chandeliers 124
dishcloth 78, 93
drapes 118, 119
fireplaces 119
furniture 100–102
gray film on furniture 102
glass, broken 93
gilt frames 121
iron 149
piano keys 123
oil paintings 121, 122
playing cards 123
porcelain 95, 124
radiators 123
silk lamp shades 122
silver 87, 333
stains 138–145
sticky marks on furniture 101
vases 122
washing machine 132
windows 117
woodstoves 120

Closet Organizer 323

Closets
avoiding damp odors 125

Clothes
care for 322–326
colorfast 131, 136
ironing 149–152
jeans too stiff 342
scorched while ironing 151
stains 138–145
washing 131
wrinkles from dryer 148

Clothes Washer, Dryer
mechanical problems . . .231–233

Clothespin
covers 147
other uses 76
Coats
drying outside 147
in winter 324
repairing raincoats 324
Cockroaches 242
Cocktail Dictionary 62
Coconut
shredded topping 60
Coffee
beans for garlic breath 39
browning gravy 54
storing 61
freezing 69
iced, sweetening 60
leftovers 60
stains 91, 109, 142
too bitter 60
when planting 266
Coffee Filter
substitute for 70-71
Coffee Grinder
cleaning 344
Coffeemaker
mechanical problems 233
to clean 84
Coins
easy grip 189
Colorfast
clothing 131, 136
Collars
ironing 151
removing rings 135, 136
Combs
to clean 315
Compact Discs
to clean 121
Companion Planting 280–281
Composter
homemade 265
Composting Tips 265

Computer
in home 306
Concrete
stains 230
wall cracks 200
Condensation
toilet 97
walls, basement 203
windows 204
Containers
kitchen 92
leaking 93
plastic, stained 89
odors 89, 102, 103
Cookies
cookie-cutter substitute 18
optimizing ingredients 18
storage 19
to prevent dough sticking 18
with chocolate chips 18
with raisins 18
Cooking
as a senior 192
ideal temperatures 77
odors 37, 125
outdoors 291–294
timer 192
while camping 287
Cooking oil
to remove paint 211
Coolers
to keep cool 287
to repair 287
Copper
finish protector 341
to clean 85, 86
Cords & Cables
electrical 216–218
to prevent pets chewing 238
Cork
as a pot handle 73
as a recipe holder 76
to clean cutlery 86

Corkscrew
substitute for 71

Corn
buttering 38
cooking 38
removing corn hairs 38
shucking 38

Cornmeal
to clean carpets 108

Cornstarch
substitute for 14

Corn Syrup
substitute for 14

Costume Jewelry
to clean 333, 334
to preserve 334

Cottage
outhouse toilet paper 289

Cottage Cheese
storage 29

Countertops
cleaning 91
stains, to prevent 75
stains, to remove 91

Couponing
best ways 73

Crackers
keeping crisp 26
restoring freshness 26
storing 26

Crawling Bugs 242

Crayons
on floors 114
on walls & wallpaper 116
stains 140
to conceal wood cracks 104

Cream
no-drip creamer 74
stationary whipping 75
whipping 28

Cream, Sour
substitute for 14

Cream, Whipped
substitute for 14

Cribs
for infant 166

Crochet
ball holder 191

Croutons
homemade 24

Crystal . . . . . *See also* Glassware

Cucumbers
ants, to repel 241
as an astringent 312
freezing 67
how to buy 39
in a sandwich 39
in the garden 266
oil paintings, to clean 122
puffy eyes, to relieve 313
to decorate 39
wax film, to remove 39

Curling
broom restoration 298

Curry Stains 144

Curtains . . . . *See also* Drapes
care of 118, 119
net, to repair 160
shower, other uses for 236
shower, to clean 96

Cushions
if sliding 107
restuffing 339
when worn 106

Cut Flowers
care of 273, 274

Cutlery
easy grip 188
to clean 86, 87
rust removal 345
silver, to clean 87

Cuts
minor, to treat 181

Cutting Board
cleaning wooden 90

Cutworms 266
Cycling 300

D

Darning
socks & gloves 162
Decals
removing from bathtub 95
Decanter
if stopper is stuck 345
Defrosting, Freezer 82
De-Icing
windshield in winter 260–261
winter car locks 261
Dental Floss
cleaning uses 90
other uses 17, 161, 332, 346
Dents
body of car 253
Desserts
recipes & advice 60
Diaper Rash 167
Diapers 166
Dishcloth, To Clean 78, 93
Dishwasher
cleaning film buildup 80
cleaning stains 81
efficiency 225
mechanical problems 233
odors 343
Distributor
for car 250
Dogs . . . .*See also* Pet Care
fleas 237
messy dog dish 239
reflective night collar 238
Doors
cupboard-door magnets 205
hinges & knobs, to tighten . .204
locks 204
recycling 205
rusty bolts 204

Doorstop
homemade 336
Downspouts 230
Drainpipe, Leaking 213
Drains 91, 97
Drapes . . . .*See also* Curtains
hooks & weights 119
prepare for cleaning 118, 119
repairing net 160
Drawers
sticky 222
loose 221
Dresses
drying outside 147
Drilling
wood or metal 220
Driving
car 256–257
in winter 259–262
on hills & mountains 256
speed 256
temporary gas-leak repair 257
with a trailer 257
Dryer
care of 147
for a few items 149
lint-free drying 147
mechanical problems 233
no-iron jean drying 148
reducing drying time 149
static-free drying 148
to fluff pillows 148
to run efficiently 226
unwrinkling clothes 148
Drying Outside
clothes 147
clothesline 146
clothespin covers 147
coats 147
delicates 147
dresses 147
rugs .111
sweaters 146
trousers 146

Dusting
plants 266, 267
ways to 107–8

Dustpan
as a vegetable scoop 72
for fence painting 208

E

Earaches
temporary relief 181

Earring Back
to replace 304

Earwigs 242

Easter
leftover chocolate 59

Eaves troughs
cleaning 282

Eggs
boiling 30, 72
brown 32
cleaning 94
freezing 68
frying 29
how to beat 31
how to buy 32
poaching 30
removing egg shells 30
scrambled-egg extender 14
separating 31, 32
slicing hard-boiled 30
stains on cutlery 86
storing 30, 31
substitute egg cup 287
substitute for 14
testing freshness 32
uses for shells 90, 268
whites
as face mask 311
beating 31
book page, to repair 337
for cut potatoes 43
freezing 68
storing 31

sunburn relief 182
whipping 31
yolks
as face mask 311
for your dog's coat 237
freezing 68
storing 31
to keep centered 30

Electric Cable
cutting & stapling 217

Electric Frying Pan 84

Electrical Cords
pet chewing, to prevent 238
safety 127
storage 216–217

Electrical, General 215–218
appliances
large 232–234
small 218, 232–234
cords, cables 216, 217
fuses, circuit breakers . . .215–216
lighting 217, 218

Embroidery
ironing 152

Energy Conservation
home 224–227

Entertaining Outdoors
buffet 291
condiment container 291
homemade drink holder 293
toothpick holder 291
using candles 292

Epsom Salts
for noncolorfast items 136

Evaporated Milk
to extend butter 28

Exercise
when house cleaning 80

Extension Cords
correct usage 216
storage 216, 217

Eyeglasses
emergency screw 304
to prevent misting 340

Eyes
relieving puffiness 313

F

Fabric
buying & storing 160
Facials, Scrubs, Masks . . .310–312
Fan, Portable
mechanical problems 234
Faucets
leaking 213–214
Feet
bathing 317
swollen 187
Felt Hats
cleaning 322, 323
Fences
painting 208
Fertilizer
homemade for garden 264
File, Metal
prevent clogging 196
Filters
air .248
gas .249
oil 248, 249
Fingernails
polishing & filing 321
to avoid dirt 339
Fireplace
homemade logs 340
safety & efficiency 226
summer accents 340
to clean 119
Fire Prevention 126
Fire Safety 127
Fish
baking 50
how to buy 50, 51
odor on hands 50
preparation 50

thawing 50
Fish, Fresh
how to cook 356
Fish, Frozen
how to cook 356
Fishing
finding worms 299
makeshift scaler 299
makeshift stringer 299
reeling without tangling 299
types of lures 298
Flatware . . . .*See* Cutlery
Flavors
substitutes for 14
Fleas
prevention 237
Flea Powder
to apply 237
Flies
fruit flies 243
to discourage 243
when camping 287
Floors
eliminate squeaking 203
linoleum cleaning 114
linoleum heel marks 114
linoleum repair 203
linoleum scuff marks 114
prevent scratching 113
registers & vents 115
remove crayon 114
remove wax buildup 114
removing scratches 113
repairing edges 203
rocking-chair marks 113
Flour
browning for gravies 53
saltshaker dispenser 72
substitutes for 15
Flowers, Cut
care of 273, 274
centerpieces 273, 275
drying 275
lengthening the stems 274

Flowers, Cut . . . .(cont'd)
quick-opening method 275
wilted 274
Fluorescent
efficiency 225
lighting 217
Flying Bugs 243
Fondue
chocolate 59
Food Coloring
substitute for 15
Food Mixers
mechanical problems 232
Food-Wrap Dispenser
use made easy 76
Footbath 317
Foot Massage
homemade 303
Footwear 326–330
Fragrance Storage 330
Freezer
defrosting 82
efficiency 64
moving 65
power loss 65
Freezing
cabbage 67
cake frosting 68
cakes 68
cheese 68
coffee 69
container types 65
cooked meats 66
dating packages 65, 66
egg whites & yolks 68
extra portions 70
fried or breaded food 67
fruit 66, 67
hamburgers 66
hard-boiled eggs 68
homemade dinners 70
ice cubes 69
leftover vegetables 67
raw meat 66

raw vegetables 67
soups, stews & sauces 66, 69
spices 69, 70
to avoid spoilage 66
tomatoes 67
tomato paste 67
waffles or french toast 68
Fridge . . . .*See* Refrigerator
Front-Door Storage 126
Frosting . . . .*See* Icing
Fruit
buying 33–35
flies 243
in salad 32
prevent bruising 74
stains 35, 145
stains on hands 35
stuffed with marshmallow 59
tips for peeling 35
to freeze 66, 67
Frying Pan
cast-iron, to clean 85
electric, to clean 84
Funnel
substitute for in kitchen 71
to separate eggs 32
Fur Coats
care of 324
Furniture
black lacquer 102
burn marks 103
candle wax, to remove 103
cane & wicker 104, 105
cat clawing, to prevent 238
cleaning 100, 101
dusting 107, 108
gray film, to remove 102
heat-mark treatment 103
leather 105, 106
nursery ideas 175
odors 102, 103
painting 222
plastic 105
polish, homemade 100
polishing 100, 101

Furniture . . . .(cont'd)
  polish remover 100
  protecting 109
  refinishing 222, 223
  repairing
    cracks 104
    drawers, sticking 222
    gouges 222
    loose joints 221
    loose knobs 222
    scratches 103, 222
    warps 104, 222
    wobbly drawers 221
  spot or stain repair 223
  staining 223
  sticky marks, to remove 101
  to make level 342
  to move 343
  upholstery care 106, 107
  water rings, to remove 101
  white spots, to remove 101
Fuses & Breakers 215–216

G

Games
  for kids indoors 172
  for kids outdoors 172–173
  storing, for kids 174, 175
Garage
  cleanup 230, 231
  door insulation 224
  parking 257
Garbage Disposer
  odors 84
  to clean 84
Garbage Raiders 245
Gardening 191, 281–284
  companion planting 280–281
  composting 265
  eaves troughs, to clean 282
  fertilizer
    homemade 264
    using sawdust 264
    using soot 264
  for seniors 191
  hose care 270–271
  lawn aerating 265
  leaves, bagging 283
  location of 276
  mulch, with newspaper 264
  pest control241–245, 265, 280–281
  pine needles 282
  planning 276, 277
  planting 278–280
  plants, to protect 283, 284
  plant support, homemade 284
  preparing to plant 277
  seeding, indoors 277
  seedlings transplanted 279
  seeds
    identifying bad 278
    protecting 280
    sowing 278
  tool storage 191, 281
  trellis, homemade 284
  vegetables 276–281
  watering 267–270
  weeds, to discourage 284
  wheelbarrow steadiness 284
  worms 265, 266, 299
Garlic
  for fleas 237
  garden bugs, to eliminate . . .265
  odor, to eliminate on hands . . .39
  odor, to eliminate on breath . . .39
Gas Filters
  for car 249
Gelatin
  softening 59
Generator
  of car 251
Gilt Frame
  to clean 121
  preserver 121
Glass
  broken, to pick up 93
  surface scratches 229
Glassware
  baking dishes, cleaning 89

Glassware . . . .(cont'd)
  crystal cleaning 89
  preventing cracks 89
  stuck glasses 89

Gloves, Rubber
  to remove 344

Glue
  missing top 221
  removal 111

Gold Chains
  repairing 332
  storing 332
  when swimming 298

Golf Bag
  as a garden tote 191, 281

Golfing
  club care 300
  glove storage & care 300
  storing balls 301

Grapefruit
  how to buy 33

Grass Stains 144

Grater
  easy to use 75, 76
  to clean 90

Gravy
  browning 54, 69
  browning flour 53
  smooth 53
  too burned 54
  too greasy 54
  too thick 54
  too thin 54
  using coffee to brown 69

Grease
  canvas shoes, to remove 326
  food, too greasy 52, 54
  on books, to remove spots . . .338
  sink 91
  splatter guard 71
  stain on leather 106
  stains 132, 140
  stains on upholstery 106
  wallpaper 200

Grocery List 74

Gum
  automotive leaks, to prevent . .257
  carpets, to remove from 111
  clothing, to remove from 140
  flies, to discourage 287
  hair, to remove from 140
  worms, to discourage 243

Gumdrops
  cake icing decoration 21

Guttering 282

H

Hair
  care for 314–317
  cleaning brushes, combs 315
  conditioner, homemade 316
  dandruff treatment 317
  dry shampoo 315
  hairband, homemade 315
  highlighting 315
  hot oil treatment 316
  if too oily 317
  mayonnaise, to use 316
  protein treatment 316
  setting lotions 315
  shampoo 314–315
  style, to maintain 316
  upholstery, to remove from . .106

Hair Spray
  to preserve kids' artwork 170

Ham
  baking 47
  how to buy 47
  leftovers . . . . *See* Leftovers

Hamburger
  fast cooking 47
  freezing . . . . *See* Freezing
  stretcher 47
  when barbecueing 292

Hammering
  into wood 219
  using spatula protector 196

Handbag
recycling 161
Handles & Knobs
painting 207, 211
Hands
chapped 182
dry .313
Handsaw 219
Hatchet
extend life 230
Hats
berets, to clean 323
felt, to clean 322
keeping cool 188
straw, to renew shine 323
windy, wearing 323
Heat Marks
on furniture 103
Hemming
adjustable 161
in an emergency 304
Herbs
storing 56
Hinges
if squeaking 204
Hockey
puck carrier 297
skate care 297
stick gliding 297
stick grip replacement 298
Hollandaise Sauce 53
Home Energy Conservation
ceiling fans, using 224
control switch 225
hot water heater 224
temperature, to set correct . . .224
thermostat 224
Home Office
and children 305–306
bulletin board 306
business-card holder 308
computer location 306
environment 305

file archives 306
location 305
setting up 305–308
stamp dispenser 307
supplies & equipment 307
Home Remedies 180–183
Home Safety 126–129
Honey
if cloudy 23
measuring 22
substitute for 15
Honeydew
how to buy 33
Hornets 243
Hosiery . . . . . . *See also* Panty Hose
extending life 325
laundering 134
rug hooking 344
storing 325
Hot Dogs
barbecue 292
Hot Water Heater
conserving energy 224
Household
insurance inventory 128
planning cleaning 80
House Painting 209
Houseplants
bugs, removing common 267
care of 266–267
fertilizer, homemade 264
growth booster 267
mending broken limbs 267
overwatering 270
splints 267
tea for plants 268
underwatered 270
watering 267, 268
watering when away 268–269
Humidifier
odor .125

I

Ice Cream
storage of 341
Ice Cubes
clear 69
dressed up 69
giant size 69
sticking 69
to remove fat 52
Ice Pack
in an emergency 183
Ice Trays
substitutes for 15
Icing
cinnamon topping 21
decorating 21
freezing 68
fudge 21
icing sugar, topping 21
keeping plate clean 21
to prevent slipping 22
too sweet 21
using mint patties 20
Ink
stains 141
Insulating
around the house 226
Insurance
household inventory 128
Iron
care of 149
cleaning 149, 150
Ironing 149–152
chintz 151
collars 151
efficiently 150
embroidery 152
in an emergency 151
preparing for later 151
ribbons 152
scorched 151
shoulder pads 151
tucks 152

when sewing 154
while traveling 152
wool blends 151

J

Jars
checking contents 75
hard to open 74, 75
Jeans
drying 148
too stiff 342
Jelly Molds
unsticking 59
Jewelry
beads, to restring 332
chains, to store 332
cleaner, homemade 333
costume, to clean 333, 334
costume, to preserve 334
diamonds, to clean 333
earring-back substitute 304
gold chains, to repair 332
organizing 332
pearls, to clean 334
ring, to remove 334
ring marks, to prevent 334
silver, to clean 87, 333
storage in kitchen 93
when swimming 298

K

Ketchup
stains 109, 144
substitute for 15
to clean copper 86
won't pour 57
Kettle
to clean 83, 218
whistling 192
Key Ring 342
Keys
easy identification 128, 129

Kids . . . . *See also* Children
  ideas and tips 164–180
Kids' Cooking
  homemade butter 171
  pancake fun 171
  porridge 171
Kids' Crafts
  birdfeeder, homemade 171
  ease, homemade 170
  finger-paint recipe 169
  paint cleanup 170
  paint organizer 169
  paint-roller, homemade 169
  paint tray 170
  paste, homemade 168
  play–dough, homemade 168
  preserving artwork 170
Kids' Games
  indoors & outdoors 172–173
  organizing games 174, 175
Kids' Rooms
  clothes, hanging 175
  nursery 175
Kids' Safety
  door opening 177
  identifying danger 177
  in the swimming pool 176
  paintbrushes 176
  phone number 176
  sliding doors 177
Kids' Shoes
  polishing 176
  slippery 175
  undoing shoelace knots 176
Kids' Toys
  sand shovel & pail 171
  storage 175
  to clean stuffed 174
Kindling
  how to make a fire 286
  if wet 286
  using fruit 340
Kitchen
  boiling alarm 74

cleaning
  countertop, cleaning 91, 92
  deodorizers 93
  dishcloth 78, 93
  dropped egg 94
  straw placemats 94
counter space, additional 294
storage
  closet 92
  cupboard tops 92
  leaky containers 93
  spices 92
  steel wool 93
Kitchen Sink
  faucet drip 213, 214
  maintenance 90, 91
  unplugging 91
Kitchenware
  can openers 90
  grater, cleaning 90
  pizza cutters 90
  plastic containers 89
  thermos, cleaning 90
  wooden cutting board 90
Kittens
  care of 237
Kiwi Fruit
  how to buy 34
  tenderize meat 46
Knees
  protect when planting . . .283–284
Knitting
  general 163
  keeping count 163
  needle storage 163
  tangle free 162, 163
Knives
  to sharpen 342
Knobs & Handles
  loose 222
  painting 207

L

Labels
    clothing 131
    parcels 342
    wood, to remove 101, 103
Lace
    starching 138
    yellowed 137
Ladder
    catchall 198
    use & safety 229
    when using 200, 229, 230
Lamps
    inserting new wires 218
Lamp Shades
    to clean silk 122
Lard
    measuring when hard 22
Latex Paint
    stains, to remove 145
Laundromat
    laundry organizing 131, 132
Laundry 131–152
    brightener 136
    children's clothes 138
    collar rings 135, 136
    delicates 137
    dissolving soap 132
    doilies 138
    drying 146–149
    general washing 131
    hard-to-clean items 136
    hard-water treatment 133
    homemade scoop 133
    hosiery 134
    jeans, softening 342
    lace, yellowed 137
    lintless 137
    noncolorfast items 136
    pillows, starching 138
    prewashing 132
    reduce suds 132
    setting colors 136
    silks 133
    socks 134
    sorting 131
    sweaters, reshaping 135
    whitening 135
    woolens 134, 135
Lawns
    aerating 265
    watering 270
Leather
    furniture 105–106
    grease stains, to remove 106
    handbags as patches 161
    mildew, to remove 142
    patent, to clean 327
    preservative 106
    shoes, to clean 326
    softener 106
    to clean 105, 106
Leaves
    bagging 283
Leftovers
    at Christmas 348
    bacon 63
    bread crumbs 23
    chocolate 59
    coffee 60, 69
    freezing . . . . *See* Freezing
    ham .63
    liqueur 61
    meat loaf 63
    pasta 56, 63
    pork .63
    potatoes 64
    rice .63
    salad 64
    shampoo 99
    tomato paste 67
    tuna salad 63
    turkey & chicken 62
    vegetables 64
Lemons
    extracting juice 34
    peels as kindling 340
    substitute for 15
    uses for rind 35

Letter Opener
  using a toothbrush 307
Lettuce
  freezing 67
  to eliminate grease 52
  when baking fish 50
  wilted 45
Lightbulb
  efficiency 225
  replacement 217, 218
Lights
  Christmas 217
  fluorescent 217
Light Switch
  for energy conserving 225
  made easy 189
  three-way 225
Lingerie, Drying 147
Linoleum
  removing heel marks 114
  removing scuff marks 114
  repairing 203
  to clean 114
Lint
  in laundry, to remove 137
Lips
  chapped 182
Lipstick
  getting the most of 322
  stains 141
  to make 321
  to store 322
Liqueur
  leftovers 61
Lobster . . . .*See* Shellfish
Locks
  for doors 204
  for your windows 204
  if frozen car door 261
  lubricants for car 253
Lubricants
  for car 250
  for car locks 253

  winter car locks 261
Luggage
  cleaning vinyl 331
  fresh smelling 187
  to identify 186
Lumber
  purchasing 219
  storing 231
Lunch Box
  containers 57

M

Magnifying Glass
  emergency 186
Mailing
  labeling parcels 342
Major Appliances
  cleaning/deodorizing 80–83
  noise reduction 229
Makeup
  stains 139
  storing 321, 322
  to remove 139, 314
Mallet
  in an emergency 196
Marble
  removing stains 123
Margarine
  to prevent creamer drips 74
Marshmallows
  as fruit stuffing 59
  miniaturizing 60
Masks, Scrubs, Facials 310–312
Matches
  making waterproof 286
  substitute 340
  to prevent flat beer 292
Mayonnaise
  conditioner 316
  substitute for 15
  to brown chicken 49

Mealworms 243

Measuring
hard ingredients 22
round items 221
sticky liquids 22

Measuring Spoons
making legible 75

Meat Grinder
to clean 84

Meatballs
to make moist 47

Meat Loaf
leftover . . . . *See* Leftovers

Meats
cooking temperatures 356
freezing, general . . .*See* Freezing
freezing, raw 66
general cooking tips 46
hamburgers, barbecued 292
hot dogs, barbecued 292
how to buy 48
roasts
carving 46
cooking tips 46
tenderizing 46
sausages, barbecued 292
tenderizing 46

Medication
administering to pets 238
easy pill swallow 181
for seniors & kids 185
medical inventory 186
opening pill bottles 185

Mending . . . .*See* Sewing

Metric
area conversions 351–352
common conversions 357
fuel conversions 354
gas conversions 354
general conversions 351
length conversions 352
meat temperatures 355–356
quick conversions 352–353
temperature conversions 355

traveling lengths 353–354
volume conversion 356
weight conversions 358

Mice 245

Microwave
cleaning 82
cooking tips 77, 78
deodorizing 82

Mildew
stains 95, 142

Milk
scorched 28
storing 27
substitute for 15
to repair fine-china cracks 88
to restore freshness 27
to sour 27
to thaw frozen fish 50

Mirrors
as a kitchen window 77
defogging 99
hiding worn spots 229
removing scratches 229
repairing worn edges 228
safety 129

Mixer
mechanical problems 232
splatters, to prevent 83

Moisturizers
for hair 316
for skin 313

Mold
bathtub 95
cheese 29
clothes 95, 142
leather 142

Moles
to discourage 282

Mops
shaking 123

Mosquitoes
bites, to relieve 182, 183
to deter 244

Moths 244

Motors, Small
  ventilation 218
Mouthwash
  to make 319
Mud Stains
  on carpet 109
  on clothing 140
Muffins
  reviving stale muffins 19
Mushrooms
  cleaning 39
  slicing 40
  storing 40
  substitutes for 16
Mussels . . . .*See* Shellfish
Mustard Stains 143

N

Nail Polish
  bottles, to open easily 321
  chipping, to prevent 321
  for net-curtain repair 160
  long lasting 321
  measuring spoons, legible 75
  quick dry 321
  remover, emergency 321
  thickening, to prevent 320
Nails
  filing & polishing 321
  removing 196, 220
  to avoid dirt 339
Neck Support
  when sleeping 186
Needle & Thread
  portable 159
Needles
  easy threading 157, 158
  keeping sharp 158
  knitting 163
  storing 158
Noise Reduction
  on major appliances 229

Nursery, For Baby 175
Nuts
  chopping easily 23
  shelling Brazil nuts 23
Nylons . . . .*See* Panty Hose
  to launder 134
  to make beach pillow 155

O

Oatmeal
  as facial scrub & mask 310
Odors
  baby spit-ups 167
  bleach on hands 41
  burned food 125
  car 255
  closet dampness 125
  cooking 37, 125
  cut flowers 274
  deodorizer, homemade 125
  dishwasher 343
  garbage disposer 84
  garlic on hands 39
  hiking boots 290
  humidifier 125
  kitchen 93
  musty 102, 103
  onion on hands 40
  painting 209
  pet urine 238
  plastic kitchenware 89
  refrigerator 82
  skunk 236
  sleeping bags 288
  small areas 125
  smoke 124
  vacuum cleaner 125
Office, Home
  setting up 305–308
Office Tips 303–304
Oil
  cooking, substitute 16
  filters, car 249

Oil . . . .(cont'd)
  motor, car 249
  paint removal 211
  spills, garage 230
  stains, pavement 231
Oil Paint
  stains 144
Oil Paintings
  to clean 121
Onion Bag
  uses for
    beach-toy holder 289
    cleaning mushrooms 39
    stuffing chicken 48
Onions
  odors, eliminate on hands . .40, 41
  peeling without tears 40
  planting 266
  storing 40
  to remove scorch stain 143
Oranges
  how to buy 34
  juice, maximizing amount 34
  mosquitoes, to discourage . . .244
  peels as kindling 340
  uses for rind 35
Outdoor Entertaining . . .291–294
Oven Cleaning 81–82
Oysters . . . .*See* Shellfish
  as fertilizer 264

P

Paint
  cleanup, for kids' crafts 170
  roller, for kids' crafts 169
  roller, to clean 210
  safety, for kids' crafts 176
  stains 144, 145, 211
  tray, for kids' crafts 169, 170
Painting 205–211
  brush storage 210
  cleanup
    brushes 209

  paint cans 211
  rollers 210
  you 211
  drips, to prevent 206
  fences 208
  furniture 222
  hardware, to prevent paint . . .211
  holes & cracks, filling 206
  houses 209
  knobs & handles 207
  lumpy paint 205
  masking-tape substitutes 208
  messy cans, reducing 206
  odor 209
  quick color check 205
  radiators 207
  rollers & paintbrushes 206
  small & awkward jobs . .206, 207
  stains, to remove . . .144, 145, 211
  steps 208
  thinner, to reuse 205, 210
  white paint 205
  windows 207, 208
Pancakes
  for kids 171
Paneling
  stains 202
  storing 231
  switch box, to add 202
  walls 202
Pans . . . .*See* Pots & Pans
Pants . . . .*See* Trousers
Pant Hanger
  for drying rugs 111
  for recipe books 76
Panty Hose . . . . . .*See also* Hosiery
  broom maintenance 115
  drying outside 147
  extending life 325
  headband 315
  repair runs 325
  storing 325
  storing onions 40
  to launder 134
  uses when camping 290
  wood smoothness, to check . .220

Parking
cooling engine 257
in garage 257
in parking lot 257
shading seat 258
Pasta
boiling 55
boiling with an egg 72
enhancing color 55
how to buy 54
leftovers . . . .*See* Leftovers
preparing sauce 53, 63
spaghetti
    cooking 55
    long match 340
sticky 55
storing 56
storing fresh 56
toothpick substitute 55
to prevent pie spillovers 20
Pastry . . . .*See also* Pies
Patio
unwanted growth,
    discourage 284
Peaches
how to buy 35
to ripen 35
Peanut Butter
for burned gravy 54
Pearls
to clean 334
Pears
stuffed with marshmallow 59
Peas
cooking 41
storing 41
Pen
ink stains 141
purse holder 191
Pencil Sharpener
substitute for 71
Pepper
to repel ants 241

Peppers
green, when baking 41
how to buy 41
Perfume
to preserve 321
when applying 321
Personal
home beauty 310–322
home body treatment 312
makeup remover 314
Perspiration
stains 142
Pests 240–246
ants 241, 242
bees 243
cats, unwanted 246
cockroaches 242
companion planting 280–281
crawling bugs 242
earwigs 242
flies 243
flies, fruit 243
flying bugs 243
garbage raiders 245
hornets 243
mealworms 243
mice 245
moles 282
mosquitoes 244
moths 244
pigeons 245
slugs 244
snails 244
spiders 244
squirrels 245
tent caterpillars 245
wasps 243
while camping 290
while gardening 281
Pet Care 235–239
bath tips 236
burrs, to remove 237
electrical-cord chewing 238
flea prevention 237
fur balls, to reduce 238–239
furniture clawing 238
hair from upholstery 106

Pet Care . . . .(cont'd)
   kittens & puppies 237
   litter box 239
   medicine, to administer 238
   messy food area 239
   safety 238
   shampoo, dry 236
   shampoo, odorless 236
   shiny coat 237
   skunk odor 236
   stains 110
   urine, to clean 110, 238
   vomit 110

Photo Album
   as a telephone book 186
   as recipe holder 77

Photographs
   black & white 343
   storage 344
   to frame 344
   to mail 344

Piano Keys
   ivory, to clean 123
   plastic, to clean 123

Pickles
   preparation 58

Pickpocket
   to prevent 187

Picnicking . . . . *See* Camping

Pictures
   when hanging 229

Pies
   crusts
     burned 20
     flaky 20
     soggy 19
   fast & easy fillings 20
   freezing 68
   fruit-pie spillovers 20
   how to cut for 5 people 19
   making pastry 19
   meringues, to cut 20

Pigeons 245

Pillows
   fluffed 148

Pimples
   to relieve 183, 311, 313, 314

Pineapples
   grow your own 272
   how to buy 35
   to tenderize meat 46

Pinecones
   as kindling 286

Pine Needles 282

Ping-Pong Ball
   repair 296

Pins
   easy pickup 159
   storage 158, 159

Pipes
   cutting 213
   frozen 212
   insulation 226
   leaking 212, 213
   soldering 213

Plants 263–281
   artificial, to clean 122
   bugs 265–267, 280, 281
   containers 272, 273
   leaves, polish & clean . .266–267
   potting 271–273
   protecting 283
   root-ball, to remove 272
   transplanting 271
   watering
     indoor & outdoor 267–271

Plastic Furniture
   care & cleaning 105

Playing Cards
   easy grip 189
   to rejuvenate 123

Plumbing 212–215
   faucet, leaking 213, 214
   pipes
     frozen 212
     leaking 212, 213
     to cut 213
     to solder 213
   sink, plugged 91

Plumbing . . . .(cont'd)
  toilet, running 214
  washer replacement 214
Plywood
  cutting 219
  storing 231
Poison Ivy
  to relieve 183
Polish
  for nails . . . . . . *See* Nail Polish
  homemade furniture 100
  homemade remover 100
Polishing
  car .253
  shoes 175, 176, 341
  wood 100, 101
  woodstoves 120
Pool
  jewelry 298
  skimmer 298
Porcelain
  cleaning items 95, 124
  sink cleaning 95
  sink repair 215
Pork
  leftovers 63
Porridge
  for kids 171
Postcards
  homemade 341
Potato Chips
  keeping crisp 26
Potatoes
  baking 42, 64
  homes fries 42
  how to buy 43
  keeping warm 42
  leftovers . . . . *See* Leftovers
  mashed 42, 64
  nutritional value 41
  peeling 41
  slicing 42
  sweet 43
  to clean grinders 84

  to clean oil paintings 122
  to clean rusty pans 86
  to clean silverware 87
  to eliminate saltiness 52
  to revive vegetables 45
  unfried french fries 43
  when planting 266
Pot-Handle Replacement 73
Pots & Pans
  baking dish, to remove rust . . .86
  boil-dry alarm 74
  cleaning
    cast-iron 85
    copper bottom 85–86
    enamel pans 84
    nonstick 85
    scorched 85
    to remove burned food 85
  double-duty cooking 75, 287
  ill-fitting lids 77
Plant Holder 272
Poultry 48–50
  chicken
    crumb coating 49
    defrosting 49
    how to buy 48
    leftovers . . . . *See* Leftovers
    roasting 49
    stuffing 48
    substitutes for 13
  turkey
    basting 50
    defrosting 49
    how to buy 49
    leftovers . . . . *See* Leftovers
    roasting 49
    stuffing 48, 49
Power Saw 219
Pretzels
  keeping crisp 26
Puddings
  chocolate mousse 59
  creamy 59
Pumpkin
  how to buy 43

Purse
leather, to clean 105
penholder 191
safety 190
vinyl, to clean 331

R

Raccoons 245
Radiators
car .248
household
efficiency, to improve 227
painting 207
to clean 123
Radishes
freezing 67
planting 266
wilted 45
Raincoats
care of 324
Raisins
for flat sparkling wine 61
to make plump 18
Razors, Disposable
to extend life 319
Recipe Books
keeping open 76
Recipe Box
for laundry labels 131
Recipe-Card Tips 76, 77
Red Wine . . . .*See* Wine
Refinishing, Furniture . . .222–223
Refrigerator
odors 82
to check seal 227
to repair 233
Registers & Vents
to keep clear 115
Remedies 180–183
Ribbons
ironing 152

Rice
burned 44
keep salt dry 57
leftover . . . .*See* Leftovers
prevent sticking 44
tastier 44
Rings
care of 334
collar, to remove 135, 136
jewelry, to remove 334
Rolls
if burned 26
restoring freshness 25
to warm 25
Roof
working safety 230
Rope
to prevent fraying 198
Roses
to last longer 275
Rubber
band as clamp 199
easy cutting 199
gloves
for moisturizing hands 313
to open bottles and jars 74
to remove 344
Rugs . . . .*See* Carpet
Rust
prevention
barbecue 293
car 253, 262
door bolts 204
shower rods 96
stains 91, 109
steel wool 92, 93
tools 195–196
umbrella 346
woodstove 120
zipper 349
removal
baking dish 86
cutlery 345
stains, on clothing 142
tools 195

S

Safety
bathtub 188
burglars, to discourage . .128, 192
car .258
electrical cords 127
emergency light 127
fire prevention 126
for children 176, 177
household inventory 128
smoke alarm 127
telephone 128

Salads
leftovers . . . .*See* Leftovers

Salt
prevent clogging 57
substitute for 16
testing saltiness 57
too salty 52

Saltshaker
for spices 72
other uses for 72
to prevent clogging 57

Sand
for oil spills 230

Sandpaper
organizing 221
renewing 220
to sharpen needles 158
to sharpen scissors 158

Sauces
freezing . . . .*See* Freezing
hollandaise 53
if too thin 53
pasta 53
spaghetti 63
storage life 53
tomato 53

Sausage
on the barbecue 292
reduce shrinking 47

Sawdust
as garden fertilizer 264

Sawing
by hand 219
by power saw 219
using clamps 219

Scallops . . . .*See* Shellfish

Scarves
storing & organizing 323

Scissors
keeping sharp 158

Scorched
gravy 54
milk .28
pots & pans 85
stains 143
while ironing 151

Scratches
floors 113
furniture 103, 104, 222

Screens
quick repair 347
to clean 118

Screwdriver
in an emergency 197

Screws
in awkward places 228
too loose 227
too tight 197, 228

Scrubs, Masks, Facials . . .310–312

Scuff Marks 114

Seeds
bad, to identify 278
indoor 277
protecting 280
sowing 278
transplanting 279

Seniors 184–192
boots on easily 190
coin grip, easy 189
cooking, general 192
crochet-ball holder 191
cutlery grip, easy 188
emergency identification 190
gardening, easy 191
home safety 192

Seniors . . . . (cont'd)
  in bathroom 188
  keeping cool 188
  light switch, easy 189
  magnifying glass 186
  medication 185, 186
  playing cards, easy grip 189
  purse holder 190, 191
  shoes 190
  telephone-book reading 186
  traveling tips 186, 192, 349
  zipping, easy 189
Sewing 154–163
  buttons & buttonholes 161
  fabric, to buy 160
  hem, adjustable 161
  invisible mending 160
  knots 157
  needles, to keep sharp 158
  net-curtain repair 160
  patterns 156–157
  pin pickups 159
  recycling/repair zippers 161
  scissors, to keep sharp 158
  seams, to cut 156
  storage 155, 156, 158, 159
  tailor's chalk, homemade 157
  threading easily 157, 158
Sewing Machine
  mechanical problems 234
Shampoo
  carpet 108
  doubling 314
  dry 236, 315
  leftovers 99
Shaving
  leg tips 318
Shaving Cream
  carpet-stain remover 109
  eyeglass misting 340
  to defog mirrors, windows 99, 255
Shellfish
  clams, shucking 51
  lobster, how to buy 51
  mussels, freshness 51

oysters
  preparing 51
  fertilizer 264
  scallops, how to buy 51
shrimp
  cooking odors 51
  substitute deveiner 71
Shirt Collars
  to iron 151
Shoes
  canvas, to clean 326
  children's 175, 176
  for seniors 190
  heel touch-up 327
  leather, to clean 326
  patent leather, to clean 327
  polishing 328, 341
  scuffs 327
  shoehorn, substitute 341
  shoelaces 176, 329
  slippery 175, 327
  squeaks 328
  storage 329
  suede, to clean 327
  tennis shoes, to clean 296
  to extend life 326
  when to buy 329
Shoppers' Guide 359
Shopping
  for singles 74
Shortening
  measuring when hard 22
  substitute for 48
Shower Cap
  as a microwave cover 78
Shower Cleaning
  curtains 96
  doors 96
  drains 97
  heads 96
  tracks 96
  walls 96
Shrimp . . . . *See* Shellfish
  substitute deveiner 71

Silk
flowers, to clean 122
lamp shades, to clean 122
laundering 133
Silver
cutlery, to clean 87
jewelry, to clean 87, 333
Sinks
bathroom
porcelain repair 215
porcelain, to clean 95
stain removal 94
kitchen
emergency plug 71
preventive plumbing 91
to clean stainless steel 90
Skin Treatments 310–314
oily, normal, dry skin 311
toners, moisturizers 312–314
Skunk Odor
from pets 236
Sleeping Bags
odors, to discourage 288
zipper rust, to prevent . . .288, 349
Slugs .244
Smoke
alarm 127
tobacco odor, to
remove 124, 125
Snails 244
Snoring
discouraging 345
Soap
as tailor's chalk 157
to last longer 320
uses for slivers 187, 320
Socks
to launder 134
Soot
buildup in chimney 121
garden fertilizer 264
stain removal 111
Soups
freezing . . . . .See Freezing

too greasy 52
too salty 52
too sweet 52
Spaghetti . . . . .See Pasta
Spark Plugs
for car 250
Spices
freezing 69, 70
how to buy 57
in saltshaker 72
storing 56, 57, 92
Spiders 244
Splinter
to remove 182
Sports Equipment 296–301
baseball 297
boating 299
curling broom 298
cycling 300
fishing 298–299
golfing 300–301
hockey 297–298
swimming 298
tennis 296
Spot Remover
homemade 139
Spray Bottles
maximizing use 72
Squeaky Floors 203
Squirrels 245
Stainless Steel
sink cleaning 90
teapot cleaning 86
Stains 109–111, 138–145
ballpoint pen ink 141
bathtubs 94
blood
carpet 109
fabric 139, 140
upholstery 106
candle wax
carpets 110
fabric 140
carpet 109, 110

Stains . . . .(cont'd)
  chocolate 109, 144
  coffee 109, 142
  concrete floors 230, 231
  countertops 91
  crayon 116, 140
  curry 144
  egg .86
  fruit 145
  fruit, on hands 35
  general 139
  grass 144
  grease
    clothing 132, 140
    leather 106
    upholstery 106
    wallpaper 200
  gum 111, 140
  ink .141
  ketchup 144
  lipstick 141
  makeup 139
  marble 123
  mildew 95, 142
  mud
    carpet 109
    clothing 140
  mustard 143
  nongreasy 139
  oil
    clothing 140, 141
    garage 230
    pavement 231
  paint 144, 145, 211
  perspiration 142
  pet accidents on carpets 110
  plastic containers 89
  rust 142
  scorch 143
  scuff marks 114
  sinks 90, 91, 94
  soot 111
  spot remover, homemade 139
  suede 139
  tar
    car 254
    clothing 142

  feet 289
  tea 87, 109, 142
  teeth 319
  tomato 89, 109, 144
  unknown origin 145
  urine 110, 238
  vomit 110
  wax 110, 140
  wine 109, 143
Stamps
  homemade dispenser 307
  that are stuck 307
  to wet 308
Static
  carpet 111
  cling, to prevent . . .148, 304, 331
  laundry 148
Stationery
  buying for home office 307
Steps
  painting 208
Stews
  freezing . . . .*See* Freezing
  too greasy 52
  too salty 52
  too sweet 52
Stickers
  removal from windows 254
  removal from furniture . .101, 103
Storage
  appliance cords, cables . .216, 217
  at front door 126
  books 337
  broom 115
  clothing 92, 175
  kitchen 92
  knitting needles 163
  lumber & paneling 231
  nails & screws 195
  paintbrushes 210
  sandpaper 220, 221
  sewing 158, 159
  shoes 329
  small toys, games 174, 175

Strawberries
  as face mask 311
  to clean 35
  washing 35
Straw Place Mats 94
Stud Finder 199
Stuffing
  chicken or turkey 48
  cushions 339
  fruit 59
  peppers 41
  turkey 49
Substitutes for
  allspice 13
  baking powder 13
  bread tag 70, 76
  butter 13
  buttermilk 13
  celery 13
  chicken 13
  chocolate 13
  chocolate frosting 14
  coffee filter 70, 71
  cookie cutter 18
  corkscrew 71
  corn syrup 14
  cornstarch 14
  cream, sour or whipped 14
  egg cup 287
  eggs 14
  earring back 304
  flavors 14
  flour 15
  food coloring 15
  honey 15
  ice trays 15
  icing decorator 21
  ketchup 15
  kitchen funnel 71
  kitchen-sink plug 71
  letter opener 307
  long match 340
  masking tape 208
  mayonnaise 15
  milk 15
  mushrooms 16
  oil, cooking 16
  pencil sharpener 71
  rope 290
  salt 16
  shoehorn 341
  shoe polish 328
  shrimp deveiner 71
  splash guard 71
  sugar 16, 188
  table for emergencies 360
  tea cozy 70
  tomato paste 16
  toothpaste 319
  toothpicks 55
  yogurt 16
Suede, To Remove Stain 139
Sugar
  brown, to soften 22
  substitute for 16, 188
  to eliminate saltiness 52
Sunburn, To Relieve 182
Sweaters
  angora 324
  drying outside 146
  recycling 163
  reshaping 135
  unfuzzing 324
Sweeping 114, 115
Swimming
  pool safety 176
  pool skimmer 298
Syrup, Measuring 22

T

Tables
  area conversions 351–352
  common conversions 357
  emergency substitutes 360
  gas consumption 354
  length conversions 352–354
  shoppers' guide 359
  temperature 355–356
  volume conversion 356
  weight conversions 358

Tar
bare feet, to remove 289
canvas shoes, to remove 326
car exterior, to remove 254
stains on clothing 142
Tea
flavoring 61
furniture, to stain 223
iced, foggy 61
leftovers 60
plants, to water 268
stains 91, 109, 142
storing 61
Tea Cozy
substitute for 70
Teakettle
to clean 86
to run efficiently 218
Teapots
to clean stainless steel 86
Teething, Babies 166
Telephone
book, easy to read 186
for office 306, 307
safety 128
Television
dusting 108
reception 345
Tennis
ball 296
shoe care & cleaning 296
Tennis, Table
dented ball 296
Tent Caterpillars 245
Tents
tips when camping 288
Thermos
to clean 90
Thimbles
use when grating 75
Thread 157–158
Tiles
cracked in bathtub 214, 215

grout cleaning 98
to clean 98
Tires
balance 251
changing 251
pressure 251
rotating 251
Toasters
cleaning 218
mechanical problem 234
Tobacco, To Remove Smoke . .124
Toilet
condensation 97
paper storage 98
ring, to remove 97
running, to stop 214
Tomatoes
buying economically 44
freezing 67
growing 280
peeling 44
ripening 43
slicing 44
stains 89, 109, 144
storing 43
Tomato Paste
freezing 67
substitute for 16
Toners 312–314
Toolbox
suggested contents 194
Tools
belt, homemade 198
chisel storage 197
clamps, rubber bands 199
mallet, emergency 196
metal-file care 196
rust, to prevent 195, 196
screwdriver, emergency 197
screws, too tight 197
spatula for hammering 196
spatula for screwing 196
wire stripper, emergency 197
wrenches 197

Toothache
  to relieve 181
Toothbrush
  as fish stringer 299
  as letter opener 307
Toothpaste
  china scratches 88
  maximizing 319
  substitution 319
  to clean brass 123
  to clean jewelry 334
Toothpick Holder 291
Toys
  bath, organizing 165
  beach carrier 289
  for baby 166
  small, storage 175
  stuffed animals, to clean 174
Travel Tips 186–187, 349
  baby-bottle holder 165
  converting mileage 353, 354
  homemade sewing kit 159
  how to pack 331, 349
  ironing tips 152
  luggage 186, 187
  pickpocket prevention 187
  plant care, when away . .268, 269
  retracing route 187
  swollen feet 187
  time-savers 187, 349
  travel arrangements 349
  with kids 178
  with trailer 257
Tree
  as baby present 180
  care of 284
  sap, removal from car 258
Trellis, Homemade 284
Trousers
  catching on shoes 327
  drying outside 146
  hemming in emergency 304
Tulips
  to last longer 275

Tuna Salad
  Leftovers . . . .*See* Leftovers
Turkey . . . .*See* Poultry
Turnip
  prevent cooking odor 37

U

Umbrella
  as car-seat shade 258
  care for 346
  patio, storage 284
Upholstery
  bloodstains 106
  cushion wear & care 106
  grease stains 106
  leather 105, 106
  pet hair, to remove 106
  pet urine, to clean 238
  rip & hole repair 107
Urine, To Remove 110, 238

V

Vacuum Cleaner
  mechanical problems 234
  odors from 125
Vases
  to clean 122
Vegetables
  cooking 45
  cooking odors, to eliminate . . .37
  freezing . . . .*See* Freezing
  gardening 276
  leftovers . . . .*See* Leftovers
  nutritional value 45
  planting 266
  quick scoop 72
  raw, freezing . . . . . .*See* Freezing
  wilted 45
Velvet
  restoring 152

Venetian Blinds
as a surprise message 347
to clean 348
Videotapes 346
Vinegar
cider, eliminate saltiness 52
remove dishwasher film 80
storage 58
wine vinegar, homemade 58
Vomit, On Carpet 110

W

Waffle Iron
mechanical problems 234
Wallpaper
cleaning 115, 116
dirt, to remove 200
edges, to join 201
getting started 201
grease spots 200
measuring for 202
peeling 201
rips & marks 201
Walls
checking condensation 203
crack widening 200
finding studs 199
holes, to fill 200, 206
paneling 202, 203
plaster, to repair 199, 200
shower 96
to protect from ladders 200
wallpapering 200–202
washing 115
Wardrobe 330–331
closet organizing 330, 331
for a business trip 304
hanger grips 330
static cling, to reduce 331
storage sachet 330
Warping
tabletops 222

Washer
replacement of 213–214
to repair loose knobs 222
Washer, Clothes
care of 132
dissolving soap 132
mechanical problems 232
reducing vibration 229
Washing . . . .*See also* Laundry
organizing for 131
Wasps 243
Water
conservation 225
hard, treatment 133, 319
marks on furniture 101
Wax . . . . *See also* Candle Wax
ashtray cleaning 122
carpets, to remove from 110
clothing stains 140
cooler, to repair leaking 287
matches, to waterproof 286
wood, to remove from 103
zippers, to unstick 326
Wax Buildup
remove from floors 114
Wax Paste
for toilet condensation 97
Wheelbarrow Repair 284
Whipping Cream . . . . .*See* Cream
White Marks
furniture 101
paneling 202
Wicker & Cane
care & cleaning 104, 105
Windows
buffing 117
cars 254, 255
dirt, cobwebs in tracks 118
frost, to prevent 117
installing locks 204
insulation 226
painting 207, 208
scratches, to remove 229
screens, to clean 118

Windows . . . .(cont'd)
 stickers, to remove 254
 sticky, to treat 204
 sweating 204
 to clean 116, 117
 windshield wash, homemade. .254
 wipers, to clean with 118

Window Screen
 to clean 118
 to repair 347

Window Tracks
 smooth sliding 118

Wine
 cork in bottle 61
 homemade wine vinegar 58
 leftover 69
 lost its sparkle 61
 rack, as bathroom towel rack . .99
 removing stains 109, 143

Winter Driving
 frost-free windows 117
 frozen locks 261
 icy windshield 254, 259–262
 ignition timing 260
 starting car 259
 stuck in snow 260

Wiper Blades
 other uses 118

Wipes
 homemade, for baby 166

Wire
 for lamps 218
 stripper, in an emergency 197
 to straighten 228

Wood
 burn marks, to remove 103
 candle wax, to remove . .103, 116
 cutting plywood 219
 doors, swelling 116
 drilling 220
 gray film, to remove 102
 hammering nail into 219
 nails, to remove 196, 220
 polishing 100, 101
 purchasing lumber 219

 sanding 220
 scratches, to conceal 103, 104
 splitting, to prevent 219
 sticky marks 101, 103
 storing, drying 231
 warps or cracks, to prevent . . .104
 water rings, to remove 101
 white marks, to remove .101, 202

Woodstoves
 fuel 120
 humidifier/deodorizer 120
 polishing & cleaning . . .120, 121

Woodwork
 cleaning 116
 removing candle wax 116

Woolens
 care of 324
 gentle bleaching 135
 shrinkage 135
 to soften 134
 washing 134

Workshop
 in a closet 195
 ladder 198
 rusty-tool prevention . . .195, 196
 suggested tools 194

Worms
 added to composter 265
 finding for fishing 299
 in garden 266
 to deter with matches 265

Wrenches 197

Y

Yogurt, Substitute For 16

Z

Zippers
 easy to use 189
 recycling & repair 161
 rust, to prevent 288, 349
 sticking 325, 326

GLOSSARY OF TERMS

NORTH AMERICAN		EUROPEAN
baby nipple	-	teat
bathtub decals	-	rubberized stick-ons
bobby pin	-	hair grip, clip
broiler	-	grill
burlap bag	-	hessian sack
caulking	-	sealant
cellophane tape	-	cellotape
clothespins	-	clothes-pegs
club soda	-	soda water
cookie	-	biscuit
cookie sheet	-	baking tray
cornstarch	-	corn flour
denatured alcohol	-	methylated spirits
diapers	-	nappies
drapery	-	curtains
eaves trough	-	guttering
faucet	-	tap
garbage cans	-	refuse sacks
garbage disposer	-	waste disposal
gasoline/gas	-	petrol
gum/Artgum eraser	-	rubber
heat liniment	-	muscle rub
hood	-	bonnet
kerosene	-	paraffin
kraft wrapping paper	-	brown paper
lard	-	shortening
latex paint	-	emulsion
liquid dish soap	-	washing-up liquid
liquor store	-	off license
lumber	-	timber
mailbox	-	letter box
milk bag	-	freezer bag
mint patties	-	after-dinner mints
pants	-	trousers
pattern "sizing"	-	starch
perlite	-	crushed seashells
plastic baggies	-	small plastic bags
plastic barrette	-	plastic hair clip
popsicle	-	lolly
potato chips	-	crisps
purse	-	handbag
registers	-	vents
rubber cement	-	modeling glue
rubbing alcohol	-	isopropyl alcohol
sachet powder	-	bath salts (powder)
screening	-	wire mesh
shower stall	-	shower cubicle
sleepers	-	baby grows
soda crackers	-	cracker biscuits
toque	-	knitted hat
Turkish towel	-	thick, soft bath towel
varathane	-	clear varnish
washing soda*	-	water softener, lime-scale remover
waxed paper	-	greaseproof
X-Acto knife	-	modeling knife
zucchini	-	courgette

*IMPORTANT: The silver-cleaning hint on page 87 refers to "washing soda." Do not use washing soda crystals. They can react with the aluminum foil, causing noxious fumes. Use powdered lime-scale remover (sometimes called water softener) sold for use in washing machines.